Patricia Zanella

Chicano Studies
A Multidisciplinary Approach

Bilingual Education Series

GARY D. KELLER, *Editor*

GUADALUPE VALDÉS, ANTHONY G. LOZANO, and RODOLFO
  GARCÍA-MOYA, editors
*Teaching Spanish to the Hispanic Bilingual: Issues, Aims,
and Methods*

JOSHUA A. FISHMAN and GARY D. KELLER, editors
*Bilingual Education for Hispanic Students in the United
States*

FLORENCE BARKIN, ELIZABETH A. BRANDT, and JACOB
  ORNSTEIN-GALICIA, editors
*Bilingualism and Language Contact: Spanish, English,
and Native American Languages*

MAE CHU-CHANG, editor
*Asian- and Pacific-American Perspectives in Bilingual
Education: Comparative Research*

GARY D. KELLER
Leo y entiendo, a Spanish-language reading program for
kindergarten through grade 3

THERESA H. ESCOBEDO, editor
*Early Childhood Bilingual Education: A Hispanic
Perspective*

EUGENE E. GARCÍA, FRANCISCO A. LOMELÍ, and ISIDRO D.
  ORTIZ, editors
Chicano Studies: A Multidisciplinary Approach

Chicano Studies

A Multidisciplinary Approach

Edited by
EUGENE E. GARCÍA

FRANCISCO A. LOMELÍ

ISIDRO D. ORTIZ

Teachers College, Columbia University
New York and London

Published by Teachers College Press, 1234 Amsterdam Avenue,
New York, N.Y. 10027

Grateful acknowledgment is made for permission to reprint the
"Corrido de Joaquín Murieta," collected by Philip Sonnichsen
and printed in "Texas-Mexican Border Music," vols. 2 and 3,
corridos 1 and 2, Arhollie Records, 1975. © by Arhoolie
Productions Inc. Used with permission. From the Folklyric LP
9004. 10341 San Pablo Ave., El Cerrito, CA 94530. For
complete catalog send $1.00

Library of Congress Cataloging in Publication Data

Main entry under title:

Chicano studies.

  (Bilingual education series)
  Includes bibliographical references and index.
  1. Mexican Americans—Addresses, essays, lectures.
I. García, Eugene E., 1946–   . II. Lomelí,
Francisco A. III. Ortiz, Isidro D., 1949–
IV. Series: Bilingual education series (Columbia
University. Teachers college)
E184.M5C455   1984   973'.046872   83-18152

ISBN 0-8077-2749-0

Manufactured in the United States of America

89 88 87 86 85   2 3 4 5 6

*This book is dedicated
to our wives, children, and parents.*

Contents

IV | Educational Perspectives   191

V | Future Chicano Studies Research   253

Acknowledgments

A volume of this kind becomes possible only with the assistance of many individuals. We are especially indebted to the scholars who contributed to the anthology. Needless to say, without their willingness to embrace our ideas this volume would not have become a reality. We are also indebted to David Sprecher, Dean of the College of Letters and Sciences at the University of California at Santa Barbara, Raymond Huerta, Affirmative Action Coordinator at the University of California at Santa Barbara, and Ms. Lupe Barba. They provided assistance at critical points in the development of the volume. Gracias.

Grateful acknowledgment is also made for permission to quote from the following works:

Ricardo Sánchez, *Canto y grito mi liberación* (Garden City, N.Y.: Doubleday, 1973), p. 87, 139. By permission of the poet.

Alurista, *Floricanto en Aztlán* (Los Angeles: Chicano Cultural Center, UCLA, 1971), poem #40; "We've Played Cowboys," in A. Castañeda Shular, T. Ybarra-Frausto, and J. Sommers, eds. *Literatura chicana: texto y contexto* (Englewood Cliffs, N.J.: Prentice-Hall, 1972), p. 31; *Dawn,* in *El Grito* ("Chicano Drama"), book 4, year 8 (1974), pp. 68–69. By permission of the poet.

Angela de Hoyos, *Chicano Poems for the Barrio* (Bloomington, Ind.: Backstage Books, 1975); "Chicano," *Revista Chicano–Riqueña,* año 3, no. 4 (1975), pp. 23–24. By permission of the poet.

Lorna Dee Cervantes, "El sueño de las flores" in *Mango,* vol. 1, no. 1 (Fall 1976), p. 31; "Grandma," *El Grito del Sol,* vol. 3, no. 3 (1978), p. 38. By permission of the poet.

José Montoya, "La jefita," "Lazy Skin," and "In a Pink Bubble Gum World," in *El espejo—The Mirror.* By permission of the poet.

Verónica Cunningham, "A woman/was raped . . . ," unpublished. By permission of the poet.

Guadalupe Valdés-Fallis, "Las muñecas cuando se acuestan cierran los ojos," *Tejidos,* vol. 1, no. 3 (1974). By permission of the author.

Estela Portillo Trambley, "If It Weren't for the Honeysuckle," in *Rain of Scorpions and Other Writings* (Berkeley: Tonatiuh International, 1975). By permission of the author.

Luis Valdez, *Pensamiento Serpentino* (San Juan Bautista: Cucaracha Publications, 1973), p. 1. By permission of the author and El Teatro Campesino.

Aurelio M. Espinosa, "La esposa infiel," *Romancero de Nuevo México* (Madrid: Consejo Superior de Investigaciones Científicas, 1953), p. 66. By permission of the publisher.

Pedro Ortiz Vázquez, "Quienes somos," *The Bilingual Review/La Revista Bilingüe,* vol. 2, no. 3 (1975), p. 292. By permission of the publisher.

El Huitlacoche, "Searching for La Real Cosa," *The Bilingual Review/La Revista Bilingüe,* vol. 5, nos. 1 and 2 (1978), pp. 139, 142; "The Urban(e) Chicano's 76," *The Bilingual Review/La Revista Bilingüe,* vol. 3, no. 2 (1976), pp. 185–86; "From the Heights of Macho Bicho," *The Bilingual Review/La Revista Bilingüe,* vol. 2, nos. 1 & 2 (1975), pp. 192–93. By permission of the publisher.

Adaljiza Sosa Riddell, "Malinche," *El Grito* ("Chicanas en la Literatura y el Arte"), book 1, year 7 (1973), p. 76. By permission of the poet.

Lorenza Calvillo Schmidt, "Como duele," *El Grito* ("Chicanas en la Literatura y el Arte"), book 1, year 7 (1973), p. 61. By permission of the poet.

Abelardo Delgado, "La Causa" and "Stupid America," in Philip D. Ortego, ed., *We Are Chicanos* (New York: Washington Square Books, 1973). By permission of the poet.

Gary Soto, "The Vision" and "A Few Coins," *The Tale of Sunlight* (Pittsburgh: University of Pittsburgh Press, 1978). By permission of the poet.

Tino Villanueva, "Que hay otra voz." By permission of the poet.

Margarita Virginia Sánchez, "Escape," in Philip C. Ortego, ed., *We Are Chicanos* (New York: Washington Square Books, 1973), p. 208. By permission of the poet.

I | The Discipline of Chicano Studies

Overview

Chicano Studies is a relatively young discipline in academic circles. It emerged in the tumultuous 1960s in large part as an attempt to systematically meet the social, cultural, and educational needs of people of Mexican descent, particularly in the southwestern United States. It became a formal field of study in the institutions of higher education when Chicano Studies departments and programs were created to pursue the systematic study of the Chicano experience in all its facets within an interdisciplinary framework. Chicano Studies now offers an opportunity unavailable to students prior to the 1960s: the possibility of pursuing a program of study in a discipline dedicated exclusively to understanding the experience of the Mexican population in American society.

Throughout the twentieth century, the experience of people of Mexican descent was a concern of some scholars. However, the creation of a discipline was not an objective. Anglo-American students of ethnic and race relations issues were primarily concerned with understanding the reasons for the perceived inability of Mexicans to assimilate into American society in the manner of other ethnic groups from Europe.

In the small community of scholars of Mexican descent, Américo Paredes, George I. Sánchez, and Ernesto Galarza recognized the need to develop an organized field study. However, throughout much of their scholarly careers, the conditions of the Mexican community and widespread discriminatory practices mandated that these scholars devote their energies to the critical and vital tasks of defending the Mexican community from intellectual attacks and of exposing and documenting the detrimental impact on their community of public and private policies and programs. Much to their credit, they courageously assumed leadership. Galarza, for example, for over a decade waged a campaign through his research against the Bracero Program, which permitted the importation of Mexican laborers into the United States in the years after World War II. His documentation of the exploitative character of the programs and its detrimental consequences contributed to the termination of the program in 1964 by the Congress of the United States.[1]

In the late 1960s the possibility of creating a discipline grew with the rising demand for the creation of ethnic studies programs throughout the country and the steady growth in the number of Chicano students and faculty on college and university campuses. This opportunity was quickly seized by Chicanos. On campuses throughout the Southwest, a foundation was laid and work began on the structure of a discipline that ultimately would house scholars and students dedicated to the development of knowledge about the experience of people of Mexican descent in American society.

As a result of these efforts the discipline of Chicano Studies is at least ten years old and students are now able to engage in a new and relevant field of study. Since its creation, scholars have examined the problems of the discipline. However, despite its age and significance, its origins, evolution, and contributions have not received much scholarly attention. In the introductory article in this volume, Carlos Muñoz, one of the leading participants in the efforts to create and develop the field, proposes to remedy the lack of attention by critically examining its creation, growth, and impact. Muñoz begins by tracing the intellectual and political roots of Chicano Studies to the demands of the Chicano student movement of the late 1960s. He reveals that the participants in the movement agreed that a field of study was urgently needed to carry out research on the Mexican population, but they often disagreed on the appropriate structure and objectives for the proposed field. Consequently, in 1969 systematic efforts were made to reconcile the competing perspectives at one of the most important conferences of the Chicano movement in Santa Barbara, California. The product of this conference, he reveals, was a statement called *El Plan de Santa Bárbara*.[2]

This document has been portrayed as the definitive statement on Chicano Studies by some scholars in the field. Muñoz challenges this contention. He argues that the document is deficient in that it leaves several critical issues unresolved. After discussing *El Plan de Santa Bárbara* and specifying some of its deficiencies, Muñoz discusses growth of the field. Since its inception, he notes, Chicano Studies has been plagued by several problems; it has often found itself attempting to survive in a hostile environment in institutions of higher education. Nevertheless, through the labors of its practitioners, it has made steady progress. It has become and remains an established, thriving, and legitimate field of study that has made and continues to make significant intellectual and social contributions.

NOTES

1. Ernesto Galarza's campaign is documented in Ernesto Galarza, *Farm Workers and Agri-Business in California, 1947–1960* (Notre Dame, Ind.: University of Notre Dame Press, 1977).

2. *El Plan de Santa Bárbara: A Chicano Plan for Higher Education* (Oakland: La Causa Publications, 1969).

1 | The Development of Chicano Studies, 1968–1981

CARLOS MUÑOZ, JR.

When compared to the typical academic discipline or field of study in the university, Chicano Studies is indeed unique. As is the case with Ethnic Studies as a whole, Chicano Studies was a product of the turbulent decade of the 1960s that witnessed the phenomena of mass student protest on university and college campuses throughout America. Student radicalism during that period was generated by the particular societal issues and politics of the time, which were characterized by mass demonstrations against poverty, racism, and a most unpopular war in Vietnam. Besides being concerned with those issues, Mexican youth were also concerned with access to institutions of higher learning that historically had systematically excluded them. They demanded from the university an education that would teach them about their people's culture and history and provide them with the knowledge and training needed to make changes in their respective communities. Chicano Studies was the direct result of their demands.

The first Chicano Studies program was created in 1968. Much has been written and published about the experience of people of Mexican descent in the United States since then. Chicano Studies itself, however, has not been a subject for serious research. What little has been written about it is for the most part polemical in nature and couched in the rhetoric of the politics of the 1960s. Although Chicano Studies has gone beyond those politics, its past and present objectives in the university remain little understood. This article critically examines the origins and objectives of Chicano Studies and places its development over time in a perspective that contributes to the understanding of its present and future status in the university.

POLITICAL AND INTELLECTUAL ROOTS OF CHICANO STUDIES

Chicano Studies was and is largely a California product, although programs were eventually established and currently exist in other states. The vast majority of the programs were founded and are located on the campuses of the Uni-

versity of California and the California State College and University Systems.[1]
There are two major reasons for this. One is the fact that the state of California
has the largest population of people of Mexican descent in the United States;
the other is that the Chicano student movement in California made Chicano
Studies its top priority and waged a constant struggle to first create and then
maintain those programs. In contrast, Chicano student organizations on campuses of universities in other states were more concerned with directing campus
resources to community programs and organizations.

Prior to the creation of the first Chicano Studies program, student groups in
California had a variety of organizational names. The more prominent were
the United Mexican American Students (UMAS), the Mexican American
Youth Organization (MAYO), or the Mexican American Student Confeder-
ation (MASC). The black civil rights movement and later the Black Power
movement raised the political consciousness of Chicano student activists, but
their direct involvement and exposure to the farmworker movement led by
César Chávez in California, and to some extent the struggle for land waged by
Reies Lopez Tijerina in northern New Mexico, compelled many in the leadership of those organizations to move in the direction of a distinct Chicano
political perspective. Involvement in local community politics further broadened their political perspectives and led to their participation in various protest
activities that directly confronted the reality of racial oppression in their
respective communities.

Their confrontation with racism resulted in a response similar to that which
was expressed by black student militants on the campus. Some began to seriously question the role of the university in the perpetuation of poverty and
racism. They questioned the process of assimilation into the dominant culture
of American society and criticized the schools and the university for their role
in contributing to the problems in their communities.

In the fall of 1967 a Chicano student group by the name of Quinto Sol at
the University of California, Berkeley, published its first issue of *El Grito: A
Journal of Contemporary Mexican-American Thought*. In an editorial, the
group directly challenged the notion that Chicanos had assimilated and criticized the ideology created by social scientists that blamed Chicanos for their
problems. They declared:

> Contrary to the general pattern of ethnic minorities in the history of the United
> States, Mexican Americans have retained their distinct identity and have refused
> to disappear into the Great American Melting Pot . . . American ingenuity has
> produced an ideological rhetoric that serves to neatly explain away both the
> oppressive and exploitative factors maintaining Mexican Americans in their eco-
> nomically impoverished condition . . . the essential message is . . . that Chicanos
> . . . choose poverty and isolation instead of assimilating into the American main-
> stream and accepting its material riches and superior culture. Formulated and

propagated by those intellectual mercenaries of our age, the social scientists, this rhetoric has been professionally certified and institutionally sanctified.[2]

The group did not call for the creation of Chicano Studies, but laid one of its founding premises: the notion that Chicanos had the responsibility to challenge the assimilationist perspective of the university that had resulted in the perpetuation of racist stereotypes of Chicanos as "simple-minded," with "limited mentality," and an "inferior, backward, traditional culture."[3] *El Grito* became the first Chicano intellectual journal in the history of the United States, and, under the editorship of Octavio Romano-V, was of paramount importance not only to the development of Chicano Studies, but to the development of writers of Mexican descent in American society.

By the fall of 1968 administrators at several campuses throughout the state of California had responded to demands made by Chicano student activists for courses about different aspects of the Chicano experience. For the most part, one or two courses were created in existing academic departments, or within interdisciplinary programs, and sometimes in special unaffiliated curricula. At the California State College at Los Angeles, students were given what was to be the first department of Mexican-American Studies; it consisted of two courses, one on the Politics of the Southwest and the other on Mexican-American History. These were taught by part-time instructors who were first-year graduate students in political science and Latin-American Studies. Although there were only a handful of university faculty of Mexican descent throughout the state and even fewer who were sympathetic to the idea of Chicano Studies,[4] the student activists were nevertheless able to generate proposals for the creation and institutionalization of Chicano Studies programs during the academic year of 1968–69 at various campuses. Their proposals reflected a wide variety of perspectives on Chicano Studies objectives.

At San Francisco State College, for example, a Department of Raza Studies within the School of Ethnic Studies was proposed that would have the following aims:

> The purpose and goal of La Raza Studies is to provide education to Chicanos and Latinos . . . excluded from the educational process. . . . The concept of education . . . involves a new understanding of education (and) . . . a powerful force in the renovation and reconstruction of the entire system of education . . . to provide the community with the resources to deal with the problems it faces. The primary resources . . . are individuals who are sensitive to the needs of their people, creative in their approach to problem solving, and equipped with the skills necessary to serve their community.[5]

At the University of California, San Diego campus, Chicano Studies was proposed within the context of a Third World college whose objectives were defined in terms of a definite radical alternative to existing academic units on that campus.

> We demand that (the) . . . college be devoted to relevant education for minority youth and to the study of the contemporary social problems of all people. To do this authentically, this college must radically depart from the usual role as the ideological backbone of the social system, and must instead subject every part of the system to ruthless criticism. To reflect these aims . . . it will be called Lumumba Zapata College. To enhance the beauty of the name, we demand that the architecture be of Mexican and African style.[6]

At the University of California, Berkeley campus, Chicano Studies was envisioned in somewhat more academic terms at the same time that a community component was stressed. Students there proposed the establishment of a Chicano Studies department with the structure of a Third World college. The college had been one of the demands of the Third World Liberation Front (TWLF) during a student strike on that campus.

> The present needs of the Chicano must be met in such a way as to provide relevant programs which will sustain self-confidence and provide a feeling of acceptance on the student's terms . . . bilingual studies must constitute a part of the University's realistic recognition of community realities and innovative academic potential . . . a part of the function of a department must be to prepare students for more advanced participation in the University outside of the Chicano Studies department . . . to develop student's abilities in a bilingual, bicultural manner . . . by focusing on an intellectual perspective of and about the Spanish-speaking communities . . . to develop . . . abilities to serve their communities . . . to develop a potential for self-fulfillment in at least two cultures.[7]

At the University of California, Los Angeles (UCLA), the proposal for Chicano Studies called for the establishment of a center as opposed to a department but with an emphasis on research. The center was to be called the "Mexican American Cultural Center" and was to develop along the following lines:

> The principal objectives of the Center are the following ones . . . to encourage and support research into all areas of knowledge relevant to the Mexican American community. . . . To assist in the development of programs and research which will focus the unique resources of this University on the problems of the Mexican community . . . To assist in the development of new curriculum and bibliographical materials dealing with the culture, history and problems of the Mexican American . . . To actively engage in furthering the involvement of the University with the Mexican American community. . . . In its role as a coordinator between community and University and as a research and bibliographical resource, the Center hopes to place this University in the forefront of institutions actively seeking solutions to the problems of the barrios of America.[8]

At San Fernando Valley State College the proposal for Chicano Studies called for a Department of Mexican-American Studies with a traditional department status. Its objectives were defined as follows:

> To study the contributions of the Mexican-American to American culture and society . . . promote better understanding among all Americans . . . train those in professions such as civil services, police or social work, education, advertising, etc. to work more effectively with . . . problems . . . aggravated by the alienation of the Mexican-American . . . encourage Mexican-Americans to seek higher education by creating a greater feeling of pride for their heritage and acquainting them with the culture that helped form their community . . . enable all students, whatever their ethnic background, to specialize in the Mexican-American.[9]

The most ambitious in terms of scope and structure was the proposal developed at the University of California, Santa Barbara. It called for a Chicano Studies Center to include a department, a research component, and a community-university component to develop cultural and "urban-change" programs with the following objectives:

> Through Chicano Studies, Chicano students intend to study and legitimize their culture heritage . . . broaden and deepen the university's educational and cultural mission by enlarging its academic program . . . serve . . . as a socializing process . . . affect the student's individual consciousness and contribute to the shaping of his sense of community . . . provide the student with the necessary technical and educational skills to interpret his social worlds . . . especially that part of the world denominated "the Third World." The end result will be that students will be able to know themselves . . . to change their community.[10]

Differences of perspective as to structure and objectives characterized the various proposed programs. There was a consensus on the relevance and need of those programs for Chicano students but there was a lack of coherence in expectations and emphasis. Some emphasized the potential for such programs to contribute to the solution of students' cultural identity crisis caused by the assimilation process. Others expected that these programs would develop into meaningful academic alternatives to traditional departments. Still others perceived such programs as training grounds for community organizers. Ideologically, the spectrum ran from those who defined Chicano Studies as curricula that would emphasize the contributions of Americans of Mexican descent to American culture and society to those who defined it as curricula that would focus attention on racism and the structure of class oppression.

In the interest of developing a more unified and coordinated effort to establish Chicano Studies and other support programs for Chicano students throughout California, a committee was formed by student leaders, faculty, and staff, who were directly involved in those programs at various campuses.

They called it the Chicano Coordinating Committee on Higher Education (CCHE). Shortly after its creation, CCHE called for a statewide conference for the purpose of formulating a plan of action or blueprint that could provide the necessary direction for the overall struggle for equal access for Chicanos to higher education. In a letter to selected student leaders, professors, administrators, and community leaders, CCHE made clear its objectives:

> The purpose . . . is to develop a "Master-Plan" for Chicanos in higher education which would at once serve as a guideline . . . and would articulate the reality of the Chicano educational situation to the established system at large . . . produce a document that can be used as a guide to recruit Chicano students, faculty, and administrators . . . to deal with support programs, curriculum, etc. . . . present the needs of the Chicano community, as it relates to higher education, not as a series of demands, rather as an irrevocable law—an objective to be reached within a given time—a tangible reality.[11]

The conference took place in April 1969, at the University of California, Santa Barbara campus and was restricted to one hundred participants. Twenty-nine campuses throughout the state of California with an active Chicano student organization sent two official student representatives for a total of fifty-eight students. The remaining forty-two official participants were from the faculty, other university staff, and community activists involved in educational programs in Chicano communities. Approximately thirty to fifty others not officially invited attended during the three days of the conference.

The conference was structured around nine workshops that were broken down into two main categories. The first category involved "technical operations." The workshops under this category dealt with recruitment, support programs, funding and legislation, Chicano Studies curriculum, and the "institutionalization" of Chicano Studies programs. The second category of workshops focused on "political operations" and consisted of workshops revolving around the questions of statewide communication and coordination, university-community relations, campus organization, and political action. The latter provided the thrust for the formation of "El Movimiento Estudiantil Chicano de Aztlán" or MECHA, the statewide student movement, while the first category of workshops furnished the impetus for the establishment of Chicano Studies programs and the strategy for the expansion of Equal Opportunity Programs (EOP) to include a focus on Chicano students. The establishment of Chicano Studies programs, however, was perceived as the key objective to the successful implementation of all the goals of the conference. In the document resulting from the workshops the participants declared:

> Chicano Studies represents the total conceptualization of the Chicano community's aspirations that involve higher education. To meet these ends, the university and college systems of the State of California must act in the following basic

areas: (1) admission and recruitment of Chicano students, faculty, administrators, and staff; (2) a curriculum program and an academic major relevant to the Chicano cultural and historical experience; (3) support and tutorial programs; (4) research programs; (5) publications programs; (6) community cultural and social action centers.[12]

The conference lasted three days and was successful beyond the expectations of the organizers. In addition to meeting the stated objectives, it resulted in the unification of all the diverse student groups under one ideological force they defined as "Chicanismo." Student activists agreed on the new name of "El Movimiento Estudiantil Chicano de Aztlán" because it underscored the concept of "Aztlán" and promoted the Chicano identity. In the spirit of unity generated at Santa Barbara, the CCHE leadership distributed the following message in a brief report after the conference:

> The three-day Chicano Conference of students, faculty, staff, and community was an historic *encuentro*. There was *hermandad,* there was *intercambio de ideas*. . . . Most important, there was work on the issues affecting higher education and Chicanos in California. . . . The conference, not an end in itself, was a strong and critical step forward. . . . (T)he ten workshops produced reports which will ultimately make up a *Chicano* master plan. . . . (I)t will be sent to Hitch, Dumke, the Regents, Reagan, et al.[13]

The "Chicano master plan" was published in October 1969 with the title of *El Plan de Santa Bárbara*. The document reflected the ideas and dialogue that had been generated in the various workshops of the conference that were in turn edited by six members of the CCHE Steering Committee.[14] The philosophical framework of the document, however, was based largely on the proposal for Chicano Studies written for the University of California, Santa Barbara campus by Jesús Chavarría, an assistant professor in the Department of History, who had been one of the principal organizers of the conference. The document stressed antiassimilation and antiracism as the point of departure for Chicano Studies. It placed the development of those programs within the context of the politics of change.

> Due to the racist character of American society . . . in the past only individual Mexican-Americans were able to obtain moderate status and success in a society dominated by Anglo-American values and institutions. . . . (T)he price of assimilation resulted . . . in a turning away from the community; . . . the community remained exploited, backward, and static. Now Chicano university students not unmindful of the historic price of assimilation, take change within the community as the point of departure for their social and political involvement.[15]

This clearly placed the development of Chicano Studies on the same terms as that of the student movement. Given that the student movement was committed to contributing to social and political change in the Chicano community, it was held that Chicano Studies should become an integral part of that process. The Chavarría proposal interpreted the aims of the student movement to be a quest to compel the university to "respond to the particular needs and aspirations of the barrio and of the colonia" on the same basis as it has historically met the needs of the dominant society. Finally, since the student movement was seeking to make changes in the Chicano community and to free Chicano cultural values and lifestyle "from the standardized criteria of Anglo-American culture," it was imperative that Chicano Studies develop both an academic and a community orientation.[16] It was reasoned that the university itself would enhance its role in the larger society and in the Chicano community by allowing Chicano Studies programs to develop in this fashion:

> In short, Chicano students are seeking an authentic freedom of expression within the university and society at large. Their call is for authentic diversification of American culture, a prospect which can only enrich the university's fulfillment of its cultural mission.[17]

The *Plan* went beyond the question of Chicano Studies and was directed at the broader question of the institutionalization of all Chicano programs. The concern was to provide a reference point for those involved in the development of proposals, the politics of negotiation with administrators, and the organization of Chicanos on campus. Specifically, it was the intent to provide a set of tactics and a strategy to be implemented at every campus throughout the state of California designed to maximize Chicano influence in the decision-making processes of those institutions. In the final analysis, however, it was not so much a final blueprint upon which to build all programs; it was more a set of recommendations and general analytical framework designed to place the development of programs in a proper perspective vis-à-vis the goals of the student movement and the rhetoric of the time.

Some of those who played an important role in both the organization of the conference and the writing of the *Plan* nevertheless perceived it as a more definitive document and indeed a blueprint. As one of the editors of the *Plan* later declared,

> The seminal statement on Chicano Studies is the *Plan de Santa Bárbara.* . . . A commonplace "defense" of those who would betray, especially for those who need to cover up their early lack of participation or their present self-interest, is to charge that the statements of the *Plan* . . . were "vague" or "romantic." They were as clear and concrete as policy statements are and as pragmatic as called for by the reality of the time . . . Obviously, years later, the implementation of objectives continuously demands increased complexity. The six year old *Plan* is as relevant as the 200 year old Declaration of Independence.[18]

In point of fact it was a significant document and it did contribute to the development of Chicano Studies and other programs at campuses where those programs were yet to be created and/or implemented, both within and outside California. Most importantly, it remains an important document of substantial historical value because it captures the mood of that time, especially among Chicano activists. But in retrospect, it was far from definitive.

What the *Plan* did not do was to define or redefine Chicano Studies curricula as outlined in earlier proposals in concrete terms or in terms that could be interpreted as an authentic alternative to traditional academic curricula. Although it argued that Chicano Studies should develop in the direction of an alternative ideological framework, it did not spell out that ideology beyond the "Chicanismo" or "cultural nationalism" rhetoric of the student movement. The result was that Chicano Studies was loosely defined as simply curricula on the Chicano experience, past and present, with a focus on the cultural aspects of that experience, although the curriculum workshop participants agreed that Chicano Studies should not become simply another academic program because it should also have a focus on community. It was hypothesized that this latter focus would provide the student with the opportunity to engage in practical learning experiences dealing with the everyday issues of his people and lead to the discovery of his people's cultural traditions, thus providing an understanding of himself and his people. In short, the rationale for Chicano Studies as outlined in the *Plan* was predicated on an inward look at the Chicano experience as opposed to looking at the external factors for the identity crisis amongst youth of Mexican descent. More precisely, the emphasis was placed on the need to develop the Chicano identity on the basis of the intrinsic character of the Chicano experience and not on the ways that experience has been shaped as a result of Chicano interaction with dominant Anglo institutions. As the authors of the *Plan* put it:

> The critical dialectics of Chicano Studies are the individual and culture which produces identity and new culture; the individual and community produces social action and change. Chicano Studies mean, in the final analysis, the re-discovery and the re-conquest of the self and of the community by Chicanos.[19]

The framers of the *Plan* were not concerned with changing the university as much as they were with applying its resources to the needs of the Chicano community. They correctly perceived the university as a generator and distributor of knowledge and hypothesized that Chicano access to the university could result in the redirection of its knowledge in the interest of Chicanos.

> The systematic character of the racist relationship between gabacho society and Chicanos will not be altered unless solid research becomes the basis for Chicano political strategy and action. Rigorous analysis of conditions must be undertaken, issues identified, and priorities determined as Chicanos adopt strategies and develop tactics for the purpose of realigning our community's structural relationship to gabacho society . . . knowledge (can be) applied through university-sponsored programs, as well as by spin-off organizations, in the Chicano community.[20]

The *Plan,* however, did not spell out how in fact the university could be compelled to produce knowledge in the interest of Chicanos.

PROBLEMS AND PROGRESS OF CHICANO STUDIES

By the time the *Plan de Santa Bárbara* was published, many of the Chicano Studies programs that had previously been in the process of creation were deeply embroiled in struggles with campus administrations over the questions of control, funding, objectives, role of students, and staffing. The response of the university was largely negative toward implementation of those programs, as they were perceived to be counter to the interest and purpose of the university. Students strikes at San Francisco State College in 1968 and at the University of California, Berkeley, in 1969 demanding Chicano and Ethnic Studies had resulted in violent confrontations between police and student protestors. Although approval of those programs had been given, it was granted out of political expediency in the interest of stabilizing the campus. It was not granted because it was believed that those programs offered a viable academic orientation. At Fresno State College the administration dealt severely with the efforts on the part of Chicano faculty to allow students and community representatives a voice in the governance of the Chicano Studies program. All the faculty was fired, and the program was temporarily shut down until the administration hired new faculty it perceived more in accord with an "academic orientation."

Chicano Studies programs were also characterized by internal divisions over emphasis and priorities. At UCLA the director of the Chicano Studies Center, a Chicano sociologist who had been recruited from Yale University, was asked to resign by MECHA on the grounds that he was pursuing the objectives of UCLA and not the students' or the Chicano community.[21] At the California State University at San Diego, Chicano faculty who up until 1973 were developing a Marxist orientation were ousted by those who represented "cultural and revolutionary nationalist concepts."[22] At the California State University at Northridge, Chicano Studies became divided over the issue of sexism that emerged over the firing of a woman faculty member.[23]

In the midst of all the political conflict that characterized the creation and implementation of Chicano Studies programs, students and faculty nevertheless made substantial progress in the area of research that eventually contributed to the definition of Chicano Studies as a distinct and legitimate academic field of study in the university. The writings that appeared in the Berkeley-based journal, *El Grito,* prior to the Santa Barbara conference, gave intellectual credence to the rhetoric and ideology emanating from the student movement that was essentially a product of the emotionalism of the time. These writings exposed the negative myths and stereotypes about Chicanos that had been generated by white academia. They were the initial critiques of social science that profoundly influenced the direction of Chicano research in the early developmental stages of Chicano Studies.

After the Santa Barbara conference, MECHA activists at the UCLA campus founded another journal named *Aztlán: Chicano Journal of the Social Sciences and the Arts*. Its stated purpose was to "promote an active quest for solutions to the problems of the barrios of America" and to "focus scholarly discussion and analysis of Chicano matters as they relate to the group and to the total American society."[24] The fact that it was named *Aztlán* reflected a commitment to the goals of the student movement and the larger Chicano struggle that was in the process of emerging throughout the southwestern United States. Specifically, it reflected a concern on the part of the editors to generate the kind of research called for by the *Plan de Santa Bárbara* to produce knowledge about the historical conditions and struggles of Chicanos that would be useful to the development of a distinct Chicano consciousness.

The primary research thrust during the early phases of Chicano Studies development came from those in the disciplines of history and the social sciences. Most were graduate students involved as part-time or full-time faculty in Chicano Studies programs while simultaneously pursuing their doctoral degrees in traditional academic departments. Some of them had been active in the formation of Chicano caucuses in the various professional associations of their respective disciplines where they promoted Chicano interests and called for new research directions that could benefit the Chicano community. These caucuses eventually merged into the National Caucus of Chicano Social Scientists. At a conference held at the New Mexico Highlands University in May 1973, a proposal was drafted to create a national professional association that could generate the "committed scholarship" necessary to "contribute to Chicano liberation."[25] It was also agreed that traditional social science research was to be discouraged within the proposed new association in favor of more critical analysis and that the goals of Chicano research would be the following:

(1) Social Science research by Chicanos must be much more problem-oriented than traditional social science; . . . scholarship cannot be justified for its own sake; (2) . . . research projects must be *interdisciplinary* in nature . . . traditional disciplines(s) . . . serve . . . to fragment our research in a highly artificial manner, and to obscure the interconnections among variables that operate to maintain the oppression of our people; (3) . . . research and action should exist in a dialectical relationship . . . in order to bridge the gap between theory and action, Chicano social scientists must develop close ties with community action groups; (4) Chicano social science must be highly *critical* . . . of American institutions . . . ; (5) . . . We must study the Chicano community . . . within the context of those dominant institutional relationships that affect Chicanos . . . research has to do with the relationship between class, race, and culture in determining the Chicano's historical experience.[26]

The National Caucus became the National Association of Chicano Social Scientists. The first annual meeting of the new association was held at the University of California, Irvine, in May 1973. Two years later at the annual meeting held at the University of California, Berkeley, the association changed its name to the National Association for Chicano Studies (NACS) in the interest of expanding its constituency to include Chicano scholars from the humanities. It became and remains the official professional association for Chicano Studies in the same context that traditional academic disciplines have developed their respective professional associations.

IMPACT OF CHICANO STUDIES

The development of Chicano Studies has been a largely uneven process. The field is characterized by a diversity of perspectives, approaches, theoretical frameworks, and methodologies. The limitations that have been imposed on Chicano Studies by a generally unsympathetic and at times hostile university have not resulted in the elimination of programs.[27] On the contrary, those programs have survived and some have even grown. Scholars of Mexican descent in both traditional academic departments and Chicano Studies programs have collectively built an impressive intellectual tradition of critical inquiry and advocacy. This tradition began with the works of the late George Sánchez,[28] Ernesto Galarza,[29] Américo Paredes,[30] and Julián Samora.[31] Prior to the creation of Chicano Studies, these men were the only visible scholars of Mexican descent in the United States engaged in serious research on the Chicano experience.

The fruit of their collective labor is beginning to show results as they are finally at the stage of producing important works based on the research they have been doing since the late 1960s. Many scholars who have been key participants in the National Association for Chicano Studies have published books that have contributed to the field of Chicano Studies, to the humanities, and to the social sciences. These scholars include Rudolfo Acuña whose book *Occupied America: The Chicano's Struggle for Liberation* was the first book published by a scholar in Chicano Studies.[32] They also include Mario Barrera, whose work *Race and Class in the Southwest: A Theory of Racial Inequality* was judged the best book of the year in 1979 in the area of ethnic and racial politics by the American Political Science Association.[33] Other scholars involved with Chicano Studies research who have also published important books in recent years are Albert Camarillo,[34] Mario García,[35] Oscar Martínez,[36] Alfredo Mirandé and Evangelina Enríquez,[37] Juan Gómez-Quiñones,[38] Félix Gutiérrez and Jorge Reina Schement,[39] Richard Griswold del Castillo,[40] Juan Bruce-Novoa,[41] and Jorge Huerta.[42] All of these works collectively reflect the fact that Chicano Studies has evolved from what was a turbulent history during its early stages of development, into an important and legitimate field of academic study in the university. Chicano Studies, in summary, has profoundly contributed to the development of a generation of Chicano intellectuals and professionals that has played a central role in promoting equal access to the advancement in higher education for students, administrative staff, and faculty of Mexican and Latino descent. This intellectual presence is making a significant impact on both the Chicano community and the larger society.

NOTES

1. There are a total of nineteen in these systems. In addition, there are some in community college and private universities, such as Claremont University. Colorado has the next highest number of programs with a total of four.

2. *El Grito: A Journal of Contemporary Mexican-American Thought,* vol. 1, no. 1 (Fall 1967), p. 4.

3. Ibid.

4. In 1968 there was only a handful of Chicano academics with a Ph.D. in the disciplines of history or the social sciences in the entire United States.

5. "Proposal for Raza Studies," n.d. Author's files.

6. Pamphlet, "BSC-MAYA Demands," n.d. Author's files.

7. "MASC Proposal for a Third World College," n.d. Author's files.

8. "Proposal for a Mexican American Cultural Center," n.d. Author's files.

9. The name of the college was later changed to its present name of California State University at Northridge. The proposal was drafted by Rodolfo Acuña and appears in its entirety in *El Plan de Santa Bárbara: A Chicano Plan for Higher Education* (Oakland: La Causa Publications, 1969), pp. 104–05.

10. Jesús Chavarría, "A Proposal for a Chicano Studies Program: The Santa Barbara Model," in Ibid., pp. 92–102.

11. Letter dated March 12, 1969. Author's files.

12. *El Plan de Santa Bárbara,* p. 10.

13. Letter, n.d. Author's files.

14. Thirty-three people served on the CCHE Steering Committee. The six editors of the document were René Núñez, Jesús Chavarría, Fernando de Necochea, Juan Gómez-Quinoñes, Paul Sánchez, and Armando Valdez.

15. *El Plan de Santa Bárbara,* p. 92.

16. Ibid., p. 93.

17. Ibid.

18. Juan Gómez-Quinoñes, "To Leave to Hope or Chance: Propositions on Chicano Studies, 1973," in *Parameters of Institutional Change: Chicano Experiences in Education* (Hayward, Calif.: Southwest Network, 1974), pp. 154–56.

19. *El Plan de Santa Bárbara,* p. 40.

20. Ibid., p. 78.

21. "Letter to the Editor," *La Gente,* Feb. 27, 1973. *La Gente* is the Chicano student newspaper at UCLA.

22. Chicano Affairs Governing Board, "Position Paper," n.d. Author's files.

23. Editorial, *La Gente,* March 1973, p. 2.

24. *Aztlán: Chicano Journal of the Social Sciences and the Arts,* vol. 1, no. 1 (Fall 1970), p. vi. The name was later changed to *Aztlán: International Journal of Chicano Studies Research.*

25. Appendix II in Reynaldo Flores Macias, ed., *Perspectives En Chicano Studies* (Los Angeles: UCLA Chicano Studies Center Publications, 1977), pp. 214–20 is a report of the conference.

26. Ibid., pp. 215–16.

27. For a discussion on the issues related to this point see Dan Moreno and Rudy Torres, eds., *The Political Economy of Institutional Change: Proceedings of the Ethnic Studies Symposium* (Irvine, Calif.: Program in Comparative Culture, 1977).

28. His best known work was: George Sánchez, *Forgotten People* (Albuquerque: University of New Mexico Press, 1940).

29. See, for example, Ernesto Galarza, *The Merchants of Labor* (Santa Barbara: McNally and Loftin, 1964).

30. Américo Paredes' *With a Pistol in His Hand* (Austin: University of Texas Press, 1958) has become a classic in the field.

31. His most recent work is: Julián Samora, *Gunpowder Justice: A Reassessment of the Texas Rangers* (Notre Dame: University of Notre Dame Press, 1979).

32. Rudolfo Acuña, *Occupied America: The Chicano's Struggle for Liberation* (San Francisco: Canfield Press, 1972). A second edition has recently been published with a new subtitle of *A History of Chicanos* (New York: Harper and Row, 1981).

33. Mario Barrera, *Race and Class in the Southwest: A Theory of Racial Inequality* (Notre Dame: University of Notre Dame Press, 1979). The award is called the "Ethnic and Cultural Pluralism Award."

34. Alberto Camarillo, *Chicanos in a Changing Society* (Cambridge: Harvard University Press, 1979).

35. Mario García, *Desert Immigrants: The Mexicans of El Paso, 1880–1920* (New Haven: Yale University Press, 1981).

36. Oscar Martínez, *Border Boom Town: Cuidad Juárez* (Austin: University of Texas Press, 1978).

37. Alfredo Mirandé and Evangelina Enríquez, *La Chicana* (Chicago: University of Chicago Press, 1979).

38. Juan Gómez-Quinoñes, *Sembradores: Ricardo Flores Magon Y El Partido Liberal* (Los Angeles: Aztlán Publications, 1973).

39. Félix Gutiérrez and Jorge Reina Schement, *Spanish-Language Radio in the Southwestern United States* (Berkeley: University of California Press, 1979).

40. Richard Griswold del Castillo, *The Los Angeles Barrio, 1850–1890: A Social History* (Berkeley: University of California Press, 1979).

41. Juan Bruce-Novoa, *Chicano Authors: Inquiry by Interview* (Austin: University of Texas Press, 1980).

42. Jorge Huerta, *Chicano Theater: Themes and Forms* (Ypsilanti, Mich.: Bilingual Press/Editorial Bilingüe, 1981).

II | History, Social Structure, and Politics

Overview

Historically, Chicanos have been seen as a rural population. The fact that at least since 1930 the overwhelming majority of the Chicano population has been concentrated in the urban centers of the country has been neglected. One result of this oversight has been that the experience of Chicanos in the cities has been neglected. Albert Camarillo takes us one step toward remedying these oversights. Camarillo offers an overview of the most significant dimensions and questions regarding the urban experience of the Chicano community in the latter part of the nineteenth century and the twentieth century. Camarillo provides for the first time some insights into the Chicano urban experience and suggests a framework for the study of Chicano urban history. This framework will help shed some light on the continuities and changes as well as the unique and shared dimensions of the Chicano urban experience in the nineteenth and twentieth centuries.

In some of the literature on Chicanos, they are often portrayed as a homogeneous class population. Such a portrayal is misleading, as Mario Barrera, one of the most prominent scholars in the field of Chicano Studies, shows in his discussion of the class structure of the Chicano community. This community, in reality, has an extensive amount of class diversity that must be acknowledged. The class structure, Barrera notes, is the product of a long historical development in the Southwest. From the latter part of the nineteenth century to the present, Chicanos have been represented in all classes that make up the class structure of the United States but not on the basis of equality with members of the Anglo population. Today, Chicanos are still represented in all of the classes comprising the class structure of American society: in the capitalist, the petty bourgeois, and the working classes. And, as in the past, they continue to lack representation on the basis of equality with segments of the Anglo population.

Throughout the latter part of the nineteenth century and the decades of the twentieth century, the contours of the Mexican community in the United States have been substantially influenced by the continual movement, both legal and illegal, of Mexican citizens across the United States-Mexico border. In his article, Juan Gómez-Quiñones examines the roots, character, impact, and recent politics of the immigration. He notes that it is an integral part of the global evolution of capitalism. Without recognition of this fact its origins, persistence, and significance cannot be adequately grasped. The immigration, he reveals, is a movement of human beings whose ability to sustain a livelihood has been made problematic. These individuals aspire to a decent livelihood, come from distinct regions of Mexico, exhibit distinct characteristics, and perform critical social, economic, and political functions that make them invaluable to some sectors of American society. Throughout the twentieth century they have been the targets of various governmental measures designed to restrict their movement across the border and of hostility from sectors of American society that have perceived Mexicans as a threat to American interests. The Mexican's presence has had profound consequences for American society and for life in the Mexican community. In the latter part of the seventies, Gómez-Quiñones reveals, their presence animated political life in the United States and stimulated debates and activities that continue in the decade of the eighties.

Lastly, Christine Sierra examines the political arrangements, practices, and processes that have set parameters in which contemporary political endeavors in the Mexican community have evolved. In contrast to Gómez-Quiñones, she asks and provides answers to two questions: What factors in the political history of Mexicans in the United States distinguish this group from other minority groups, especially white ethnic groups and blacks? and, How have these factors affected the organizational history of Mexicans in the United States?

In the political history of the Mexican community, she notes, four factors have set the context within which contemporary Chicano political development evolves. These are: (1) the status of Mexicans in the United States as a "people of conquest"; (2) the nature of Mexican immigration to the United States; (3) the nature of the Mexican work experience; and (4) the organizational experience required by Mexicans as an ethnic group in the United States. Each of these factors helped to shape the antecedent conditions to Chicano political development. The conquest of the Mexican population, for example, led to three processes of political significance: the usurpation of Mexican land rights, the replacement of Mexican institutional structures and procedures with Anglo-American ones, and the suppression of the cultural autonomy of the Mexican population. Combined with the other factors it assured that the political development of the Mexican population would not be identical to the course of political development blazed by immigrant groups from Europe.

Together with the preceding articles, Sierra's article provides insights into the unique and critical aspects of the Chicano experience, the diverse nature of the Mexican population and the factors that have shaped its existence in American society. And, it exemplifies, as do the other articles, the kind of research recently conducted and currently being pursued by scholars in Chicano Studies.

2 | Chicanos in the American City

ALBERT CAMARILLO

"That extraordinary vessel, the American melting pot, is bubbling once again," a cover story in an issue of *Time* magazine claimed. The article further stated that Chicanos, and Hispanic Americans in general, "as America's latest great wave of immigrants . . . are learning another hard lesson: latecomers start at the bottom."[1] The *Time* perspective on Chicanos[2] as the "last group in" for the race of social mobility in the United States characterizes the public's and much of the scholarly community's misunderstanding of the historical reality of this ethnic group. On the one hand, this perspective on Mexican Americans beclouds and negates the centuries of historical influences that have shaped the contemporary status of the group. On the other hand, this application of standard assimilation theory to the Chicano case places the group squarely within the traditional historical framework, one that focuses primarily on the integration of immigrant groups, usually Europeans, into mainstream American society. Chicano history thus becomes simply the story of another immigrant group awaiting its turn to experience the "American dream" of upward social mobility. The study of Chicano history must be analyzed beyond the scope of the twentieth century and beyond the framework of assimilation theory. Furthermore, the Chicano historical experience, in order to be placed in a larger national perspective, must also be compared with that of the other major ethnic and immigrant groups in United States history.

The intent of this article is, therefore, twofold. The primary objective is to provide a framework for the study of a national Chicano urban history by outlining the major historical questions and patterns for the nineteenth and twentieth centuries; and, secondarily, to provide some brief comparative generalizations between Chicano, black, and European immigrant urban history. One may, of course, pose the question: Why focus on Chicano "urban" history, when not until 1930 did a majority of the Mexican population in the United States live in cities? Throughout the nineteenth century a large percentage of the Mexican population continued to inhabit their pueblos, many of which became the growing American cities of the Southwest. These expanding cities and barrios provide, therefore, the best context in which to study the socioeconomic, political, and cultural contact that occurred between Anglos and Mexicans over time. The patterns that evolved in the cities, moreover, are more clearly discernible than those which occur elsewhere. Yet, these experiences of urban Chicanos vis-à-vis the dominant society are parallel to those experienced by rural Chicanos. The cities, finally, are the centers where both Anglos and Chicanos come to reside with greater frequency each decade. It is, therefore, more appropriate to focus on the urban context, where the great majority of Chicanos—about eighty to ninety percent—and other Americans live today, and to trace the historical experience of these city dwellers.

ORIGINS OF DOMINANT-SUBORDINATE RELATIONSHIPS IN THE NEW AMERICAN SOUTHWEST, 1848–1900

Perhaps the central question for examining Chicano urban history in the nineteenth century is, How and when do patterns of dominant-subordinate relationships between Anglos and Mexicans manifest themselves during the period following the Mexican-American War? For the purpose of this article, suffice it to say that prior to the war initial economic penetration by Americans and conflictual racial attitudes were already well-established. However, it is not until after 1848, when Americans begin to systematically colonize the Southwest through immigration and steady economic development, that distinct patterns of dominant-subordinate relationships occur between the two groups. These relationships are particularly evident in those existing Mexican pueblos that began to experience rapid transition into urban barrios as the young American cities began to expand in, near, and around them.

The socioeconomic and political status of future generations of Mexican Americans was formed during the closing decades of the nineteenth century as Chicanos were relegated to a subordinate position within the developing new American Southwest. Clearly, throughout the Southwest by the turn of the century a structure of dominant-subordinate relationships had been established for Chicanos as an ethnic minority group. To understand the development of the racial and class subordination of Mexicans during the second half of the nineteenth century, four related historical processes must be analyzed. These processes are: (1) land loss and economic displacement; (2) political powerlessness; (3) barrioization; and (4) proletarianization. Directly influencing each of these processes in the new American Southwest was the development of a racial order that had historically maintained the exclusion and subordination of nonwhite peoples.

Land Loss and Economic Displacement

From the beginning, colonization and settlement of the present-day Southwest by the Indian-mestizo-mulatto people from Mexico was based on a pastoral economy. Vital to the continuation of this precapitalist, semifeudal economic system was the Mexican ownership of land, both private and communal. From Texas to California, the pastoral economy and subsistence agriculture had left an indelible stamp on the society of the far northern frontier of New Spain and Mexico. Although the development of the pastoral economy varied to some degree in each province of northern Mexico—from large private landholdings in California, to smaller rancho land ownership in Texas, to patterns of communal landholdings in New Mexico—livestock raising remained the primary organizing force in Mexican society. The occupational structure as well as the social and political structures of society were directly linked to the continuation of a pastoral form of production. Everything from the *compadrazgo* system of godparent relationships to patterns of patron leadership were greatly influenced by the traditions and occupational activities associated with the Mexican pastoral economy. Needless to say, therefore, the Mexican land loss in the decades following the Mexican-American War, which resulted in the destruction of the pastoral economy, had far-reaching repercussions for Chicanos in the new American Southwest. Loss of Mexican-owned ranchos and pueblo communal lands altered the nature of the economy, radically changed the land tenure and land-use system, and eventually led to the economic exploitation of the Mexican people. Once the subdivision of rancho and pueblo lands had begun, the dominance of the emerging economic system of American capitalism in the once-Mexican region was a foregone conclusion. The process of land loss and displacement of the Mexican pastoral economy was fairly complete throughout the Southwest by the 1880s.[3]

For the Chicanos who inhabited the old pueblo areas within the growing American cities, the loss of Mexican-owned land created a series of negative influences upon their lives. The loss of rancho lands in the hinterlands, the loss of communal pueblo lands for family livestock raising and subsistence gardening, and the introduction of American capitalism in the region initiated many disruptive forces within the pueblo populations: occupational dislocation, economic impoverishment, residential segregation, and political powerlessness.

Political Powerlessness

Land loss and economic displacement occurred simultaneously with Mexican political powerlessness. The efforts by Anglo Americans to divest Mexicans of their land and to remove them from institutions of political control were mutually supporting. In order to wrest political control from the traditional Mexican patron and his mestizo constituency, Americans had to undermine the politico's economic influence. As the Mexican leaders' and their followers' economic status began to decline and as the Anglo population continued to increase, the balance of political power began to shift. Once Anglos acquired more political influence at the territorial, state, and local levels, the process of

Mexican land loss and political decline increased. The traditional Mexican leadership began to dissolve and Anglos gained increasing control of the political and judicial apparatus. Consequently, Chicanos throughout the Southwest exercised less control over their political destiny. By the last two decades of the nineteenth century Mexicans from Texas to California, with the possible exception of parts of New Mexico, had been excluded from the political process. For the most part Chicanos in the cities of the Southwest became a leaderless, disenfranchised, and politically powerless sector of the population. In different cities throughout the region the Mexican population would be denied meaningful participation in the political structure due to gerrymandering, racial exclusion from political parties, poll taxes, loss of leadership, minority voter status, and other reasons.[4]

The process of political powerlessness that evolved at different times in different cities shaped the political reality of Chicanos from that point. Together with economic displacement, increasing impoverishment, and lack of political-judicial representation, Chicanos fell victim to a system that placed them at the bottom of society. This subordinate status in the developing American urban society throughout the Southwest was perhaps best reflected in their barrioization and residential segregation.

Process of Barrioization

As early as the 1850s in some towns and as late as the 1880s in others, the forces of political powerlessness, economic displacement, and growing racial separation combined to create a new reality for people of Mexican descent in the Southwest. Although rural Chicanos shared much the same status as their urban counterparts, those Chicanos who remained in the old pueblo areas faced the full impact of being a racial minority group in a dominant white society. The process by which the once Mexican pueblos became urban barrios was a complex one. This barrioization process was most visibly characterized by increasing Chicano residential segregation, but it also involved the sociocultural and political accommodation of Mexican people to their new reality. Barrioization, furthermore, was the result of the larger developments of Americanization, urbanization, and racial-cultural separation occurring throughout the region. The loss of political representation and steady economic decline accelerated the process.

Several types of barrioization unfolded within the cities of the Southwest during the second half of the nineteenth century. Los Angeles, for example, experienced a type of barrioization common elsewhere. The old pueblo area, known to Anglos as Sonoratown, became a central-area barrio within the American city which began to expand around it. Increasingly hemmed in by business and residential development in the growing city, Chicanos remained within this area of settlement which had been the home of mestizo peoples for over one hundred years. Another type of barrioization, characteristic of Santa Barbara and San Antonio for example, was the development of contiguous American sections of a city next to the old pueblo settlements. Residential segregation between the two distinct sections of the cities was clearly drawn from the beginning of substantial Anglo immigration. As the demographic and numerical balance shifted toward the Anglo community, contact between the two groups was further minimized. A third type of barrioization can be classified as geographic isolation and economic strangulation. This type occurred in southern California, and perhaps elsewhere, when Anglos decided to locate their settlements away from but near the old Mexican pueblos. American business and political interests drew economic development away from the old pueblos and neglected and harrassed the nearby Mexican communities; for example, Anglos enacted laws designed to disrupt Mexican pastoral activity and sociocultural life styles. As a result, the pueblo settlements began to experience population decline and economic strangulation. Some, like Old Town San Diego, lost much of their cohesiveness as a Mexican town by the turn of the century; others, like Agua Mansa and La Placita in the San Bernardino Valley of southern California, ceased to exist in the twentieth century. A fourth type of barrioization was characterized by Chicano communities that continued to maintain numerical superiority over Anglos, but had lost the economic and political control of their towns. Such places as Santa Fe, New Mexico and El Paso, Texas are examples of cities where the controlling Anglo minority lived in the small "American" sections of the town yet were able to keep Mexicans segregated through political and law enforcement practices. Oftentimes the Anglo elite of these towns ruled in consort with the Mexican elite, the latter usually more concerned with personal gain than with providing representation and leadership for the Mexican majority.[5]

Although the process of barrioization was characterized by socioeconomic segregation, which negatively affected Chicanos, there were positive elements of barrioization as well. At a time when many external negative forces threatened the very existence of Chicanos' urban society, Chicanos accommodated to their new reality by reestablishing their ethnic, cultural cohesiveness as a group and by creating new sources of organization. Throughout the Southwest, Chicano mutual aid associations, Mexican patriotic organizations, and Spanish-language newspapers provided some of the necessary societal unity that was so crucial to Chicanos during a period of disruption.[6]

Proletarianization of the Chicano Working Class

The poverty reflected in the urban barrios throughout the Southwest during the nineteenth century was the direct result of occupational dislocation and land loss. As the pastoral economy was steadily replaced by the spread of American capitalism the occupations in which Mexicans were once engaged became increasingly obsolete. With each passing decade more and more displaced Chicano workers entered the expanding urban labor market as unskilled, semiskilled menial workers. By the 1890s the pattern of employment for Chicanos was becoming well-established. Men worked in a variety of low paying, unskilled jobs in service industries, transportation, and construction. Women were also drawn into work outside the home for the first time in substantial numbers; they became cannery workers, domestics, and laundresses. In addition, a common employment pattern that developed during the late nineteenth century was the periodic migration of urban Chicano families to the farmlands for seasonal agricultural harvests.[7]

Elsewhere in the Southwest, Chicano workers in the cities increasingly occupied the lowest levels of the occupational structure. This was particularly evident in many California cities where, for example, the Chinese exclusion movement created a greater need for menial labor. In the other areas of the Southwest, Texas for example, the low status of the Chicano work force was shared by blacks. The Chicano working class by the turn of the century, therefore, had become an impoverished, predominantly unskilled, menial work force that had little or no chance for upward occupational mobility—Chicanos were fixed to the bottom of the socioeconomic structure.[8] The proletarianization process—the dislocation from pastoral occupations, the loss of a land base, entry into the capitalist labor market, and occupational immobility within the lowest strata of the occupational structure—that significantly shaped the making of the Chicano working class affected both native and foreign-born Mexicans and continued into the twentieth century.

The processes of land loss, economic displacement, political powerlessness, and proletarianization during the second half of the nineteenth century together shaped the contours of Chicano urban history. From the beginning of continuous contact between Mexicans and Anglo Americans and in all subsequent interactions between the two peoples conflictual race relations played a crucial role. As Anglo-American hegemony in the Southwest was established, antagonistic racial attitudes laid the basis for the development of subordinate-dominant relationships that continued in the decades after the Mexican-American War. The subordinate racial status of Chicanos was supported and reinforced by their class status. As a group of poor, unskilled workers cemented to the bottom of the occupational structure, Chicanos had entered an increasingly stratified system based on class and race within the capitalist labor market of the urban Southwest.

In my opinion and in the opinion of other scholars, a fundamental question for future research in Chicano history—and for the history of other racial minority groups—thus becomes, How and in what ways have race and class determined the status of Mexicans in the United States society? The task of the historian, both professional and student, is, however, complicated by the lack of information needed to place Chicano urban history within a larger historical framework. Writing Chicano history necessarily entails filling in gaps in the urban, economic, and social historiography of the Southwest and viewing this regional history within the broader context of United States history.

THE TWENTIETH CENTURY: 1900 TO WORLD WAR II

The study of twentieth-century Chicano urban history is perhaps best viewed from two perspectives. First, it is essential to analyze what major socioeconomic, political, and demographic continuities from the nineteenth century persist into the twentieth century. Likewise, it is important to understand the changes that took place after 1900. Second, by examining these continuities and changes in Chicano urban history one must determine whether the racial and class stratification of Chicanos is perpetuated and more firmly established in American society during the twentieth century. Or, do Chicanos, like many European immigrant groups, begin to experience avenues of social and occupational mobility which provide them means of escaping their subordinate socioeconomic status?

In order to analyze these fundamental questions about Chicano urban history, one must examine some of the major developments of the period: (1) growing complexity of Southwestern urbanization; (2) dramatic economic development in the cities; (3) differential population and economic growth within the region; (4) migration of both native-born and foreign-born whites to the cities; and (5) Mexican migration to the cities throughout the United States (the immigration of foreign-born as well as the rural to urban migration of native-born). In studying these historical developments it is useful to look at Eric Lampard's model for analyzing components of urbanization. Lampard's framework has been adopted by historian Ricardo Romo for his study of Chicano urban history during the early twentieth century in the Southwest. However, while Lampard's model is useful in providing insight into the larger framework of twentieth-century urbanization, it is inadequate for examining patterns of continuity and change in Chicano urban history between nineteenth-century origins and twentieth-century developments.[9]

By the twentieth-century certain nineteenth-century developments, such as Mexican land loss and political powerlessness, had run their course. Other patterns such as barrioization and proletarianization were, however, still evolving due to changes occurring during the new century. To examine more effectively the Chicano urban experience during the early twentieth century, it is necessary to analyze three important developments: (1) new and continuing processes of barrioization; (2) patterns in the racial and class stratification of the expanding urban labor market; and (3) relationships of Chicanos to the institutional and political structures of cities.

Barrioization

The new and continuing processes of twentieth-century barrioization involved more than simply urban residential settlement of Mexican people. Much like its nineteenth-century origins, barrioization during the 1900s was indeed a complex process that included social and cultural adjustment to a new urban environment, an environment that usually segregated Chicanos from the mainstream of American society. Barrioization involved occupational as well as social adjustments, especially for the many newcomers to the urban barrios who had migrated from an agrarian society either in Mexico or in other parts of the Southwest.

By using barrioization as a framework of study within the larger framework of urbanization, historians can examine the urban social history of the groups and can trace continuities of Chicano barrio life from the nineteenth century. In addition, it allows one to gauge the changes that occur in the twentieth century. By focusing on the subprocesses which make up the complex phenomenon of barrioization, the historian can better relate the social, cultural, and organizational activity of Mexican Americans to the residential and demographic configurations of their communities in any given city. The complexities of Chicano urban social history are only now beginning to be understood more fully and await further investigation by scholars.

During the first three decades of the twentieth century, the dramatic increase in the Mexican population in the United States, because of immigration from Mexico, had profound impact upon urbanization and barrioization. Although barrioization was undergoing significant change during the early twentieth century, one fundamental pattern from the nineteenth century persisted—the vast majority of urban Chicanos continued to live in impoverished, residentially segregated areas in the southwestern cities. Three types of barrioization occurred during the first four decades of the twentieth century that reflect the continuing and newer processes of Chicano urban settlement. Each type, it must be remembered, was shaped by different local as well as regional economic and cultural-racial factors.

In most major urban locales throughout the Southwest during the early twentieth century, the old pueblo-barrios still contained the majority of the Mexican population. Sociocultural life, the Spanish language, ethnic shops and restaurants were maintained in those "old Mexican sections" of many young but growing American cities. It was natural, then, that such cities as Los Angeles, San Antonio, San Francisco, El Paso, Tucson, and others would attract tens of thousands of new arrivals from Mexico. The large numbers of new residents to the old pueblo-barrios, together with the continued urbanization of southwestern cities, began to change the character of these historical areas of Mexican settlement. Some began to expand outward from the boundaries of the old barrios as population increase and the growth of the contiguous Anglo sections of the city pushed Chicanos out. This growth-displacement effect resulted oftentimes in the suburbanization of Chicano barrios away from the city center or in the expansion of settlement in and around the old barrio. This pattern of barrioization was greatly influenced by the work-settlement factor, for proximity to employment and availability of low cost housing was a primary consideration for locating in any city.[10]

Two additional types of barrioization began to evolve during the early twentieth century as thousands of new Mexican residents settled in communities where no prior Chicano barrio or colonia had existed. The creation of new urban barrios can be differentiated by region. First, in many of the newer, expanding cities in the Southwest, Chicano barrios soon developed as thousands of people came to these urban areas in search of employment. In cities like Houston, Dallas, San Diego (New Town), San Jose, and Phoenix the origins of their contemporary barrio populations date from the pre-Depression period. In addition, in booming southwestern cities, such as Los Angeles, where a central barrio had existed for several generations, other smaller barrios were established throughout the greater metropolitan areas.

A second type of barrio development occurred outside the Southwest. By World War I small ethnic enclaves of Mexicans began to appear in cities in the Midwest, the Great Lakes, and the Northeast. The manpower shortages during the First World War and the increased restrictions placed upon immigration from Europe during the early 1920s created a greater demand for Mexican labor. The small but growing barrios of Kansas City, Omaha, St. Louis, Chicago, Detroit, Minneapolis, and Bethlehem, Pennsylvania, for example, were created as Mexican workers were recruited by northern industrialists seeking additional pools of unskilled labor. In other cases, agricultural interests from the Midwest recruited Mexican labor during the seasonal harvest periods and many workers decided to remain in nearby cities instead of returning to the Southwest. The urban barrios of the midwestern and Great Lakes states, some originating as labor camps, steadily expanded. These barrios were typically located near the sources of employment for which Mexicans were initially recruited—meat packing plants, railroad yards, steel manufacturers, and other facilities of commerce and industry. Although the great majority of the Mexican population remained in the Southwest, the group was becoming for the first time a national rather than a regional minority.[11]

The Persistence of Racial and Class Stratification

Twentieth-century barrioization clearly reflected the continuing racial and class separation of Chicanos from the mainstream of American urban society.

Impoverishment, residential segregation, educational segregation, and many other forms of racial discrimination were part of the daily lives of most Mexicans in the United States. Also evident was the racial and class stratification of Chicanos within the expanding labor market in the cities. Their subordinate class status as workers continued to reinforce their subordinate status as a racial minority and vice versa.

The predominant patterns of labor-market participation of Chicanos during the first four decades of the twentieth century were characterized by the following: (1) occupational immobility; (2) predominance within the menial, semiskilled-unskilled sectors of the occupational structure; and (3) exploitation of workers, particularly through the disproportionate use of contract labor and other abusive practices. These trends were the product of Chicano proletarianization originating during the late nineteenth century. Although these same patterns persist in the twentieth century, the creation of new jobs and new forms of racial-class domination helped solidify the existing stratification of Mexicans within the capitalist labor market.

The differential economic development of cities in the United States where Chicanos formed part of the labor force determined the range of employment opportunities available to them. In smaller cities, for example, Chicano males continued to work as unskilled-semiskilled workers in the construction, maintenance, and transportation industries as well as in the seasonal agricultural harvests. Chicanas and children participated in these seasonal agricultural migrations but also worked in the agricultural-related industries (canneries and packing houses) and in service industries (as domestics, laundresses). In the larger cities, where increasing industrialization and diversification of the urban economy was rapidly taking place, the growing number of Chicano workers discovered that newer types of employment were also available to them. Thus, while Mexican workers continued to labor in the more traditional occupations open to them, they were also incorporated into the various manufacturing, textile, light and heavy industrial sectors of the expanding urban labor market. Though a small percentage of Chicanos were able to achieve skilled or low white-collar status, the vast majority of workers in both new and older occupations were restricted to the lowest strata of the occupational structure. This subordinate class status was further reinforced by such employer practices as racial and sexual wage differentials (a lower wage paid to Chicanos and Chicanas than paid to white workers who performed the same function), the contract labor system (an exploitative system most common in the construction and transportation industries), and suppression of Chicano labor unionism.[12]

In several cities in the Southwest, Chicanos became the backbone of the unskilled labor force. In many other areas they formed part of the growing working class composed primarily of European immigrants (first and second generation) and blacks who had migrated to northern cities and who later migrated west to California. But Chicanos, unlike their white counterparts, were virtually locked into the bottom of the occupational structure. Upward occupational mobility for the great majority of workers prior to World War II was almost unattainable whether one was fifth generation native-born or first generation of foreign-born parents.

Obviously, research into the status of Mexican workers in the United States is needed. Of those studies already completed and those in progress, most research indicates that the aforementioned patterns of the Chicano working class were clearly the dominant ones before World War II. Questions of occupational mobility—intergenerational and intragenerational—and the relationships between class and race within the urban labor market should continue to guide future studies.

Relationships of Chicano Communities to Urban Institutions

A subordinate working class status together with the process of barrioization shaped, to a great extent, the urban Chicano experience during the twentieth century. In order to further understand these developments in Chicano urban history, it is useful to explore the relationships between Chicano communities and the dominant political and societal institutions. To focus on Chicano voter participation in the political structure per se would be of little use since Mexican Americans still remained outside the mainstream of municipal politics. The nineteenth-century pattern of Chicano political powerlessness manifested itself in the absence of widespread naturalization rates among immigrants and in the reluctance of the native-born to participate in electoral politics. (Most of the organizational efforts by Chicanos during this period were directed toward the establishment of mutual aid, civil rights, and labor union organizations instead of traditional party politics.) In studying the relationships between Chicano communities and the dominant political-societal institutions, it is important to determine how these institutions affected the lives of Chicanos in different cities. For example, city governments together with chambers of commerce or boards of realtors often established gerrymandered ethnic political districts and created restrictive real estate convenants that forbade the sale of property to racial minorities in certain sections of a city. City planners, in addition, often established zoning ordinances which dictated where workers could and could not live; the creation of new zoning ordinances frequently resulted in the dislocation of Chicano and other working class families from urban core areas. These formal and informal practices perpetuated racial residential segregation and restricted the geographic mobility of nonwhites. To cite another example, in many cities during the 1920s city social welfare and private charitable agencies initiated "Americanization" programs for Mexicans. When attempts to force Mexicans to discard their cultural and familial traditions failed, these welfare agencies began to define the "Mexican problem" in terms of nonassimilation and welfare relief dependency. By 1930, as the federal government initiated its program of massive deportation of Mexican people from the United States, these same welfare agencies played a vital role in the success of the federal deportation drive. Other areas of research into the impact of societal institutions on the lives of Chicano urban dwellers—the educational system and law enforcement agencies in particular—must be examined. How the relationships evolved between these institutions and Chicanos may help explain why Mexican Americans have historically decried the institutional neglect of their communities and why their experience with municipal institutions has not, for the most part, been a positive one.[13]

POST-WORLD WAR II ERA

Very little research has been conducted in Chicano history for the decades since World War II. In order to fill in basic gaps in historical information, historians and other social scientists have necessarily focused on nineteenth-century roots and early twentieth-century developments; this helps to explain the obvious lack of scholarly research for the more recent period. Thus, perhaps the most appropriate way to deal with Chicano history in our contemporary era is to pose some central questions that provide continuity of research for the pre- and post-war periods.

A basic area of research concerns the occupational status of Chicano workers. Do substantial numbers of Chicanos move up into skilled and white-collar occupations after World War II or does the racial and class stratification of earlier periods continue? Are the rates of intergenerational mobility for second- and third-generation children of foreign-born Mexican parents similar to those for European immigrants and for Anglo workers in general? What impact does the development of a changing urban economy—one becoming less tied to an unskilled, labor intensive work force—have on Chicano workers? Does access to labor union participation alter the occupational opportunities available to Mexican-American workers? Lastly, what factors account for the rise of a small, but identifiable Chicano middle class? Among the few studies that examine the nature of Chicano occupational patterns during the period there is disagreement. While some studies have claimed that the occupational gap between Mexican Americans and Anglo workers is decreasing, other studies have indicated that Chicanos are still distinctly occupationally disadvantaged vis-à-vis nonminority workers.[14]

Another important area of research in post World War II Chicano urban history is the continuing process of barrioization. Do most Chicano urban dwellers remain residentially confined to barrios? Or, do the ongoing trends of metropolitanization and suburbanization of Mexican-American families begin to break down the historic concentration in the urban barrios? To what extent is geographic mobility into Anglo communities realized by Chicanos? Have new patterns of Chicano barrioization developed during the last four decades?

Answers to these questions are particularly important for Chicanos in the Southwest, for they have been the most rapidly urbanizing group in the region since the 1940s. Clearly, anyone who travels through the urban Southwest must conclude that the barrios are not disappearing. In fact, one might conclude with a great deal of accuracy that Chicano barrioization is dramatically increasing once again due to many factors.[15]

A third area of future research concerns Chicanos and the political system. In recent years the numbers of Mexican-American elected officials have increased as have governmental programs in the barrios. Yet several fundamental questions need to be examined to determine whether the political status of Chicano communities significantly has changed. Have Chicanos as an ethnic constituency been able to influence partisan politics at the municipal and state levels? What role has the new middle class played in urban politics during the period? Are programs implemented by the city, state, and federal governments directed toward the roots of problems in the barrios? In what ways did the urban revolt of Chicano communities during the late 1960s and early 1970s reflect their socioeconomic and political conditions? As a rapidly growing minority, will Chicanos play an increasingly more important role in traditional politics or will historic political practices (gerrymandering, neglect by the two political parties, lack of ethnic representation) militate against their becoming as important a political force as their numbers would indicate?[16]

Lastly, all the aforementioned areas of Chicano urban historical research that must be explored have been influenced by the continuing phenomenon of immigration from Mexico. Undocumented Mexican workers in the United States, the great majority of whom became urbanities, have been conservatively estimated at between four and twelve million. Undoubtedly these millions of Mexican urban dwellers have had a great impact on the processes of barrioization, the occupational structure, the economy, and other aspects of urban society. Admittedly, very little is known specifically about the impact of Mexican immigration both within Mexican-American urban communities and within United States society in general. Contemporary Chicano urban history, like the urban history of the early twentieth century, will be incomplete without an examination of the continuing influence and impact of mass migration north from Mexico.[17]

CHICANOS, BLACKS, AND EUROPEAN IMMIGRANTS IN THE AMERICAN CITY: SOME BRIEF COMPARATIVE PERSPECTIVES

In placing Chicano urban history within a larger national historical perspective, it is imperative that the Chicano case be compared with that of other major ethnic and immigrant groups. At a time when white ethnic communities are rapidly disappearing from American urban landscapes, the Chicano barrios continue to expand in the inner cities and throughout the metropolitan districts. The immigrant ghettos of American cities during the late nineteenth and early twentieth centuries have lost their ethnic distinctiveness through geographic mobility, social mobility, and assimilation of later generations. In the persistence of its unique ethnic environment the "perpetual" barrio shares much in common with the "enduring" black ghetto. Chicanos also share with black Americans a distinctive history of restricted occupational-social mobility. While one cannot argue that some economic gap between Chicanos and blacks and the dominant white society has not been bridged, unemployment, underemployment, welfare relief, and other unmistakable historical indices of disadvantaged socioeconomic status still characterize these two largest minority groups in the United States.

Though Mexican Americans and black Americans occupy roughly the same status in United States society, their historical evolution as ethnic minorities is significantly different. Two major developments separate their experiences within the urban historical context. Imported as slaves, Afro Americans were first introduced to cities by slaveowners and were attracted to the northern cities during the great post-Civil War migrations. The origins of their urban experience were, therefore, shaped as they entered the cities as newcomers. The origins of the Chicano urban experience, conversely, was initiated in their native pueblos as Americans began to enter them and established urban centers in the Southwest. A second major divergence in the experience between the two groups is that black settlement in American cities has grown from natural increases in the population and from rural to urban migration. The Chicano population in American cities has also expanded due to these factors, but continued immigration from Mexico has been the main reason for rapid Chicano urbanization during the twentieth century.[18]

Chicano urban history, influenced greatly by immigration from Mexico, certainly has parallels with the history of European immigration to the United States, which cannot be detailed in this paper. Yet, Chicano urban history diverges from the history of European immigrant groups in American cities in many ways. Historical origins in the present-day United States, restricted social mobility patterns, perpetual urban barrios, recurrent waves of immigration as well as other factors separate Chicano urban history from that of traditional immigrant urban history. Undoubtedly, however, the overriding difference between the case of Chicanos and European immigrants has been the extent of historic racial and class stratification that continues to characterize the Chicano urban reality today.[19]

Detailed comparative analyses between Chicano urban history and that of blacks, other racial minorities, and European immigrants will provide an exciting and fascinating area of future research. The first task of historians is, however, to document more thoroughly the history of Chicanos in the American city. Only then will scholars be able to examine the history of the nation's soon-to-be largest minority in light of United States urban history in general.

NOTES

1. October 16, 1978, pp. 48–50.

2. The terms Chicano, Mexican, and Mexican American are used interchangeably in this study. Anglo or Anglo American refers to Americans of European descent.

3. For useful overviews, see the following: Rodolfo Acuña, *Occupied America: The Chicano's Struggle Toward Liberation* (San Francisco: Canfield Press, 1972); David J. Weber, *Foreigners in Their Native Land: Historical Roots of the Mexican American* (Albuquerque: University of New Mexico Press, 1973); Rodman Paul, "The Spanish Americans in the Southwest, 1848–1900," in John G. Clark, ed., *The Frontier Challenge* (Lawrence: University of Kansas Press, 1971). See also, Leonard Pitt, *The Decline of the Californios* (Berkeley: University of California Press, 1966); Albert Camarillo, *Chicanos in a Changing Society: From Mexican Pueblos to American Barrios in Santa Barbara and Southern California, 1848–1930* (Cambridge: Harvard University Press, 1979); David Montejano, "Race, Labor Repression, and Capitalist Agriculture: Notes from South Texas," Institute for the Study of Social Change, Working Paper Series #102, University of California, Berkeley, 1977.

4. Pitt, *Decline of the Californios;* Camarillo, *Chicanos in a Changing Society;* Robert Rosenbaum, "Mexicano vs Americano: A Study of Hispanic-American Resistance to Anglo-American Control in New Mexico Territory, 1870–1900" (Ph.D. dissertation, University of Texas, Austin, 1972); Dale S. McLemore, "The Origins of Mexican American Subordination in Texas," *Social Science Quarterly,* vol. 53, no. 4 (March 1973), pp. 656–70.

5. Richard Griswold del Castillo, "La Raza Hispano Americana: The Emergence of an Urban Culture Among the Spanish Speaking of Los Angeles, 1850–1880" (Ph.D. dissertation, UCLA, 1974); Albert Camarillo, "The Development of Chicano Urban Society in Southern California, 1848–1930" (Clark Memorial Library Publications, UCLA, 1979); Terry Lehman, "Santa Fe and Albuquerque, 1870–1900: Contrast and Conflict in the Development of Two Southwestern Towns" (Ph.D. dissertation, Indiana University, 1974); Mario T. García, "Obreros: The Mexican Workers of El Paso, 1880–1920" (Ph.D. dissertation, University of California, San Diego, 1975).

6. Griswold del Castillo, "La Raza Hispano Americana"; Pitt, *Decline of the Californios;* Félix Gutiérrez, "Spanish-Language Media in America: Background, Resources, History," *Journalism History,* vol. 4, no. 2 (Summer 1977), pp. 125–56; Nancie Gonzales, *The Spanish Americans of New Mexico* (Albuquerque: University of New Mexico Press, 1971).

7. Camarillo, *Chicanos in a Changing Society;* García, "Obreros"; Alwyn Barr, "Occupational and Geographic Mobility in San Antonio, 1870–1900," *Social Science Quarterly,* vol. 50, no. 3 (Sept. 1970), pp. 396–403; Joseph F. Park, *The History of Mexican Labor in Arizona During the Territorial Period* (Tucson: University of Arizona Press, 1971); Griswold del Castillo, "La Raza Hispano Americana"; Montejano, "Race, Labor Repression, and Capitalist Agriculture."

8. Tomás Almaguer, "Class, Race, and Capitalist Development: The Social Transformation of a Southern California County, 1860–1910" (Ph.D. dissertation, University of California, Berkeley, in progress); Camarillo, *Chicanos in a Changing Society;* Barr, "Occupational and Geographic Mobility in San Antonio"; García, "Obreros."

9. Eric E. Lampard, "Urbanization and Social Change: On Broadening the Scope of Relevance of Urban History," in Oscar Handlin and John Burchard, eds., *The Historian and City* (Cambridge: MIT-Harvard University Press, 1963); Ricardo Romo, "The Urbanization of Southwestern Chicanos in the Early Twentieth Century," *New Scholar,* vol. 6 (1977), pp. 183–208.

10. Pedro Castillo, "Mexicans in Los Angeles: 1890–1920" (Ph.D. dissertation, University of California, Santa Barbara, 1978); Ricardo Romo, "Mexican Workers in the City: Los Angeles, 1918–1928" (Ph.D. dissertation, University of California, Los Angeles, 1975); García, "Obreros"; Camarillo, *Chicanos in a Changing Society;* Romo, "The Urbanization of Southwestern Chicanos."

11. Mark Reisler, "The Mexican Immigrant in the Chicago Area During the 1920s," *Journal of the Illinois State Historical Society,* vol. 16 (Summer 1973), pp. 148–58; Louise A. N. Kerr, "Mexicans in Chicago, 1920–1970" (Ph.D. dissertation, University of Chicago, 1975); Paul S. Taylor, *Mexican Labor in the United States,* vol. I–II, no. 1–10 (Berkeley, Calif.: University of California Press, 1928–34); Francisco Rosales, "Mexicans in the Harbor: East Chicago, 1918–1928" (Ph.D. dissertation, University of Indiana, 1975); Julián Samora and Richard A. Lamanna, *Mexican Americans in a Midwest Metropolis: A Study of East Chicago* (UCLA, Graduate School of Business, 1967).

12. Mario Barrera, *Race and Class in the Southwest* (North Bend, Ind.: Notre Dame University Press, 1979); Camarillo, *Chicanos in a Changing Society;* Taylor, *Mexican Labor;* Juan Gómez-Quiñones, "The First Steps: Chicano Labor Conflict and Organizing, 1900–1920," *Aztlán,* vol. 3, no. 1 (Spring 1972), pp. 13–50; Victor S. Clark, "Mexican Labor in the United States," U.S. Department of Labor, bulletin no. 78 (1908); George I. Kiser, "Mexican American Labor Before World War II," *Journal of Mexican American History,* vol. 2, no. 2 (Spring 1972), pp. 122–42; Herbert Patterson, "Post World War I Mexican Exploitation in Arizona" (Ph.D. dissertation, University of Arizona, 1974).

13. Gilbert González, "The System of Public Education and Its Function Within the Chicano Communities, 1920–1930" (Ph.D. dissertation, UCLA, 1974); José Limón, "El Primer Congreso Mexicanista de 1911: A Precursor to Contemporary Chicanismo," *Aztlán,* vol. 5, nos. 1, 2 (1974), pp. 85–118; Alonso S. Perales, *El Mexicano Americano y Politica del Sur de Texas* (San Antonio: Naylor Co., 1931); Camarillo, *Chicanos in a Changing Society;* Abraham Hoffman, *Unwanted Mexican Americans: Repatriation Pressures During the Great Depression* (Tucson: University of Arizona Press, 1973).

14. Useful sources for the post-World War II period include: Leo Grebler, Joan Moore, and Ralph Guzmán, *The Mexican American People: The Nation's Second Largest Minority* (New York: The Free Press, 1970); Tim Kane, "Structural Change and Chicano Employment in the Southwest, 1950–1970," *Aztlán,* vol. 4, no. 2 (Fall 1973), pp. 383–93; Bernon Briggs, Walter Fogel, and Fred Schmidt, *The Chicano Worker* (Austin: University of Texas Press, 1977).

15. Some of these questions can be superficially analyzed by examining the data found in Grebler et al., *The Mexican American People.*

16. See, for example: Biliana C. S. Ambrecht and Harry P. Pachon, "Ethnic Political Mobilization in a Mexican American Community: An Exploratory Study of East Los Angeles, 1965–1972," *Western Political Quarterly,* vol. 27, no. 3 (Sept. 1974), pp. 500–19; F. Chris García, "Manitos and Chicanos in Nuevo Mexico Politics," *Aztlán,* vol. 5, nos. 1, 2 (1974), pp. 177–88; Ralph Guzmán, "The Function of Anglo-American Racism in the Political Development of Chicanos," *California Historical Quarterly,* vol. 50, no. 1 (Sept. 1971), pp. 34–42; Mario Barrera, "The Study of Politics and the Chicano," *Aztlán,* vol. 5, nos. 1, 2 (1974), pp. 9–26.

17. Dick H. Reavis, *Without Documents* (New York: Condor Publishing, 1978); Jorge Bustamante, "The Historical Context of the Undocumented Immigration from Mexico to the United States," *Aztlán,* vol. 3, no. 2 (Fall 1972), pp. 257–82; Leo Grebler, *Mexican Immigration to the United States: The Record and Its Implication* (Los Angeles: UCLA, Graduate School of Business, 1966); Julián Samora, *Los Mojados* (South Bend: University of Notre Dame Press, 1971); Arthur Corwin, "Mexican Emigration History, 1900–1970, Literature and Research," *Latin American Research Review,* vol. 8, no. 1 (Summer 1973), pp. 3–24.

18. Some useful sources for comparative analysis include: Stanley Lieberson, *Ethnic Patterns in American Cities* (New York: Free Press, 1963); Tamotsu Shibutani and Kian Kwan, *Ethnic Stratification: A Comparative Approach* (New York: Collier Macmillan, 1965); Gerald D. Suttles, *The Social Order of the Slum: Ethnicity and Territory in the Inner City* (Chicago: University of Chicago Press, 1968); August Meier and Eliot Rudwick, *From Plantation to Ghetto,* 3rd ed. (New York: Hill and Wang, 1966); Allan Spear, *Black Chicago, 1890–1920* (Chicago: University of Chicago Press, 1967); David Katzman, *Before the Ghetto: Black Detroit in the 19th Century* (New York: Warner, 1973); Gilbert Osofsky, *Harlem: The Making of a Ghetto 1890–1930* (New York: Harper & Row, 1966); George Grob, *The Black Migration: The Journey to Urban America* (New York: Weybright and Talley, 1972); Karl Taeuber and Alma Taeuber, *Negroes in Cities* (Chicago: Aldine, 1967).

19. The following selected studies are useful in beginning to make comparisons between Chicanos and European immigrant groups in the city: David War, *Cities and Immigrants* (New York: Oxford University Press, 1971); Oscar Handlin, *Boston's Immigrants* (Cambridge: Harvard University Press, 1959); Humbert S. Nelli, *The Italians of Chicago, 1880–1930* (New York: Oxford University Press, 1970); Otto Feinstein, ed., *Ethnic Groups in the City* (Lexington, Mass.: Heath, 1971); Nathan Glazer and Daniel Moynihan, *Beyond the Melting Pot* (Cambridge: MIT Press, 1967); John Hope Franklin, *Ethnicity in American Life* (New York: Anti-Defamation League, 1971); Salvatore La Gumina and Frank Cavaioli, *The Ethnic Dimension in American Society* (Boston: Holbrook Press, 1974); Stephan Thernstrom, *The Other Bostonians* (Cambridge: Harvard University Press, 1973).

3 | Chicano Class Structure

MARIO BARRERA

Nationalism is a political orientation that emphasizes the common identity and common interests of a group of people who see themselves as sharing a similar historical experience and cultural orientation. The 1960s was a period during which nationalism dominated political discussion among Chicano activists. Thus, it is not surprising that the political statements that came out of the 1960s tended to stress the necessity for political unity and the development of an ideology that all Chicanos could rally around. One of the clearest expressions of this was in the formation of El Partido de la Raza Unida, an organization that in its very name expresses the nationalist hope for unity of the Chicano people.

The political documents of the late 1960s and early 1970s all demonstrate this orientation to one extent or another. Some quotes from "El Plan de Aztlán," developed at the first National Chicano Youth Liberation Conference in Denver in 1969, make the ideological direction clear:

> El Plan Espiritual de Aztlán sets the theme that the Chicanos (La Raza de Bronce) must use their nationalism as the key or common denominator for mass mobilization and organization . . . Our struggle . . . must be for the control of our barrios, campos, pueblos, lands, our economy, our culture, and our political life. El Plan commits all levels of Chicano society—the barrio, the campo, the ranchero, the writer, the teacher, the worker, the professional—to La Causa.
>
> Nationalism as the key to organization transcends all religious, political, class and economic factions or boundaries. Nationalism is the common denominator that all members of La Raza can agree upon ("El Plan de Aztlán," 1971, pp. 4–5).

The *Plan de Santa Bárbara,* which provided the basis for the development of Chicano Studies programs, shared most of the same orientation, and at one point states that "Cultural Nationalism is a means of total Chicano liberation" (Chicano Coordinating Council, 1969, p. 51). In describing the content of proposed and actual Chicano Studies programs, the *Plan* emphasizes the study of the "community" but not of divisions that may exist in that community.

As time passed, however, more people began to question this broad nationalist conception and to feel that it perhaps represented a romanticized or unreal picture of the Chicano community. This critical position came partly out of the experience of having to face the real divisions that exist in Chicano communities, and that often are reflected in political conflict. La Raza Unida Party, for example, found in its own home base in Crystal City, Texas, that upwardly mobile Chicanos in the community often worked at cross purposes with the majority of poorer Chicanos, or at best cooperated in a half-hearted manner (see Shockley, 1974; Navarro, 1974).

Out of these experiences came the growing perception that Chicanos were not necessarily all struggling for the same things, and that these different orientations among the different segments of the Chicano community might have their roots in the different situations in which Chicanos found themselves. Some observers started to try to understand these divisions by paying more attention to class differences within the Chicano community but experienced or encountered confusion. One common source of confusion, however, is that the term "class" as it is currently used in the United States does not always have the same meaning. Thus we must first look at the definition of the term before applying it to the Chicano.

TWO APPROACHES TO CLASS

The Strata Approach

Most American social scientists who use the concept of class use an approach in which classes are seen as strata, or layers. The classes are seen as stacked one on top of the other, much as sedimentary rock strata are in the study of geology. They are identified by ranking them from lower to upper, as in middle class, upper middle class, lower class, and so on. The most common indicator used for ranking the classes is wealth, usually expressed as annual income. Related characteristics such as occupation and level of education are also used, as these are related to income.

Some sociologists who use this same general approach rely on indicators of honor or social status in addition to or in place of income to do their ranking. In this case the researchers attempt to find out how people in a particular community rank the different social groups in that community in terms of status; they then use those rankings to describe the class structure. (See Davis, Gardner, and Gardner, 1941, for a classic example of this approach applied to the American South.)

In another variation of this approach, people are asked to identify themselves in class terms, by telling the researcher whether they think of themselves as upper class, middle class, and so on. This variation thus relies on subjective factors of self-identification rather than on objective factors such as income to do the ranking.

Some variation of the strata approach has usually been used to study Chicano communities. What is probably the most extensive study ever done on

Chicanos, for example, makes use of a very simplified form of this approach. According to the authors of this study, "The multiple indicators of social class used in studies of entire communities are inappropriate for the analysis of our survey data from Los Angeles and San Antonio. Instead, income is here taken as the major indicator of class position . . . income (is) the most general means for the acquisition of most types of status" (Grebler, Moore, and Guzmán, 1970, p. 325). The authors of the only textbook yet to appear on Chicano political behavior use a similar approach, dividing Chicanos into a middle class and a lower class, although they also use the term "working class" to mean the same thing as lower class (García and Gárza, 1977, p. 18). Most Chicano authors use the term "class" in more or less the same way.

The Marxist Approach

There is another way to approach the study of social classes which is quite different from the strata approach. In the Marxist tradition, a class is a group of people who have a similar relationship to the process of production in a society. The process of production is that process by which all of the goods and services are produced that people use in their daily lives, such as food, houses, appliances, and so on. Each society has a particular class structure depending on the way in which such goods are produced and on the way in which the work force is organized.

In a society like the contemporary United States, Marxists generally identify three major classes. Capitalists constitute one class, defined as those people who actually own the means of production, such as tools, factories, and money to be invested. This class also hires people to work for them, and are thus involved in buying labor power. A second class consists of the *workers;* these people do not own the means of production and sell their labor to capitalists. This class includes the so-called white-collar workers, such as clerks, secretaries, and salespeople, as well as blue-collar workers who work in shops and factories. A third class is the *petty bourgeoisie,* for whom no term exists in English. These are people who neither buy nor sell large quantities of labor, and who make a living basically by being self-employed. The owners of a mom-and-pop grocery store or an independent barber shop represent typical members of this class.

This way of defining classes differs from the strata approach in that a person's class standing does not depend primarily on income. Therefore, some members of the working class, such as plumbers or electricians, have higher incomes than many members of the petty bourgeoisie, while others do not. There is a relationship between income and class standing, of course, but it is a general or statistical relationship and does not always hold.

What are the advantages of using a Marxist rather than a strata approach to class? There are two major advantages. The first of these is that the Marxist classification tends to group people together on the basis of their interests more than the strata approach does. The reason for this is that people's interests are determined to a large degree by their relationship to the process of production. Workers generally have an interest in higher wages, in organizing unions and establishing collective bargaining, in shortening the work week, in having laws passed that deal with occupational safety, and so on. Capitalists, on the other hand, have an interest in keeping wages low, in preventing unions from organizing, in lengthening the work period, and in avoiding laws that regulate working conditions. The petty bourgeoisie have an interest in preventing the large corporations from swallowing up their small business, as they are constantly threatening to do. According to Marxist analysis, the petty bourgeoisie are always in danger of being ground up between the two largest classes in capitalist societies, the workers and the capitalists.

The second major advantage is that the Marxist concept of class is tied to a particular theory of how societies change over time, and especially of revolutionary change. The strata approach, on the other hand, is completely descriptive and atheoretical. According to classical Marxist analysis, major social changes take place through conflict between the major classes in a society. The major classes are seen as always being in a state of either potential or actual conflict, because of their different interests. Therefore, it is argued that the Medieval feudal system in Europe broke down when the emerging class of merchants and businessmen were able to ally themselves with the oppressed class of serfs to overthrow the landlords who were the dominant class at the time. Likewise, Marx foresaw a potential for revolutionary change in capitalist societies when the emerging class of workers became strong enough and enlightened enough to overthrow the ruling class of capitalists. The Marxist theory of historical social change was not adequate as it was originally formulated and has been modified and revised since then, but Marxists feel that it captures enough elements of reality to serve as a basis for a more complicated and sophisticated theory.

One of the major problems that has emerged in recent years for people using the Marxist approach to class has been how to deal with a group that does not seem to fit any of the traditional classes. In advanced industrial societies like the United States there has developed a segment of the population that is sometimes referred to as "educated labor." Typically, these are college-educated people who work in large bureaucratic organizations in managerial and professional positions, including engineers, scientists, lawyers, teachers, supervisors, analysts, and a large number of other occupations. Such people are not capitalists in that they do not own the means of production and do not themselves hire labor. They are not self-employed, as are the petty bourgeoisie. While they sell their labor in much the same way that the traditional working class does, they typically have much greater independence on the job than do ordinary workers. Thus their relationship to the process of production is somewhat different from manual and white collar workers. Some researchers have referred to these employees as the "new working class." Others have called them the "new petty bourgeoisie." Still other writers believe that they constitute an entirely new class, which they call the "professional-managerial class," or PMC (Ehrenreich and Ehrenreich, 1977), a class typical of advanced capitalist society. In this essay, educated labor will be treated as constituting a separate and distinct class.

Another problem that particularly concerns American Marxists is that people whom they consider workers do not necessarily think of themselves as members of a working class. The same is true to various degrees of other classes in the United States as well. The usual response to this situation is to point out that there is often a difference between people's own interests and their perception of the interests. To the extent that members of a class perceive their common interests and begin to organize themselves around those interests, that class is said to have a high degree of class consciousness. One of the most common reasons that is given for a low degree of class consciousness among American workers is that the extreme ethnic and racial diversity of the American working class has diverted the worker's attention from their common interests. In Marxist terminology, a class that is conscious of itself as a class and organizes itself politically along class lines is said to be a "class for itself." A class which has the objective characteristics of a class in the sense of having common interests and a common relationship to the process of production but does not see itself as a class is spoken of as a "class in itself."

SIMPLISTIC APPROACHES TO CHICANO CLASS STRUCTURE

Once we get beyond the questions of classes in general to the question of how Chicanos fit into the American class structure we encounter even more confusion and disagreement. One overly simplistic answer that is encountered is that Chicanos are not part of the class structure at all but are somewhat outside of it. Writers who pursue this line of thinking usually argue as if racial divisions were the only important lines of cleavage in the U.S. social structure. The cultural nationalist approach that was mentioned earlier in this article is a good example of this type of analysis. Chicanos are seen as united or at least potentially united as a people in opposition to the dominant Anglo population. The interests of Chicanos are treated as if they were defined solely along racial lines, with no internal class divisions. Often the Anglo population as well as Chicanos are depicted as a featureless, classless group. It is not uncommon to hear spokespersons for American blacks deal with social and political questions in similar black and white terms.

A second kind of mistake that is made is to discuss Chicanos as if they were only part of the working class. It is not uncommon to hear sectarian and dogmatic Marxists come up with this kind of formulation, although this usually happens more often in speeches and conferences than in published articles or documents. The usual intent of this formulation is to downplay ethnic and racial differences in order to try to create a political movement based strictly on class. While it is true that most Chicanos are members of the working class, as are most Anglos, it is misleading to ignore the class diversity within the Chicano community. In particular, ignoring class divisions among Chicanos makes it difficult to understand some of the political dynamics that take place in the community.

HISTORICAL DEVELOPMENT OF CHICANO CLASS STRUCTURE

The existing class structure of Chicano communities is a product of a long historical development in the Southwest (see Barrera, 1979, for a fuller description of this process). While it is impossible to go into an extended description of this development here, a brief summary will give us some basis for understanding the patterns that exist today.

Settlements of Spanish-speaking people had existed in the area that we now call the Southwest for a considerable time before the coming of the Anglos, so that a class structure already existed in the area before the Mexican-American War (1846–48). While there was some variation from place to place, in most areas there was a class of landlords who controlled much of the land suitable for grazing and agriculture. These were the *patrones,* and while they owned the means of production they were not full-fledged capitalists because the economy of the area at that time was not thoroughly capitalist. In many ways it was connected to and influenced by the European capitalist economies, but much of the agricultural and other production was strictly for local use and was not intended for a national or international market. Much of it, in other words, was a subsistence economy. The landlords generally were also more interested in maintaining their privileges and way of life than in constantly building up and reinvesting a large amount of capital for constant growth in the manner of true capitalists.

There was a much larger class of people who either worked outright for the patrones or tended their land and flocks under some kind of sharecropping or shareherding arrangement. This was the class of *peones,* who were not a working class in the modern sense because they were generally not free to move around and sell their labor in a well-established labor market such as is typical of capitalist economies.

There were other classes as well. There were smaller groups of independent or semiindependent small farmers, small merchants, and artisans (skilled workmen who owned their own tools). In some areas there was also a class of Indians who were kept in a slave-like existence by the Spanish-speaking settlers.

This arrangement began to change as elements of the United States economy began to penetrate the area more rapidly in the early part of the nineteenth century. With the Mexican-American War and the incorporation of the Southwest into the United States, changes in the class structure accelerated, although again there was considerable regional variation. Areas such as southern Colorado and northern New Mexico were among the slowest to change, while northern California changed very quickly under the impact of the Gold Rush.

In those areas where Chicanos were the most concentrated and where the Anglo economy penetrated least rapidly, a kind of mixed economy developed that retained much of the older pattern for a considerable length of time. In some cases, Anglos simply moved in and themselves became like patrones with relationship to the workers, although they were capitalist in their orientation to the market and to reinvesting for growth.

Throughout the Southwest in the second half of the nineteenth century, however, the capitalist class structure of the United States was replacing the older pattern. This affected the various elements of the Chicano community in various ways, depending on their class status and other conditions. In most places it appears that the Chicano patron class was forced out of existence or drastically reduced (see Pitt, 1970, and Camarillo, 1979, for California). In New Mexico, however, because of the heavy concentration of Chicanos there and the relatively slow Anglo economic penetration, a significant number of the traditional patron families were able to hold on to some of their land and other wealth. As the economy became more and more capitalist in nature, they were forced to become capitalists in order to be able to compete under the new ground rules. However, while some of these families were able to fit themselves into the new capitalist orientation, as a group they have had to accept a position subordinate to the Anglo capitalists who came to dominate the economic and political scene in that area.

The Chicano Working Class

During the same time period there began to develop a Chicano working class, with several components that included agricultural workers, urban blue-collar and service workers, and white-collar workers. The agricultural workers developed out of the old peón class as southwestern agriculture was shifted to a capitalist basis. This was a gradual process, however, and it was some time before workers on the land were able to achieve the same kind of mobility that industrial workers have under capitalism. Various forms of peonage continued to exist in such places as South Texas until at least the 1920s. Once Chicano agricultural workers loosened their ties to individual agricultural employers, many of them were forced into what might be considered the opposite situation, that of a migrant labor force, moving from crop to crop as the demand for labor changed. This change in labor patterns occurred in the 1910s and 1920s as trucks and automobiles came into common use and as southwestern agriculture boomed with irrigation and the development of the Rio Grande Valley in Texas, the Salt River Valley in Arizona, and the Imperial Valley in California. The spread of the sugar beet industry in Colorado, Wisconsin, California, and other western and midwestern states also contributed to this development.

During the 1910s and 1920s this agricultural working class also expanded rapidly with the influx of large waves of immigrants from Mexico, and it became more of a mixed Chicano and Mexicano labor force. Since then the number of agricultural workers has declined as machines have increasingly replaced hand labor. However, Chicanos and Mexicanos have continued to be heavily represented in this sector of the working class. Women, while always constituting a minority of the agricultural workers, have long been represented in the fields. It has not been at all uncommon to find whole families working side by side, especially in the migrant labor force.

Chicanos have also traditionally been strongly represented in two lines of work that are not agricultural but that also are not typical urban industries. One of these is mining in which the Spanish-speaking settlers of the Southwest had been engaged for many years before the coming of the Anglos. The other is railroads, which expanded dramatically in the 1860s and 1870s as the transcontinental lines swept across North America. In the cities, Chicanos found employment in construction and road work, in cement factories, and in metal processing plants. In 1928, a survey of 695 California industries found Chicanos well represented in low-paying jobs in laundries and in food processing plants as well as in service jobs as maids and cooks (*Mexicans in California,* 1930).

During the Second World War, with its accompanying labor shortages, Chicanos and Chicanas were able to gain entry into many urban industries from which they had been excluded earlier. While some of these workers lost their jobs after the War, they established a foothold in these industries, which they have retained and expanded since.

By the early part of the twentieth century, there had also come into existence a small but significant group of Chicano white-collar workers. These were typically clerks and salespeople who were hired by the urban merchants to deal with their Spanish-speaking customers. If not for their ability to play this kind of "go-between" role, it is likely that Chicanos and Chicanas would have been excluded from the ranks of the white-collar workers for a much longer period of time.

It is important to keep in mind that as Chicanos became increasingly incorporated into the different parts of the working class, they were still not on the same footing with Anglo workers. Chicano workers were discriminated against in several different ways. One has already been mentioned, that is, the persistence of semi-peonage working conditions, especially in agriculture. There was also a very strong dual wage system throughout the nineteenth century and into the early part of the twentieth. Under this system, there was a "Mexican wage" that was paid to all Chicano workers in a particular line of work, and this wage was always lower than the wage paid to Anglo workers doing exactly the same work. It was also true that there were "job ceilings" in effect, under which a Chicano worker could only rise so far in the type of work done. It might be possible, for example, for a Chicano or Chicana to do unskilled or semiskilled work, but not skilled labor. Later on, when the ceiling was raised higher to allow Chicanos to do skilled labor, they were prevented from doing supervisory work. Such job ceilings still exist, although at a higher level than in earlier times.

The Chicano Petty Bourgeoisie

In his studies of various parts of the Southwest in the 1920s and 1930s, researcher Paul Taylor documented the existence of a Chicano petty bourgeois class, although he did not refer to it in those terms. Among the small business establishments he found in such places as Dimmit County and Nueces County in Texas were garages, shoe repair shops, groceries, dry goods stores, bakeries, restaurants, filling stations, tailor shops, and barber shops. Another study found 446 Chicano-operated grocery stores in El Paso in 1920 (M. García, 1975, p. 145).

In some ways, the Chicano small independent businessman found himself as limited as the Chicano worker did. Generally, the Chicano business enterprises were severely limited in capital and were confined to serving a Chicano clientele. Stores on the Anglo side of town, on the other hand, served both an Anglo and a Chicano clientele, and, as pointed out earlier, often hired Spanish-speaking clerks specifically to relate to Chicano customers.

The significance of the Chicano petty bourgeois class has always extended beyond their small numbers or their economic impact on the community. Generally they have been viewed by the dominant Anglo power-holders as the more "responsible" element in the community, and they have been sought out when it was felt necessary to have a spokesperson or representative from the barrio side of town. They have thus served as contact persons or brokers, transmitting information from one side to the other and providing input, accurate or inaccurate, about what the Chicanos in the community are thinking about a particular issue. In playing this role they have often earned the distrust of working class Chicanos, while not gaining full acceptance or equal power from their Anglo counterparts (see, for example, Watson and Samora, 1954).

The Chicano Professional-Managerial Class

There has also existed for a considerable period of time a small number of Chicanos who occupied such professional positions as lawyers, doctors, pharmacists, teachers, and ministers. With the exception of teachers and ministers, most of these professionals appear to have been self-employed and would thus come under the heading of petty bourgeoisie. More recently, however, and especially since the 1960s, there have come into existence a much larger number of Chicano administrators, health workers, middle managers, college faculty, mental health counselors, government employees, and other typical members of a professional-managerial class. There have also been more Chicano lawyers and medical personnel working for community clinics, legal aid agencies, immigration counseling centers, and so on. As their numbers have increased, these professionals have formed a variety of associations and political interest groups, in order to have regular contact with each other. Increasingly, moreover, they have come to take over the "go-between" role that the traditional Chicano petty bourgeoisie have played with respect to Anglo power-holders and the Chicano community at large.

THE NATURE OF CLASSES IN THE UNITED STATES

Once conclusion that emerges from a historical perspective is that Chicanos are and have been for some time represented in all of the classes that make up the class structure of the United States. An equally compelling conclusion is that Chicanos have not been represented in those classes on the basis of equality with members of the Anglo population. Thus we can say that American classes are not homogeneous, but rather seem to be broken up into unequally treated parts on the basis of race. These different parts of each class can be referred to as *class segments*. Other kinds of segments also exist within classes, such as those based on sex, but here I am only concerned with divisions based on race and ethnicity.

The segmented nature of American classes no doubt goes part of the way toward explaining why class consciousness has usually been at fairly low levels in the United States, especially for the working class with its very mixed character. The greatest degree of class consciousness is to be found in the capitalist class, which is also the most homogeneous, being made up almost entirely of middle-aged Anglo males.

The existence of class divisions within racial and ethnic groups such as Chicanos also helps to explain why such groups rarely attain the kind of unity that is sought by political organizations such as La Raza Unida Party. While commonalities of culture and life experiences serve to provide strong bonds among such groups, the existence of different classes with their divergent interests provides one important source of division.

THE CONTEMPORARY CLASS STATUS OF CHICANOS

Some idea of the relative distribution of Chicanos in the different classes can be gotten from looking at figures from the United States Census, although they are highly imperfect. One reason for the imperfection is that census figures are not exact, and are generally considered to undercount poorer people and minorities. Another reason is that the way in which people are classified changes from one census to another. Also, the job categories that are used by the federal government do not correspond exactly to Marxist conceptions of class. However, census figures do give us a rough idea of distribution among classes, if they are interpreted cautiously.

In table 3.1, percentage figures are given for the two census years of 1930 and 1970, so that a comparison can be made. They are also broken down separately for men and women, because the figures differ considerably by sex. The data for 1930 are based on a census classification of "Mexican gainful workers ten years and older." The 1970 data are for Spanish-surname workers 16 years and older. While these definitions differ, they probably measure fairly similar groups as long as we look only at the Southwest (Texas, New Mexico, Arizona, Colorado, and California).

Capitalists and petty bourgeoisie are to be found in the first two census categories, "managers, proprietors and officials" and "farm managers"; "professional and technical workers" are mostly members of the professional-managerial class. All of the other categories correspond to the working class, with "clerical" and "sales" making up the white-collar workers and "craftsmen," "operatives," and "laborers" making up the blue-collar workers. Farm workers and service workers are also members of this class, and they are among the lowest paid workers.

Male-female differences are apparent from the table, with men being relatively concentrated among managers and both skilled and unskilled workers. Women, on the other hand, form a disproportionate part of the white-collar workers and the service workers. All of these patterns were true in 1970 and 1930.

Table 3.1: Occupational Distribution of the Chicano Population for the Southwest, 1930 and 1970, by Sex (in percentages)

	MALE		FEMALE	
	1930	*1970*	*1930*	*1970*
Managers, proprietors & officials	2.8	5.2	2.4	2.4
Farm managers	9.8	0.9	1.0	0.1
Professional & technical	0.9	6.4	2.9	7.6
Clerical	1.0	6.6	5.8	27.8
Sales	2.4	3.9	4.3	6.1
Craftsmen & foremen (skilled)	6.8	20.8	0.6	2.2
Operatives (semiskilled)	9.1	25.4	21.9	23.1
Laborers (unskilled)	28.2	12.1	2.8	1.5
Farm laborers	35.1	8.1	19.7	3.0
Service workers	4.0	10.5	38.4	26.2

Data for 1930 are for "Mexican gainful workers 10 years and older." Data for 1970 are for Spanish-surname workers 16 years and older.
Sources: U.S. Census Reports, 1930 and 1970.

Certain important trends emerge when we compare the data for 1930 and 1970. One of the most striking is the overall decline in the proportion of farm laborers and farm managers. These trends also hold true for the Anglo population, as machines have steadily replaced farm labor and as agribusiness has replaced smaller farms. Some of the most important occupational gains for Chicanos in the forty-year period have been in the skilled-worker and white-collar-worker categories. However, representation continues to be quite low at the professional and managerial levels.

Overall, the trend from 1930 and 1970 was for the degree of occupational segregation to break down to some extent, and thus for Chicanos to become more evenly represented in the different classes. In other words, the degree to which unequal segmentation exists is less now than it was in 1930. Of course, whether these trends will continue in the future or even whether they continued from 1970 to 1980, is still unclear. It is also not clear whether the relative decline in segmentation will mean that Chicanos will become more class conscious in the future and less race conscious.

If we had to make some very rough estimates, and take into account the fact that more Chicanos than Chicanas work for wages outside the home, we could say that capitalists and petty bourgeoisie together represent around 4 to 5 percent of the Chicano population. Another 6 to 7 percent are in the professional-managerial class, while the rest, close to 90 percent, are in the working class. Again, it should be emphasized that the economic and political role of the non-working-class Chicanos in the community is much out of proportion to their numbers.

SOME FINAL ISSUES

Here I want to touch on two or three questions that are related to a class analysis of the Chicano community. One has to do with the question of undocumented workers and how they fit into the picture. Undocumented workers from Mexico and other Latin-American countries frequently settle in the same areas as Chicanos born in the United States, and often become part of the same Spanish-speaking communities. Should they be considered as fitting into the American class structure in the same way that Chicanos do? No one has analyzed this matter in detail. While it is true that most undocumented workers have typical working class occupations, and are discriminated against as are Chicanos, they also occupy a somewhat different status in some respects. The fact that their legal standing is questionable makes them very vulnerable to exploitative employers, and they are frequently preferred by employers who want to hire nonunion workers at extremely low wages and under the worst working conditions. It is not uncommon for employers to use them as strike breakers, or to engage in other unscrupulous practices such as calling the immigration service just before the workers are to be paid. For these various reasons, it may be possible to consider that undocumented workers are themselves a subordinate class segment in the United States. Another alternative would be to see them as a subordinate segment within a larger Chicano/Mexicano class segment. Perhaps future research will help clarify this problem, but it is very difficult to come up with any kind of reliable information on undocumented workers.

Another question has to do with the future community role of Chicano members of the professional-managerial class. Currently many of these professionals work for community agencies. Those who do not often deliberately orient their work toward serving the Chicano community. Most of these professionals are relatively young; moreover, they have generally been influenced by the Chicano Movement of the 1960s and 1970s to one degree or another. Given their level of education and technical skills they are in demand to serve in the "go-between" role that was mentioned earlier in this article. Clearly, this group is in a strategic position with respect to the general Chicano community, and the political positions they take and the way they structure their work activities could have an important influence on the future of the growing Chicano population. As time has passed the tendency has been for conservative influences to become stronger for this group, for two reasons. One is that the Chicano Movement has declined in recent years, so that there is less activity and less pressure on the professionals from a politically progressive direction. At the same time, as these young professionals have begun to move upward to some extent in the bureaucracies for which they work, they have been increasingly tempted to adopt the organization's perspective as their own. Since the overall role of the professional-managerial class in the United States is to provide the technical expertise to keep the capitalist system functioning smoothly, there is a real danger of cooptation of this group. If the group was to become largely coopted, they would then be functioning to control the Chicano community more than to bring about desirable and fundamental changes for that community. The danger is particularly great because cooptation is usually a subtle process. It is not necessary to consciously "sell out," to become literally a "vendido," for one's work to be, in effect, coopted. At this point in time it may be that the only counterforce acting against cooptation is the formation of Chicano-based professional associations and political groups, which have a strong community orientation, and which can maintain a constant vigilance against being coopted. These groups currently are important political battlegrounds for contending conservative and progressive forces.

A final question concerns the future political direction of the Chicano struggle as a whole, and how it is affected by the class structure. At the time this is being written there is a great deal of confusion and indecision about future political directions. The goals of the remaining Chicano Movement have not changed; they are still centered on the struggles for racial equality and for community self-determination. However, there is a greal deal of disagreement about how to work toward these goals. With the decline of La Raza Unida Party beginning around 1973, there has been less opposition than ever to working within the Democratic Party, and to identifying closely with politicians, such as former California Governor Jerry Brown, who are perceived as being sympathetic to Chicano causes. The Democratic Party is still seen by many Chicanos as a progressive political force, in spite of the fact that its differences with the Republican Party have steadily decreased since the 1930s. In adopting this approach, the effect is to more or less ignore class as an important political factor, since neither of the major parties is eager to discuss class questions in the United States.

An alternative approach would be to identify classes and class interests openly, and for progressively oriented Chicanos to seek a political alliance with progressive elements among Anglo workers and members of the professional-managerial class, as well as with blacks and other minority members of the same classes. This approach would structure itself along class lines and downplay racial and ethnic identifications and interests. Presently it is usually only the more dogmatic and sectarian Marxist-Leninist groups that strongly advocate this approach.

A third approach would be to attempt to build a new movement on the basis of racial/ethnic identification, as did La Raza Unida Party. This approach deemphasizes class lines in an effort to achieve political unity among all Chicanos. La Raza Unida Party activists found this to be a difficult task, particularly since Chicanos do not form local majorities in most parts of the Southwest. The attraction of this approach is that many Chicanos will respond more readily to political appeals based on ethnic identity than to class-based appeals.

It may be that the most successful political strategy for the future will combine certain elements of the above approaches. The most logical strategy would seem to be one in which a Chicano political organization would be built on the basis of ethnic/racial issues such as bilingual education, affirmative action in employment, community-based health clinics, antipolice harassment of Chicanos, and equitable immigration policies. At the same time, however, the leadership would be sensitive to the class nature of American society and would actively seek to create a working coalition with progressive black, Native-American, Anglo, and Asian-American groups. By pursuing such a strategy, it might be possible to acknowledge the reality of racially based class segmentation in the United States while simultaneously building a political movement that would emphasize rather than obscure class divisions.

REFERENCES

Barrera, Mario. *Race and Class in the Southwest.* Notre Dame: University of Notre Dame Press, 1979.

Camarillo, Albert M. *Chicanos in a Changing Society: From Mexican Pueblos to American Barrios in Santa Barbara and Southern California,* 1848–1930. Cambridge: Harvard University Press, 1979.

Chicano Coordinating Council on Higher Education. *El Plan de Santa Bárbara.* Oakland: La Causa Publications, 1969.

Davis, Allison; Gardner, Burleigh; and Gardner, Mary. *Deep South.* Chicago: University of Chicago, 1941.

Ehrenreich, Barbara, and Ehrenreich, John. "The Professional-Managerial Class." *Radical America,* Part I, March–April, 1977, pp. 7–31; part II, May–June, 1977, pp. 7–22.

"El Plan de Aztlán." In *Documents of the Chicano Struggle.* New York: Pathfinder Press, 1971.

García, F. Chris, and de la Gárza, Rudolph. *The Chicano Political Experience.* North Scituate, Mass.: Duxbury Press, 1977.

García, Mario. "Obreros: The Mexican Workers of El Paso, 1900–1920." Ph.D. dissertation, University of California at San Diego, 1975.

Grebler, Leo; Moore, Joan; and Guzmán, Ralph. *The Mexican-American People.* New York: The Free Press, 1970.

Mexicans in California. Report of Governor C. C. Young's Mexican Fact-Finding Committee. San Francisco: State Building, October, 1930.

Navarro, Armando. "El Partido de la Raza Unida in Crystal City." Ph.D. dissertation, University of California at Riverside, 1974.

Pitt, Leonard. *The Decline of the Californios.* Berkeley: University of California, 1970.

Shockley, John. *Chicano Revolt in a Texas Town.* Notre Dame: University of Notre Dame Press, 1974.

Taylor, Paul. *An American-Mexican Frontier: Nueces County Texas.* New York: Russell and Russell, 1971 (originally published 1934).

Watson, James, and Samora, Julián. "Subordinate Leadership in a Bicultural Community." *American Sociological Review,* August 1954, pp. 413–21.

In Eugene E. Garcia, ed. Chicano Studies:
A Multidisiciplinary Approach.

4 | Mexican Immigration to the United States, 1848–1980: An Overview

JUAN GÓMEZ-QUIÑONES

Immigration, legal and undocumented, is both an economic and political phenomenon that must be viewed historically. In the past, large-scale population movements have been a major feature of capitalist economic development. Recently, however, immigration has come to have critical economic, social, and political ramifications for the industrialized nations of Western Europe and the United States.

The economic crisis of capital in the 1970s focused increased attention on the significance of international labor migration, and the issue of immigrant workers developed into a public crisis. In several nations it was characterized by strong overtones of xenophobia directed against undocumented workers, particularly in the United States, where the influx of Mexicans has expressed capitalism's need to recruit and integrate a labor force.

Historically, the worldwide process of labor recruitment has involved the migration of rural laborers to rising centers of industrial production, facilitated by workers displaced as a result of the growth of commercial agriculture. This mass population movement occurred simultaneously with the incorporation of existing regional markets into new national economies made possible by the historical development of a capitalist economy. Plunder generated by conquest and commercial capitalism in the sixteenth and seventeenth centuries created a generalized money economy that provided the initial accumulation of wealth needed to finance the investments necessary for the industrial revolution of the eighteenth century. In the nineteenth century, the expansion of industrial and financial capitalism brought remote nations and colonies under the influence of a world capitalist economy governed by laws of value and uneven development and marked by cyclical upswings and crisis. This integration of national markets and industrial expansion in advanced capitalist countries accelerated in the twentieth century. Concurrent with it was the development of a single world market.

The internationalization of capital gave impetus to the integration of

56

national and colonial labor markets into a world market. In turn this led to international labor migration. As in the case of the migration of labor from rural regions to industrialized areas, international labor migration was spurred by the relative length and availability of employment and the wage levels and working conditions in the area of out-migration vis-à-vis that of immigration.[1]

IMMIGRATION AND POLITICAL ECONOMY

Immigration is the result of changes in the structural relationship between workers and the organization of the means of production and the uneven development of geoeconomic sectors, regions, and countries. It occurs because of the decomposition of the agricultural sector, structural unemployment, and the differential between nominal and real wages in regions and countries. In capitalism, the most advanced forms develop at the expense of the less advanced. This appropriation of the labor force, and hence, of the productive potential of less developed nations, is significant to the formation of capital.[2] Given this process there is no orchestrated conspiracy but the unfolding economic and political logic of capital. Consequently, immigration is not only circumstantially related to economic development, but is a direct structural characteristic of the present capitalist mode of production affecting both its advance and retardation.

A stimulant to the process of economic, technological, social, and integrative expansion are the continual efforts by the owners of capital to maintain and increase the overall rate of profits on their investments. In industry and agriculture, increasing the productivity of the worker increases the possibilities for the appropriation of surplus value and the profits realized from the sale of products of labor and investment. At the same time, technological improvements in production, spurred by increasing competition, result in a long-term trend for the average rate of profit to decline as larger investments in machinery and physical plant (variable capital) are necessary. Immigration has an impact on this trend by increasing the capital available and also by prolonging current technology.

Lack of development or decomposition in one place cannot be isolated from the acceleration of development elsewhere. They are parts of a dialectical whole of which a concrete manifestation is the immigrant worker. Immigrant labor provides for capital's growth through the profit derived as a result of a wage differential that temporarily counteracts the falling rate of profit. This labor is used to cushion the cyclical reactions of capital by slowing the rate of inflation.[3] From immigrant workers, capitalists obtain higher profits by paying lower wages and intensifying and prolonging the productivity of each laborer. Furthermore, the cost to the economy for the maintenance and social reproduction of the worker is practically nil. The worker is used at the peak of his productive years and replaced at small cost. Importantly, the immigrant workers profit not only the employer but all capital in general. In many ways, such laborers give up wages to survive; they subsidize the purchasing power of others, and many benefit from what savings they accumulate. The immigrant also provides political benefits.

Immigration is a means by which capitalism can regulate the labor market and the supply of workers as it undergoes economic cycles of high and low demand for labor. Periodic booms and busts are structural characteristics of the capitalist economy and result from overproduction in relation to the demands and purchasing power of consumers. This stems from the distribution of wealth, the policies of those who have ownership of the means of production in capitalist society, and international capitalist competition. Since the production of goods is not determined by the actual social needs of the population but by competition among the owners of production for profit, commodities periodically accumulate beyond the purchasing power of the population. When lack of demand finally reaches a critical point, profits and investment opportunities decline and production is reduced resulting in large unemployment. In facing this recurrent situation, immigration provides the system with elasticity.

Immigrant workers function as part of the reserve labor force. In times of high demand for labor, this reserve can be drawn upon to meet increased production. During periods of recurrent stagnation, they can readily be eliminated from participation in the labor force since they lack legal protection and are the last unionized. The presence of immigrant workers is also ideologically exploited by capitalism. In periods of economic crisis, antagonism heightens between labor and owners; and, immigrant workers are made to serve as scapegoats for public discontent through deliberate manipulation to prevent antagonism toward those actually responsible for the crisis.[4]

IMMIGRATION FROM MEXICO

Throughout the twentieth century, the following variables have generally been identified as influencing Mexican migration: agricultural productivity and agricultural commodity prices in Mexico; agricultural productivity and the rate of capital investment in the United States; and farm wages in both countries. Thus, at the core of Mexican immigration has been the question of individual or family subsistence. In other words, the situation of low wages and high prices in Mexico and higher wages and greater employment in the United States affect each other. These, in turn, relate to the economic and political relationship of Mexico to the United States as it has developed historically.[5]

The causes underlying Mexican immigration to the United States can be traced to disparities in the formation and integration of the national economies of the two nations. During the colonial period, these disparities were reflected in the economic infrastructure, relations and ownership of production, and class structure. During the early nineteenth century the United States was able to rapidly integrate its regional markets into a national economy controlled by national rather than foreign capital. United States capital controlled internal commerce and facilitated manufacturing and industrial production. Conversely, the relations and ownership of production characterizing Mexico at the time of its independence impeded the integration of regional markets into a national economy. Control of commerce and other productive resources was largely in foreign hands or in the hands of those elements whose interests were in maintaining the status quo.[6] Possibilities for the development of a viable national manufacturing sector were limited.

These weaknesses slowed national integration and made it difficult for Mexico to resist foreign economic penetration, political coercion, and military conquest. The ruling elites could neither consolidate nor pursue effective, consistent policies of national development and, to a large extent, they viewed the majority of the population as social and political chattel. In time, over half the national territory was lost to the United States in the invasion of 1846–48 and by the sale of La Mesilla in 1853. When the integration of a national economy occurred, control of major productive resources was in the hands of foreign North-American and European capital. Mexican ownership of production was marginal, controlled by a bourgeois comprador class that was subordinate to foreigners.[7]

Migration was stimulated by economic conditions in the rural areas of the Mexican north and northern-central regions and by the rapidly growing demand for labor during the development of the southwestern United States. The construction of North American-owned railroads, linked to the United States in the 1880s and 1890s, facilitated the movement of Mexican labor on an increasingly massive scale. Mexican workers and their families migrating to former Mexican territories in Alta California, Nuevo Mexico, Texas, Arizona, and Colorado joined the resident Mexican inhabitants and nonwhite workers at the bottom of the labor force. There they and their descendants continued to face extreme exploitation and intense national and racial chauvinism, which reflected historical patterns of social conflict within the United States. Concurrently, Mexican workers, as a consequence of class exploitation and national oppression, struggled to organize for the defense of their economic and national interests.

Mexican immigration was not "extra" labor. It was fundamental to the economic structure of the United States because of its occupational distribution. By providing lower cost goods and services, Mexican immigration subsidized the economy of the United States. It was a means for the state to manipulate wages, inflation, and unemployment to the advantage of the owners of capital. Importantly, the United States has gained the benefit of the Mexican worker's productivity and Mexico's resources.

Over time, from the nineteenth through the twentieth century, the relationship between Mexico and the United States became one of interdependency advantageous to the United States and disadvantageous to Mexico. The United States has influenced the economic development of Mexico in a variety of ways. Historically, it has directly appropriated resources. In contemporary times, this has been accomplished through labor immigration, direct investment, loans and interest on loans, and through political understanding between the two countries.

Mexican migration has generally consisted of the migration of labor, which, historically and economically has formed a continuous phenomenon. In the 1920s there was a forcible division into legal and nonlegal entry, which was the result of an expanding and changing capitalist economy.[8] Other aspects stem from the distinctiveness of Mexican immigrants, the transcrossing of a particular border, and the existence of a large Mexican resident community.

Historically, advances in productive capacity have been reflected in the growth and movement of human populations. The development of capital has given rise to continuing population growth and migration on an international scale. In the most basic sense, such migration represents the transfer of a labor force on an international scale, an internationalization of the labor market. In this context, immigration, the movement of a labor force, represents a fundamental link between national labor markets and a manifestation of their relative degree of interdependence.

The Mexico-United States border region represents the area of convergence, conflict, penetration, dependence, and interdependence of the national economies, state authorities, nationalities, and cultural characteristics of the two countries. While United States' claims to the present political boundary were established through military conquest and coercion in 1848 (the Treaty of Guadalupe Hidalgo), an effective administrative frontier was not functionally realized until the second and third decades of the twentieth century.

The particular characteristics of the United States-Mexico border zone encompass the following:

1. In geographical terms the border is a large area. From Tijuana-San Ysidro in California to Matamoros-Brownsville on the Gulf of Mexico, the political line of demarcation covers close to 2,000 miles. It encompasses the states of California, Arizona, New Mexico, and Texas on the United States side, and the states of Tamaulipas, Nuevo León, Coahuila, Chihuahua, Sonora, and Baja California on the Mexico side. The border is devoid of major natural obstacles impeding movement. It has common geographic features such as natural resources and a dry climate. Similar crops and industry have been developed on both sides.
2. The border area has a dynamic, evolving, popular biculture with con-

tinuity, roots, and influences from both sides. Similar language, music, architecture, folklore, food, and other cultural aspects of the Mexican communities on both sides have made the political dividing line a porous one in social, cultural, and political terms; these features also have an impact on the non-Mexican population.

3. The border represents a juncture between an affluent, developed capitalist economy and a lesser developed dependent economy. One aspect of this disparity is the brutal exploitation of one economy and society by the other and the degeneration of one people by the other.

4. The border area was, and is, a continuous area of United States and Mexican interpenetration with continually increasing population. The border is the juncture for contiguous economic, social, and political features.

5. The border is the major staging area for Mexican emigration which is facilitated by access to transportation and the relative ease of the border crossing. The existence of a large resident Mexican community on the United States side acts as a cushion for the migratory experience.

The particular characteristics of the Mexico-United States border region reflect the disparities the two countries have experienced in the process of formation. This disparity has been especially acute in economic terms on both sides of the political boundary, and particularly in the increasing migration both to the northern Mexican states and to the Southwest. More recently, the migration has been increasing to the Midwestern United States.

Mexican immigration has been closely tied to the economic dominance of Mexico by the United States, dominance which has helped maintain the Mexican economy in an underdeveloped state. Additionally, among the U.S. Mexican community, the continuous immigration has reinforced Mexican culture, and of course, has added to the growth of the population.

Some distinctive characteristics of this immigration are:

1. Since the settlement of the Southwest by mestizos, and particularly from the nineteenth century to the present, migration northward from Mexico has been a continuous and ongoing process.

2. The intensity of the immigration process has been interdependent on the economic and political relations between Mexico and the United States. It has expressed itself according to regional and local preferences.

3. Migration across the Mexican border has been of three types: permanent, periodic, and temporary; it either has been legal or undocumented.

4. Mexico, in the last decades, has supplied a larger number of permanent visa immigrants to the United States than any other single country.

5. Migrations occur over a lengthy border area free of basic natural obstacles to impede movements.
6. More than other immigration groups, the Mexican immigrant has been used as a scapegoat for the periodic cycles of economic depression and the failure of capital enterprise and the United States government to remedy these.

In general, Mexican immigrants share specific attitudes. The commonly stated reasons for immigration are lack of employment and low wages. Immigrants display a strong desire for their eventual return to Mexico, as do the majority of undocumented immigrants. Studies suggest that Mexican migrants are dissatisfied with their status at home and seek to change it. Immigrants are individuals with initiative who "plan" into the future, are willing to take risks, and are not submissive to authority or tradition.

In addition to attitudinal commonalities, immigrants also share objective ones. In comparison to other immigrants and to the general population in Mexico, Mexican immigrants are younger than those from other countries, they are less skilled, and both males and females immigrate. Consequently, existing characteristics of the Mexican community in the United States are continuously reinforced and strong social and economic ties with Mexico persist. It is not uncommon for Mexican immigrants to have relatives who emigrated to the United States with whom they retain family ties. Among legal immigrants, the breakdown by scxcs is nearly equal. Among undocumented women, immigration is increasing (15 percent of the annual total); however, males continue to be the overwhelming majority. Women originally migrate as dependents of males, but they do not remain dependents in many cases. Although the pattern has been changing in recent years, traditionally, the lower educational and skills levels of the Mexican immigrants meant that they would be disadvantaged vis-à-vis European immigrants, native-born whites, blacks, and United States-born Mexicans. However, since 1950, there has been increasing diversity in the skills and educational levels of Mexican immigrants. Mexicans who immigrate come from the lower income half of their home communities, but not the lowest sector.

The specific pattern of occupational and sectoral distribution of immigrant workers in the United States economy has been problematic due to the difficulty in obtaining statistical information. This is because the majority of Mexican immigrant workers have been undocumented. The only contemporary "hard" source of data available until recently was that compiled on deportees by the Immigration and Naturalization Service (INS). Studies by independent researchers and by United States and Mexican government agencies have indicated general patterns. While immigrant workers have located in most sectors of the economy occupying a wide range of occupations, and nearly all occupational categories are represented, it is clear that the majority have concentrated in low paid marginal occupations in agriculture (45 percent), industry (21 percent), commerce (14 percent), the service sector (9 percent), and other (1 percent). Over the years, agriculture as a source of employment has declined and other sectors have increased. Between 11–14 percent of those in industry and construction have held skilled, blue-collar jobs.

Specific occupational areas of high concentration of Mexican workers have included assembly and light manufacturing in the plastics, electronics, garment, and furniture industries, general labor, and construction. In hotels and restaurants, they have worked as busboys, waiters, maids, dishwashers, and in domestic service, gardening, and agricultural labor. Although declining in absolute number due to mechanization, Mexican agricultural workers (immigrant and United States-born) constitute the largest sector of that work force. Mexican immigrant workers are particularly concentrated in jobs that have been considered unattractive, demeaning, dangerous, dirty, temporary, or comparatively poorly paid—these are referred to as Mexican work. Many jobs for immigrants generally require little skill or knowledge of English.

The geographic origin of the immigrant population has had varied significance. What knowledge there is was derived from braceros and permanent legal immigrants, from recent surveys of legal immigrants and of undocumented workers. In the majority, immigrants come from Chihuahua, Coahuila, Durango, Zacatecas, Guanajuato, Querétaro, Aguascalientes, parts of San Luis Potosí, Jalisco, and Michoacán. The northern and west coast Mexican states have provided a significant amount of Mexican immigrants. The urban-rural origins have always been mixed, especially since the Mexican Revolution of 1910. In earlier decades, the flow of rural origin immigrants predominated. In recent years, up to 1980, the urban flow has increased. Immigration is selective, according to region and location, and it occurs from some regions and communities, not from all.[9]

Settlement patterns in the United States have shifted over the years. About 90 to 95 percent of the immigrants in the 1910–29 period chose the United States Southwest. This proportion was reduced in the 1955–64 period to 85 percent. In the Southwest, Texas was by far the area of greatest attraction in the earlier years.[10] California gained importance after the 1920s, but even at the end of the twenties many immigrants who eventually chose California intended originally to settle in Texas. Arizona was also an important destination from 1910 to 1924. In this period Arizona outdrew California in total immigrants.

Settlement preferences changed in the post-World War II period.[11] California became increasingly the favorite destination and attracted nearly 56 percent of the immigrants in the 1960–64 period; Texas was second; Arizona, New Mexico, and Colorado received fewer immigrants than other states. Significant for the future is that areas in the Midwest, such as Detroit and Chicago, have yearly drawn more and the Pacific Northwest has been drawing more immigrants since 1950. In the 1970s the majority preference was California, Texas, and Illinois, but there also persisted a wide dispersal. The majority have preferred urban destinations.

Mexican immigrants, documented or not, have been in the forefront of labor organizing; both groups have also been used to break strikes. In this they appear no different than other workers in regard to union propensity. During the seventies, roughly 10 percent of Mexican workers were union members as compared to 22 percent for the United States labor force as a whole. The single, more important obstacle to their unionization remains the attitude of organized labor. Mexican labor has generally been considered complementary rather than competitive to other labor, that is they supplement rather than displace other workers.

CYCLES OF LABOR NEEDS AND IMMIGRATION LAWS

Although Mexican migration to the north obviously occurred prior to the war of 1846, from the middle of the nineteenth century, starting with the 1849 California Gold Rush, through the twentieth century Mexican immigration to the United States became important as a component of United States capital development.[12] This broad span of time has specific periodization: from 1848 to 1910, 1910 to 1929, 1930 to 1940, 1941 to 1965, and 1966 to 1980. These periods are related to labor needs, quantity of immigration, and United States immigration laws. Recruitment of labor has been concurrent with harassment. Particularly severe persecution occurred from 1920 to 1921, 1932 to 1933, 1953 to 1954, and 1974 to 1980.[13] The latter period is marked for having been particularly virulent and longer. Undocumented immigration in the seventies was heavier than in the past, and police agencies were more active and efficient.

Legislation pertaining to Mexican immigration has tended to reflect the overall need of the United States economy for Mexican labor.[14] The principal function of immigration laws has been to regulate and control the process of immigration—the supply of labor. Enforcement of these laws has also reflected the attitudes and economic situation of the United States as a whole and the Southwest in particular. The Department of Labor, the Department of Agriculture, the State Department, and police agencies have worked in conjunction with organized interest groups to invoke policy and practices that have affected migration patterns and Mexican labor on both sides of the border.

Prior to 1882, no federal restrictions or quota laws regulating immigration existed. Two basic liberal concepts determined this open door policy: the United States was to be an asylum and a place of opportunity for all, and migrants of any nationality would be absorbed into the giant labor force of this society. In short, the need was for mass labor without restriction.

The economic organization and relations of production of the 1848–1910 period reflected a need for labor. Also evident at this time was the large-scale penetration of the Mexican economy by foreign-owned industries and the accelerated development of the United States Southwest. As a consequence of foreign economic penetration, the Mexican economy became more intensely linked to the international economy and increasingly felt the effects of international economic cycles. Periodic economic recessions caused growing inflation and unemployment. After 1900 this general economic situation in Mexico resulted in an uprise of agrarian revolts, political opposition to the Porfirio Díaz regime, labor stoppages and strikes, and state repression.

In Mexico the economic tribulation of the working class coincided with the economic development of the United States Southwest, where industrial and agricultural development attracted immigration from Mexico. Several factors contributed significantly to the increase. One was United States federal legislation, another was the building of a railway system, a third was the lessening of European and Asian immigration. In 1902 Congress passed the Newlands Reclamation Act, which provided federal funds for the construction of large-scale irrigation and reclamation projects throughout the Southwest. With vast amounts of irrigation and with plentiful cheap labor, the arid desert lands of the Southwest were ideal for the cultivation and production of high profit citrus fruits and vegetables.

Basic aspects of labor regulation and institutional racism were visible in legal and political practice by 1882.[15] The United States Congress in 1882 passed the Chinese Exclusion Act, which underscored the increasing racism of the United States population, the racist sentiments of North-American labor, and the tendency to scapegoat nonwhites. In 1883 the first general United States immigration law was enacted. It established a head tax and provided for the exclusion of certain categories of people who, because of one liability or another, could not work and would be a charge to the state. In 1885 Congress passed the first Alien Contract Labor Law.[16] Its primary goal was to prevent employers from importing "cheap foreign labor" that would replace Anglo workers. The law prohibited direct contracting of foreign workers. This was enforced with regulatory discretion. Eventually, the U.S. government signed the Gentlemen's Agreement of 1907 with Japan, severely restricting Japanese immigration.

Three events explain why immigration from Mexico reached a height during the period 1910–29: (1) the Mexican Revolution of 1910, (2) growth and expansion in the U.S. Southwest, and (3) increased labor demands caused by World War I. In 1910 a social and political upheaval in Mexico had significant

effects in shaping the current modern Mexican state and society. More immediate, however, it affected the process of immigration greatly. Intense internal
warfare dislocated the fragile economy. Agricultural production fell drastically
as did production in other sectors; unemployment and poverty increased.
Laborers were forcibly recruited from the factories and countryside into the
armies. With the constant mobility of armies facilitated by the railroad system,
warfare and economic disruption added to the mobility of the working class.
As fighting intensified, the movement northward did also. People began leaving
Mexico in large numbers mainly in search of security and subsistence. Many
Mexicans on losing sides of the battles left for fear of reprisals. It has been
estimated that over 330,000 Mexicans emigrated between 1910 and 1917, an
average of 53,000 annually.[17]

On the American side of the border, in contrast to Mexico, the economy of
the Southwest was flourishing due to technological advances and the toil of
Mexican workers. Further, labor shortages induced by World War I offered
opportunities for Mexican workers within industry and services. Some Mexicans were employed in relatively skilled occupations. They held jobs as core
makers, machinists, mechanics, finishers, job press workers, painters, and
upholsterers.

With the expanding economy and markets, and with the concurrent need for
workers, the recruitment of Mexican workers became a business. Employment
agencies were created whose sole assignment was the recruitment of Mexican
labor.[18] These agencies recruited from various parts of the interior of Mexico.
The largest agencies worked for the railroads. They sought out potential workers and furnished them with food, clothing, and transportation to the United
States. Once the workers arrived on the job, the railroad companies deducted
the travel expenses from the workers' salaries to pay the agencies.

In 1917 Congress passed an act that required a literacy test for immigration
and provided for the exclusion of persons over sixteen years who did not read
English or some other commonly used language. Though industry needed lit-
erate workers, agriculture did not. Thus, in 1918, the commissioner general of
immigration waived this requirement for Mexican laborers. This action established two significant precedents. The practice was initiated whereby immigration laws were relaxed when it became advantageous to import Mexican workers, and restrictive provisions were enforced when it appeared necessary to
exclude Mexicans from immigrating on a permanent basis. Between 1920 and
1921, 100,000 Mexicans were returned to Mexico.

Shortly after, European and Asian immigration was further decreased as a
result of the restrictions established by the Exclusion Law of 1921 and the
Quota Act of 1924.[19] This legislation established a quota system that numeri-
cally restricted immigration on the basis of a national origin formula that allocated numbers of visas to specific nationalities. The concern was for racial and

ethnic balance within United States society. However, Mexico was not limited by the quota. United States immigration policy had a dual posture; the 1917 act represented qualitative regulation, the 1924 act embodied quantitative restrictions.

Needing a large pool of low-cost labor to expand the rising economic empire of the Southwest, industrialists continued to encourage the movement of Mexicans into the Southwest. The owners and growers sought, and eventually secured, an abundant supply of labor and a constant industrial reserve to turn to as markets and needs expanded. The desire for Mexican labor was no longer restricted to the Southwest. Capitalists in the Northwest and Midwest also began hiring Mexican labor. As a segment of Mexicans went into the interior of the United States, the southwestern companies stepped up their recruitment, thus creating an extensive Mexican labor pool on both sides of the border.

Throughout the decade of the 1920s, the population of Mexican immigrants continued to increase. This period saw the greatest flow of Mexicans into the United States. Approximately 427,000 were admitted legally from 1920 to 1929. Two situations in Mexico sped the flow—the Cristero Rebellion and the increase in means of communications.[20] The prevailing negative social and economic condition of Mexico and the wage differential between Mexico and the United States continued to spur immigration. In 1925 agricultural workers in most parts of Mexico could not earn a subsistence wage; their purchasing power was one-fourteenth that of North American workers.

Anglo capitalists argued that Mexico was a natural source of cheap abundant labor supply, and thus, Mexican immigration was an economic asset to United States economic growth.[21] The Department of Agriculture asserted that Mexican labor was essential for reclamation projects. Lastly, the State Department contended that the application of the quota system to the American republics, such as Mexico, could hinder foreign policy efforts of Pan Americanism, that is, the policy of hegemony over Latin America.

The debate on the exclusion of Mexican immigration was reopened in the years from 1926 to 1930. At this time immigration from Mexico had increased both in number and relative to total immigration. A large-scale anti-Mexican campaign was opened. Racists argued that Mexicans were a danger to the cultural and genetic fabric of United States society.[22] Three major arguments for restricting further Mexican immigration emerged: (1) Mexican labor displaced Anglo workers and kept wages low, (2) the benefit derived from a cheap labor force was a short-term gain, and (3) Mexican nationality posed a threat to the "white race" since Mexicans were biologically inferior. These views were, in turn, supported by allegedly "objective scientific studies." Thus, by the twenties, the basic arguments against Mexican workers were developed.[23]

In 1924 the Border Patrol was created and thereafter expanded both in personnel and in budget appropriation for deportation work along the Mexican border.[24] This action marked a dramatic change in the situation of the Mexican worker. His status changed from being one among many immigrant workers whose entry without an official visa would be incidental, to that of a fugitive of the law who had to systematically hide in order not to be apprehended and sent back to Mexico. Thus, the concept and condition of an "illegal worker" was introduced into the relations of labor. This modified the pattern of interaction between the worker and his community. The division between legal and "illegal" worker and legal and "illegal" Mexican became increasingly operationalized from the thirties to the seventies. The fear of being "caught," apprehended, or reported presented one more dimension to the disadvantage of the Mexican worker.

In 1929 a new form of administrative control over immigration went into effect. The State Department instructed its consular officers in Mexico to enforce the restrictions of existing legislation and curtail immigration. The principal method was to combine the 1917 act with the 1885 Alien Contract Labor Law public charge clause.[25] This meant that if an immigrant applied for a visa stating that he did not have a secure job, the public charge provision excluded him, while if he said that a job awaited him in the United States, his admission was denied because of the violation of the Alien Contract Labor Law. Through the Act of 1929 it became a felony for anyone to enter the country illegally and further provided a more severe punishment for the ones who returned after being deported. This act toughened the situation for the future.

During the 1930s, workers experienced increased unemployment, labor strife, and politicalization both in Mexico and the United States as a result of world-wide economic depression. The flow of Mexican immigration subsided as unemployment, caused by the Depression, increased in the United States. While wages sunk to subsistence level or below, Mexican and migrant workers were displaced by other segments of the Anglo society. In contrast, subsistence was somewhat easier in Mexico. To diffuse the frustration of this country's labor sector and public opinion in general, Mexican workers were used as scapegoats.[26] A policy was implemented to repatriate them. This was yet another in a series of massive deportation movements of Mexican workers. Some Mexicans returned to Mexico of their own accord. However, both repatriation and voluntary returns were the results of a systematic campaign against Mexicans by local authorities and private agencies. Methods used to repatriate Mexican workers included persuasion, intimidation, violence, and forced repatriation.[27] Through these methods approximately 500,000 people left the country.

After the Depression, the importation of Mexican labor again became desirable. This country's preparation and mobilization for the impending World War II meant methods were implemented to encourage migration and employment of Mexican workers on a large but temporary basis. Now, however, there was only a slight interest in large-scale legal and permanent Mexican immigration.

Although the Mexican economy was developing, this did not mean full employment or substantial wage increases for its population. World War II stimulated industry in the United States and the need for laborers of all types; Mexican immigration was thus resumed. The renewed interest in securing Mexican labor gave rise to the Emergency Farm Labor Program.[28] Known as the Bracero Program, it was established through the 1942 Bilateral Agreement between the United States and Mexico. It gave U.S. business and government more regulation over Mexican labor. In June 1942 the State Department and the Mexican government signed an agreement for the importation of 50,000 Mexican workers.

Some main provisions of the agreement were that Mexican workers were not to be used to displace U.S. workers but to fill proven shortages; recruits were to be exempted from military service; workers' roundtrip transportation expenses as well as living expenses en route were guaranteed; hiring was to be done on the basis of a written contract between the worker and the employer; and the work was to be exclusively in agriculture. Additionally, braceros were to be free to buy merchandise in places of their own choice, housing and sanitary conditions were to be adequate, and work was to be guaranteed for three-fourths of the duration of the contract.

The Bracero Program did much to stimulate immigration. In fact, it marked the beginning of large-scale undocumented immigration as known in contemporary times, and it strengthened certain specific structures of immigration. This program meant an infrastructure was created through formalized bilateral agreement for agricultural labor and the resumption of large-scale importation of Mexican workers for temporary jobs. Concurrent with the formalized programs, undocumented immigration also increased. On the one hand, Mexican workers could save time and expenses by avoiding official channels, and on the other hand employers could avoid the red tape of the Bracero Program. They could even pay lower wages.[29] However, immigration through permanent visa also increased in the forties to a total of 54,500 for the decade. Although Mexican labor was welcomed, the attitudes toward people of Mexican origin did not change. Racial conflict occurred in parts of the Southwest, especially in Los Angeles during the forties.

As undocumented immigration from Mexico increased and the economic recession of the fifties occurred, a new current of anti-Mexican immigration developed. In 1954, attempts were made to curtail illegal Mexican immigration. The stage was set for what came to be known as "Operation Wetback," a campaign that sought to deport the maximum number of undocumented workers. Assisted by federal, state, and county officials, along with the FBI, army, navy, and supported by aircraft, special units, and public sentiment, the Border Patrol launched its most extensive campaign against a highly vulnerable Mexican labor force. The effort established a new benchmark in employee relations.[30] Increased police surveillance and militarization became a part of labor regulation. Yet, through the decades of the fifties and sixties, the open and shut gate mechanism of labor recruitment and deportation continued to operate.

The years 1955–65 were a high point of United States capitalism despite the setback of the Korean War and recurring recessions. Constant demand for Mexican labor caused the internal migration from the interior of Mexico to the north to rise dramatically. This was concurrent with a continued rise in undocumented immigration. As the economy of Mexico became more dependent on the United States, a greater number of Mexican workers entered this country's labor force in general. Further as the economy changed, Anglo workers left marginal and semiskilled occupations that Mexicans came to occupy. The importance of agriculture to employment declined, other sectors of the economy, such as manufacturing and services, grew. Consequently, Mexican workers moved from seasonal to more permanent occupations. Between 1953 and 1956, the Bracero Program increased greatly reaching a total of 445,000 workers in the Southwest and Michigan.[31] By 1959, 25 percent of this country's southwestern work force was Mexican.

During the fifties and sixties, the bracero agreement was amended and extended several times. On July 13, 1951, Public Law 78 was signed authorizing further employment of Mexican workers. Beginning in 1955, congressional legislation extended it six more times, until it was finally terminated on December 31, 1964. The bracero agreement had proven an effective instrument for depressing wages and conditions, but less so in retarding immigration. As the Bracero Program ended, a new immigration law was passed in 1965. Becoming effective in 1968, it restricted legal immigration from the western hemisphere.

The early seventies were characterized by a growing recession, high inflation, unemployment, and a real threat of economic depression. A threat of an insurmountable wave of "illegal" migration from Mexico was fomented by politicians, the INS, and certain organized interest groups hoping to evoke anti-Mexican sentiments in the general public. Immigrants were blamed for the country's economic ills. Hysterical propaganda was directed at the undocumented worker; public pressure led to a search for national legislative solution. And, a new element against illegal immigration was introduced: the argument for national security.

The choices available in the 1980s are still problematic. Abrupt total cessation of immigration and/or removal of immigrants would cause unforeseeable economic dislocation to the economies of the United States and Mexico.[32]

To rationalize, formalize, and legalize mass immigration, a program that has existed up to 1980, would not be politically feasible for the United States nor desirable for Mexico. Other policy options have invariably entailed a "control" feature since it is the "noncontrol" feature of immigration that has drawn the most attention. Increased immigration ceilings would address labor needs to raise civil rights concerns. Though Mexico is of special concern to the United States, special higher ceilings for Mexico could be problematic.

Greater vigilance at the border is preferable to direct police agency intervention at the worksite, if a choice had to be made; however, the "cost" would fall on the individual workers. Greater vigilance would also require both United States' and Mexico's participation; the latter may have domestic political consequences for Mexico.

To punish employers or workers would entail a large surveillance force or another computing system for monitoring the public; increased punishment and surveillance would increase discrimination and engender opposition. A more benign approach would be equal and fair wages and work rights for all workers. Amnesty provisions in and of themselves are not immigration options; they have been a juridical response to the phenomena of resident undocumented workers already in the United States. They are sensible and fair but do not present an option for addressing continuing immigration. Creating employment at the source has been the most attractive policy voiced, but this option is fraught with as many ambiguities as other options. Development is a long-term answer but not a short-term remedy.

Strictly bilateral decisions involving the United States and Mexico or organizations and persons from these countries have not included migration from other countries. On the other hand, unilateral action by the United States may not be effective and has potential adverse consequences.

In reviewing immigration policy options, there is no single policy alternative to the immigration issue.[33] Several elements have to be accounted for in concert over time. According to a recent poll, over 70 percent of the United States population want to halt all further immigration of "foreigners." The trend now is toward tighter regulation and enforcement of immigration, greater police power in the area of immigration, and greater selectivity of immigrant workers for specific needs. Concurrent with increasing concern over immigration, there is also increasing awareness of the importance of the Mexican and Hispanic populations in the United States.

THE RECENT POLITICS OF MEXICAN IMMIGRATION

Immigration has been important to this country's Mexican community because of its effects in a number of crucial areas. It increases the numbers in the community—increasing its rate of growth and speeding geographic distribution.

Immigration has an impact on jobs and wages in an indeterminate manner, but it also increases the total economic wealth of the community. It strengthens the urban concentration and blue-collar sector of the United States Mexican community; it has an impact on class stratification by making working-class interests more salient; it affects interethnic relations, and relations with blacks and other Latino groups in particular; it strengthens Mexican culture and it countervails assimilation, forcing the question of identity and culture to be recognized concretely; it promotes the Spanish-language media in the United States and thus the national and international communication system of the community, and finally it increases and taxes political resources. It also internationalizes concretely the radius of U.S.-Mexican community political concerns because of its impact on international relations. Politically, immigration redraws and redefines the battle line, specifically on issues of social justice.

Exploitation and attacks on the most fundamental rights of entire peoples are not unique to the United States. What is unique to the United States is a historically evolved expression of nativism, chauvinism, and racism. This has been inseparably linked to economic, social, and political domination by a small complex of special interests over the welfare of the vast majority of producers in the United States and the world. This feature of United States society has been expressed consistently and most notably around the issue of immigration.

Immigrants in the United States have been part of a vast army of labor. They include the descendants of indigenous inhabitants of the Americas, African peoples, and succeeding generations of Europeans and Asian immigrants whose combined efforts have generated wealth and industrial power in the United States. During periods of economic crisis, the anger of the unemployed and potentially unemployed is diverted from industry and government to immigrants and minority nationalities. This has taken an especially virulent form when, as in the seventies, it has been possible to combine both elements—nationality and immigrant—into a single campaign. The 1970s campaign against so-called "illegal aliens" was only one more attack. Similar attacks were mounted in 1919 (the Palmer Raids), the 1930s (the Repatriations), and the 1950s (Operation Wetback), which used virtually the same tactics and rhetoric.[34]

Research is part and parcel of immigration politics. Academic immigration research has frequently supported repression and hysteria through questionable research methods and conclusions. In some instances it has been opportunistically motivated. Contrary to what the public often has been led to believe, objective studies, based upon research in the field that investigated the impact on social services, cost versus undocumented workers' contribution in tax payments and salary deductions, have refuted negative research. The most significant research has focused on immigration policy, and the most informative is that which is considered from a context of political economy and provides specific data.[35] Up to 1980, the precise impact on employment displacement, conditions of work, and levels of worker organization was not statistically clear.

The ramifications of official policy proposals and immigration research for Mexicans in the United States and in Mexico are major. Yet, autonomous and comprehensive research has not been readily forthcoming from the Mexican community. From the perspective of the United States government, efforts have focused primarily on proposals for a more restrictive immigration policy with its attendant suggestions for implementation and enforcement while insuring a labor supply. The Mexican government and its allied researchers put forth material to support a negotiated compromise with the United States that will maintain the escape valve, maintain the flow of remittances, and secure concessions from the United States. By the late seventies, the Mexican government, through its Department of Labor, had launched studies of thousands of residents who had previously worked in the United States, the most ambitious research effort to date.

Progressive sentiment in Mexico did not develop quick enough to substantially support the human and class rights of undocumented workers and to vigorously reject the chauvinism and anti-Mexican bias underlying the policies of the United States government and labor organizations in regard to undocumented workers. The Mexican government has found itself in a difficult position, caught between its economic dependence on the United States and multinational financial interests, and the natural indignation of Mexican people and worsening conditions in Mexico. However limited and burdened with unresolved contradictions, public awareness in Mexico is crucial to full international public discussion.

The political situation of Mexican communities within the United States has been a difficult one. Majority public opinion has little sensitivity to their situation; the public views Mexicans, citizens or not, as alien. Given these attitudes, there is little public sympathy evoked by gross violations of Mexican people's civil and human rights. Faced with attacks and attempts at diversions and divisions, the Mexican community has sought to unite and seek support. There have been groups whose interests coincided with the interest of Mexican peoples on the issues of human rights and immigration. Among these have been civil rights organizations, a few persons from the black and Asian communities, and a few progressive sectors of the trade union movement. Also included among allied supporters have been those who have the most to lose, merchants and small to medium manufacturers and agriculturists. Up to 1980, a functional coalition had formed comprised of United States Mexican organizations, business interests, and interested parties in Mexico.

Undocumented workers have covert networks of support among themselves.[36] Significantly, undocumented workers, supported by legal residents, have on occasion resisted raids and deportations at the work place. These are acts that many would not have believed possible. Furthermore, they developed embryonically at least one organization, Comité Obrero en Defensa de Indocumentados/das en Lucha (CODIL), of their own; and there also was the National Committee to Unionize Undocumented Workers in the United States, and the International Brotherhood of Workers. Significantly, sectors of the labor movement, Farm Labor Organizing Committee (FLOC), United Farm Workers of America (UFWA), International Longshoremen and Warehouse Workers Union (ILWWU), International Ladies Garment Workers Union (ILGWU), and the United Auto Workers (UAW), have begun to support unionization of undocumented workers due to the recognition that if Mexicans are present in the United States labor force, they should be unionized. The most important sources of organizational support were Centro de Acción Social Autónoma (CASA) and the Mexican American Legal Defense and Education Fund (MALDEF). The key battles have been those of public opinion, juridical, legislative, and legal defense. Lawyers and allied researchers have been successful in a number of important cases pertaining to the defense of undocumented workers. Strong support from elected and national organizational leadership also has been most important. The defense of the undocumented worker has not been without cost to this country's Mexican community.

Since the turn of the century, when individual and mass deportations occurred, organizations and individuals have sought to defend the victims. Eventually, there developed a complex of leadership and of organizations known in the Mexican community for their devotion to the defense of the undocumented workers. Included among these have been legal defense groups, advocacy groups, service centers, church committees, and so forth.[37] Equally noted, however, was the political opportunism of individuals and organizations that occurred during 1977, years after the campaign in defense of the undocumented had begun.

The destructive potential of this unprincipled alliance was fully realized at the National Chicano/Latino Conference on Immigration and Public Policy held at San Antonio, Texas, October 28–30, 1977. The conference sought to unite organizations opposed to repressive immigration policies around a program of national mobilization against the Carter Plan. It was used, however, as a forum to promote individual leaders and legitimize the Trotskyite, Socialist Worker Party (SWP). This was accomplished through manipulation, which turned effective organization control of the conference over to the SWP.

The result was a rigged and packed conference allowing the SWP to secure its proposals. The major effect was to derail the organizational potential of the conference and temporarily defuse possibilities for national mobilization against the Carter Plan. True to pattern, the SWP and their allies abandoned their organizational initiative against the Carter Plan after gaining their real objective of national publicity. Authentic opponents of repressive immigration policies have learned to be wary of attempts by elements intending to use the momentum generated by popular struggles. Though efforts in defense of the undocumented workers did not altogether cease, the conference marked the high tide of resistance in the seventies. It seriously retarded coordinated national action in the United States. In contrast, the International Conference for the Full Rights of Undocumented Workers was an event of potential significance. Held in Mexico City in 1980, it involved labor representatives from both the United States and Mexican organizations. The conference issued a bill of rights of undocumented workers, a general platform on migrant workers, and laid out strategy and tactics. The conference was a benchmark whether or not it achieves even partial success in its plans.

As has happened in previous deportation crises, as repression intensifies, so does resistance. Activity in defense of the undocumented workers has consisted of conferences and mass demonstrations, advocacy before local and federal governments, and the forming of organizations and coalitions. The human rights position developed as a result of specific organizing and propagandizing drives dates from 1968. Ideologically and organizationally, in 1977 this political position solidified into four basic demands:

1. oppose repressive legislation
2. cease raids and deportations of the undocumented worker
3. unconditional amnesty for the undocumented worker
4. full human amnesty for the undocumented worker[38]

The legislative process in the United States has been of central importance in these demands, for it is in the congressional arena that immigration positions are enacted into law, modified, or shelved. A major factor influencing the outcome has been the cumulative pressure of public opinion and political strength brought to bear on legislators by proponents and opponents with electoral and organizational resources.

Another position was represented by the proposals of Mexican and U.S. government advisors grounded in partial denunciation of the injustices suffered by undocumented workers and put forth as developmental solutions. These proposals called for a program of United States economic and technical assistance to the Mexican government in establishing a program to foment large-scale agricultural production or light industry in rural areas of high outmigration. Along with a projected increase in employment were the regulatory schemes of various types of guest worker programs. Such development and guest worker programs could have the effect of actually increasing Mexican economic dependency on the United States and detracting from the potential organized strength of workers.

The Mexican government's position appeared to have coalesced around the concept of some type of an international state government. This was the result of the very limited options available within the context of the basic structural dependency of the Mexican economy on the United States. The Mexican position was not, however, clear. The topic of a temporary worker program was mentioned. The Mexican government may not have had a specific plan, but it adopted a posture of benign oversight while it sought time and lobbied for a favorable agreement. The Mexican government did have a broad policy consensus. It favored development, rather than exporting of workers; it favored employment rather than unemployment, and therefore, continuing immigration; and it supported human and civil rights for immigrants.

Upon inspection, neither government had a precise and elaborate programmatic position or had publicly offered one in the late seventies. The lack of precise government programs was due to the interrelationships encompassed by the issue. The undocumented workers phenomena was complex, and any solution involved costs that neither government wished to incur. Both governments sought to gain time as they made administrative adjustments that would lessen the magnitude of the phenomena without major formal overt agreements or concessions. Each government sought to outmaneuver or outpressure the other on the immigration question as they related it to other issues while publicly denying that relationship. Both societies stand to gain and lose by the phenomena in a complex configuration of ways. However, to establish control there must be flexible legalization of what occurs and more productive development in Mexico and higher wages. Given the nature of the relationship between the United States and Mexico, the major burden falls on the United States.

NOTES

1. Alejandro Portes, "Migration and Underdevelopment," *Politics and Society,* vol. 8, no. 1 (Fall 1978), pp. 1–48.

2. Karl Marx, *Capital,* vol. 2 (Moscow: Foreign Language Publishing House, 1962).

3. Portes, "Migration and Underdevelopment," pp. 39–40.

4. For discussions of this phenomenon see, Jorge A. Bustamante, "The Historical Context of Undocumented Mexican Immigration to the United States," *Aztlán: Chicano Journal of the Social Sciences and the Arts,* vol. 3, no. 2 (Fall 1972), pp. 257–81; and Mauricio Mazón, "Illegal Alien Surrogates: A Psychohistorical Interpretation of Group Stereotyping in Times of Economic Stress," *Aztlán: International Journal of Chicano Studies Research,* vol. 6, no. 2 (Spring 1975), pp. 305–24.

5. Richard Fagen, "The Realities of U.S.-Mexican Relations," in Antonio Rios-Bustamante, ed., *Mexican Immigrant Workers in the United States* (Los Angeles: Chicano Studies Research Center Publications, UCLA, 1981), pp. 139–51.

6. Michael Meyer and W. Sherman, *The Course of Mexican History* (New York: Oxford University Press, 1979).

7. Lawrence Cardoso, *Mexican Emigration to the United States, 1897–1931* (Tucson: The University of Arizona Press, 1980), pp. 1–12.

8. Bustamante, "The Historical Context," and Julián Samora, *Los Mojados, The Wetback Story* (Notre Dame, Ind.: University of Notre Dame Press, 1970).

9. Wayne Cornelius, "Outmigration from Rural Mexican Communities," in *The Dynamics of Internal Migration* (Washington, D.C.: Smithsonian Institute, 1976); Ira Dinerman, "Patterns of Adaptations Among Households of U.S. Bound Migrants from Michoacan, Mexico," *International Migration Review*, vol. 12, no. 4 (Winter 1978), pp. 485–501; Jorge Bustamante, "Undocumented Migration from Mexico: A Research Report," *International Migration Review*, vol. 11, no. 2 (Summer 1977), pp. 149–78.

10. Abraham Hoffman, *Unwanted Mexican-Americans* (Tucson: University of Arizona Press, 1973).

11. Ibid.

12. Bustamante, "The Historical Context."

13. J. Craig Jenkins, "The Demand for Immigrant Workers: Labor Scarcity or Social Control," *International Migration Review*, vol. 12, no. 4 (Winter 1978), pp. 514–35; and William Preston, Jr., *Aliens and Dissenters: Federal Suppression of Radicals, 1903–1933* (Cambridge, Mass.: Harvard University Press, 1963).

14. Jenkins, "The Demand for Immigrant Workers," discusses these developments.

15. See, Roger Daniels, *Politics of Prejudice* (New York: Atheneum Publishers, 1968).

16. Ibid.

17. Cardoso, *Mexican Emigration to the United States*, pp. 53–54.

18. Carey McWilliams, *North From Mexico* (New York: Greenwood Press, 1968), pp. 178–79.

19. Cardoso, *Mexican Emigration to the United States*, pp. 47–54.

20. Ibid., pp. 83–95.

21. Ibid.

22. Ibid., pp. 119–32.

23. Ibid., pp. 132–40.

24. Clifford Alan Perkins, *Border Patrol: With the U.S. Immigration Service on the Mexican Boundary, 1910–54* (El Paso: Texas Western Press, 1978).

25. Hoffman, *Unwanted Mexican-Americans*.

26. Mazón, "Illegal Alien Surrogates," pp. 305–24.

27. Hoffman, *Unwanted Mexican-Americans*, pp. 116–31.

28. Ernesto Galarza, *Merchants of Labor: The Mexican Bracero Story* (Santa Barbara: McNally & Loftin, 1964).

29. Ibid.

30. Juan R. García, *Operation Wetback: The Mass Deportation of Mexican Undocumented Workers in 1954* (Westport, CT.: Greenwood Press, 1980), and Manuel García y Griego, *The Importation of Mexican Contract Laborers to the United States,*

1942–1964: Antecedents, Operation and Legacy (San Diego: Center for U.S.-Mexican Studies, University of California, San Diego, 1980).

31. Galarza, *Merchants of Labor.*

32. Jorge A. Bustamante, "The Immigrant Worker: A Social Problem or a Human Resource," in Ríos-Bustamante, ed., *Mexican Immigrant Workers.*

33. For a discussion of the most recent governmental proposals, see Wayne A. Cornelius, "The Reagan Administration's Proposals for a New U.S. Immigration Policy: An Assessment of Potential Effects," *International Migration Review,* vol. 15, no. 4 (Winter 1981), pp. 769–78.

34. Hoffman, *Unwanted Mexican-Americans,* and García, *Operation Wetback.*

35. Manuel García y Griego and Leobardo F. Estrada, "Research on the Magnitude of Mexican Undocumented Immigration to the United States: A Summary," in Ríos-Bustamante, ed., *Mexican Immigrant Workers,* pp. 51–70; Víctor Villalpando, "Abstract—A Study of the Impact of Illegal Aliens on the County of San Diego on Specific Socioeconomic Areas," in Ríos-Bustamante, ed., *Mexican Immigrant Workers,* pp. 103–10; and David North and Marion F. Houston, *Illegal Aliens: Their Characteristics and Role in the U.S. Labor Market* (Washington, D.C.: Department of Labor, 1976).

36. The networks of immigrant workers, in particular female immigrant workers, are discussed in Margarita Melville, "Mexican Women Adapt to Migration," in Ríos-Bustamante, ed., *Mexican Immigrant Workers,* pp. 119–26.

37. Luis R. Negrete, "La lucha de la comunidad mexicana por los derechos humanos de los trabajadores emigrantes," in Ríos-Bustamante, ed., *Mexican Immigrant Workers,* pp. 161–68.

38. Ibid.

5 | Chicano Political Development: Historical Considerations

CHRISTINE M. SIERRA

Analysis of a group's political development often involves an examination of the group's political behavior, as it chooses to organize in various ways, drawing from a myriad of approaches. Yet, the exercise of choice, of deciding between alternatives, takes place within a larger context. That context consists of the structured political relationships developed over time between the group and the political system.

This study of Chicano political development provides an overview of such structural considerations: those political arrangements and processes, drawn from early periods of Chicano history, that have set the basic parameters in which contemporary political endeavors evolve. Identified as key factors are the following: (1) the nature of Mexicans' entry into U.S. society, (2) the nature of Mexican immigration, (3) the nature of the Mexican work experience, and (4) Chicano experiences with ethnic organizational structures. Political ramifications flow from each of these factors, producing a political history that sets apart the Mexican experience from the experiences of other minority groups in the United States.

HISTORICAL CONDITIONS FOR CHICANO POLITICAL DEVELOPMENT

"People of Conquest"

Contemporary political developments evolve from conditions of the past. Several factors can be identified as setting the broad parameters within which contemporary Chicano political development evolved. The first factor to note is that Mexicans in the United States constitute a "people of conquest." A defining characteristic that allows Robert Blauner to distinguish between immigrant minorities and "colonized" minorities is the nature of the group's *original* entrance into society.[1] The fact that Mexicans (and their land) became a part of the United States by conquest distinguishes Mexican political history from that of other ethnic and racial groups with the exception of the American Indians. Mexicans' "special" relationship to the land of the Southwest prompted one social scientist to state that Mexicans resemble more the "typical minority in Europe than . . . the typical European minority in the United States."[2]

That part of Mexican territory originally known as the Spanish borderlands provided the arena in which the full force of Anglo-American expansionist ideology, the relentless search for natural resources, and the malignant growth of cultural animosities[3] finally collided and burst forth in a bloody war. The Mexican-American War of 1846 ended "officially" with the signing of a treaty on February 2, 1848. However, as Carey McWilliams observes, "it becomes quite apparent that the Mexican-American War was merely an incident in a conflict which arose some years before and survived long after the Treaty of Guadalupe Hidalgo."[4]

The terms of the Treaty of Guadalupe Hidalgo of 1848 made America's belief in "manifest destiny" that much more real and concrete. Mexico ceded to the United States a vast territory, which included the present-day states of California, Arizona, New Mexico, Utah, Nevada, and parts of Colorado. Mexico also accepted the Río Grande as its border with Texas, which had become part of the United States through "annexation" in 1846.[5] Shortly thereafter, "by the use of high pressure methods already painfully familiar to the Mexicans," yet another "bite of Mexican territory" was secured for the United States.[6] The Gadsen Purchase added parts of New Mexico and southern Arizona to the newly "acquired" lands, whose mineral wealth in gold, silver, and copper had not yet been fully recognized by either the Americans or Mexicans.

The territorial conquest of "El Norte de México" laid the foundation for the future political development of Mexicans in the United States. One political scientist characterizes the conquest as pushing Mexicans in the United States "into a permanent posture of defense."[7] The political significance of the conquest crystallizes when one looks at three resultant processes: the usurpation of land rights, the supplanting of Mexican institutional structures and procedures with Anglo-American ones, and the suppression of cultural autonomy.

All citizens of Mexico who resided in the ceded territory were to become U.S. citizens if, within one year after ratification of the Treaty of Guadalupe Hidalgo, they had failed to leave the area. Carey McWilliams states that "only a few thousand Mexican nationals, perhaps not more than 1,500 or 2,000, took advantage of this provision; the rest became citizens-by-default."[8] Citizenship "by default," however, provided few long-lasting guarantees of anything, especially of rights to the land. There were essentially three ways in which land was confiscated from Mexicanos in the Southwest. First, Mexican land grants were vaguely defined and could not be defended on ownership grounds under Anglo-American land laws. Second, through the imposition of high taxes and various swindling schemes, land passed from Mexican owners to Anglo hands. Third, squatters coming from the east began taking over the land—"and the better land at that!"[9] Arturo Madrid vividly brings to life these various processes by stating:

> From the Matamoros haciendas near the Gulf of Mexico to the Petaluma ranchos off San Francisco Bay the landholding ricos were forced off their holdings. . . . Those who survived the armed violence fell victims to the Land Law of 1851, which permitted settlers to stake out claims on land which "to the best of one's knowledge" was unused. Those who resisted the squatters impoverished themselves in the courtrooms and backrooms of the new legal system, confused by judges and commissioners, outmaneuvered by plaintiffs, swindled by lawyers. Those who won the legal battles lost their lands to moneylending, tax manipulating entrepreneurs who flooded the West after the Civil War. The few survivors, extended token and symbolic political and social recognition, became the models for the "fantasy heritage" of Silver Dons, gay caballeros and Spanish conquistadores created at the turn of the century by publicists for the railroads and land companies and nurtured by . . . romanticizers of the Southwest.[10]

Whether their land was secured from them legally or illegally, Mexican settlers, rich and poor alike, "doubted a government that would not protect their person" or safeguard their property.[11]

The territorial conquest also brought a change in the institutional structures and procedures of the Southwest. Mexican laws and governmental structures and procedures, no matter how feebly enforced or followed in the borderlands,[12] were the legitimate foundations upon which Southwest society rested. Moreover, as one historian points out, although sparsely populated, the urban centers of the Mexican Southwest had achieved self-sufficiency and "were regarded by the urbanites in Mexico City as outposts of civilization on the edge of the frontier."[13] That self-sufficiency was accomplished within a Mexican legal governmental framework. The supplanting of Mexican laws and governmental bodies by those from an Anglo-American tradition "drove home" the political significance of the conquest. No doubt the use of Anglo-American laws to appropriate Mexican land highlighted this transformation.

Annexation by conquest is not the only historical experience that Mexicans and American Indians share. Both minority groups had their rights specifically safeguarded by treaty provision. The Treaty of Guadalupe Hidalgo gave Mexicans the right to retain their language, religion, and culture. Both McWilliams and Acuña emphasize that the treaty contained explicit guarantees to insure Mexican cultural autonomy. However, in reality, "no provisions were made . . . for the (legal protection and) integration of the native peoples as a group, as a society."[14]

No treaty on earth, however, could have prevented those cultural and racial animosities, rawly exposed during the Mexican American War, from becoming institutionalized in the very fabric of Southwestern society. "Anti-Catholic, anti-mestizo (the racial mix of Spanish and Indian), and anti-Indian prejudices of Anglo Americans helped to channel Mexican political development even further into a permanent posture of defense."[15] The right of conquest gave way to the imposition of other "rights"—of Anglo racial and cultural superiority—which were felt by the "native" Mexican population and became an integral part of the political experiences of Mexicans in the United States.

THE NATURE OF MEXICAN IMMIGRATION

The "special" relationship that exists between the United States, Mexico, and the Southwest sets apart Mexican immigration from that of other ethnic groups. It is this factor as well which carries implications for Mexican political development in the United States. The simple fact of Mexico's proximity to the United States generates the theme of continuity that underlies the distinctive feature of Mexican immigration, particularly in the early twentieth century. In a historical and geographical sense, the theme of continuity develops from the fact that the southwestern part of the United States once belonged to Mexico. The fact that the American Southwest, at its "birth," contained a "native" population of Mexicans influenced the nature of initial population movements from Mexico to the U.S. side. Several scholars have noted this influence by characterizing Mexican "immigration" as truly a process of "migration" instead.

Sociologist Rodolfo Alvarez refers to those who composed the first massive population movements to the United States from Mexico (during the period of approximately 1900 to 1930) as the "Migrant Generation." He asserts that although these people were in a legal sense "immigrants," they were not in a sociological and cultural sense. As they left the political upheaval in Mexico in search of the economic rewards American capitalist agriculture promised them, they did not enter a "fresh social situation where they were meeting the host society for the first time," as an ethnic or racial group. Alvarez explains that their entrance into the United States was already "predefined by the well established social position of pre-1900 Mexican Americans as a conquered people (politically, socially, culturally, economically, and in every other respect)." This situation differed to some extent from the experiences of the first-generation immigrant arrivals from Europe to the eastern shores of the United States. In some ways, Alvarez maintains, European immigrants entered, as a group, a relatively less defined social situation, as opposed to Mexicans. "Their place in the social hierarchy was, in a sense, freshly negotiated according to what the group as a whole could do here."[16]

The social and cultural milieu of the Mexican communities in the Southwest provided newcomers from Mexico with a basis for familiarity and rapid adjustment into a new environment. At the same time this process was occurring, the dominant "host" society viewed the "migrant generation" basically in the same fashion it viewed the Mexican Americans who had been living in the Southwest long before the 1900s. All were the "same"; all were Mexican.[17]

The political significance of these two simultaneous occurrences lies in the fact that the seeds of internal divisions among Mexicans, on nationality and citizenship grounds, were planted. Organizations emerged in Mexican communities that reacted to the anti-Mexican animosities embedded in the Southwest, so well reinforced by the national atmosphere of nativist sentiment permeating the 1920s. Nurtured by the class divisions already forming among Mexicans in the American Southwest, organizations emerged that stressed their American orientation over their Mexican roots.

The League of United Latin American Citizens (LULAC) evolved out of southcentral Texas in the late 1920s. Its middle-class members stressed their American citizenship and "American values" in ways that would indeed set them apart from the vast flow of Mexican migrants desperately in search of the "better life" in the land to the north.[18] Ironically, then, those forces that lent the American Southwest a historical continuity with Mexico eventually gave way to undercurrents of division and discontinuity, which began to take shape in the early 1900s.

As previously mentioned, the special nature of Mexican "immigration" brings to attention the theme of geographical continuity as well. Once a part of "El Norte de México," the Southwest, especially in the early twentieth century, physically resembled the northern portions of Mexico, for "wars do not alter the facts of geography."[19] To some extent, the resemblance still persists. As McWilliams observes, "one can travel from Chihuahua to Santa Fe with scarcely any feeling of abrupt change in the physical environment."[20]

Geographical continuity provided the Mexican migrant with a relocation experience very different from that of the European immigrant. Emigration from Europe involved traversing an enormous physical obstacle, the Atlantic Ocean, while attempting to survive the miseries time and space inflicted upon the passenger.[21] The crossing represented "a severance . . . an abrupt transition" of the utmost importance.[22] The land entered was different from the land left behind. It was "foreign" to the immigrant in countless ways.

Relocation for the Mexican migrant meant a gradual transition within the confines of a familiar environment. No less important or significant than the European experience, the relocation process for Mexicans, however, did not entail a severe severance from the land of origin. To be crossed was a border described by McWilliams as "one of the most unrealistic borders to be found in the Western Hemisphere."[23] Across much of the territory between the United States and Mexico, the border was no more than an imaginary line. In those areas where the Río Grande separated the two nations, the river could be crossed fairly easily during most of the year—a reality that still exists. In addition, not until the 1930s was an official transaction required to enter the United States, a stark contrast to the European experience of Ellis Island.[24]

The notion of permanence highlights an additional distinction between Mexican migration and European immigration. As Dinnerstein and other historians point out, some first-generation European immigrants came to the United States with intentions of returning home once they had made some economic gains. Some, in fact, were able to do so. Yet for most, the force of circumstances rapidly made a return to the Old Country a virtual impossibility.[25] For Mexicans, however, the proximity of Mexico to the United States and the railroad system built between the two countries made a return to Mexico both feasible and real. Thus, Mexican migration has really entailed a back and forth movement of people. It encompasses permanent, temporary, and intermittent migrations, patterns that are still evident today.[26]

An examination of the special nature of Mexican immigration yields some additional political observations. Rising from the theme of historical continuity is the observation that, to a large extent, Mexican politics remained a frame of reference for Mexicans in the United States. Despite a once-common social science conclusion that Mexicans "show no political interest," interest in political events was indeed evident in Mexican communities of the Southwest. Interest, in many cases, however, focused on political occurrences in Mexico, especially during the period of the Mexican Revolution of 1910. Spanish-language newspapers followed the developments of the revolution closely,[27] and political clubs in the United States took sides over which faction to support.[28] Moreover, organizational ties developed between political groups in Mexico and groups in the United States. The party founded by the Mexican revolutionary Ricardo Flores Magón established its first headquarters in the United States in San Antonio, Texas. Known as *El Partido Liberal Mexicano* (PLM), it sought to organize Mexican laborers on both sides of the border.[29] Another organization that followed a similar strategy was *El Congreso Mexicanista,* which emerged in Laredo, Texas in 1911.[30]

Present-day realities necessitate a continuation of interest in Mexican politics. Although different in content and expression, interest in economic and political developments in Mexico persists in Chicano communities. Mexican immigration, the policies of U.S. twin plants along the border, and issues such as the appointment of a U.S. ambassador to Mexico continue to serve as catalysts to Chicano political involvement.[31] The historical link of political interest between Mexicans on both sides of the border continues to exist.

The proximity of Mexico to the United States has historically allowed for constant migration between the two countries. It has also provided for the perception of the Mexican population by U.S. authorities as "movable." The implementation of deportation and repatriation measures are of fundamental importance in the political history of Mexicans in the United States. From 1926 to 1939, approximately one million people were repatriated to Mexico, voluntarily and involuntarily.[32] The United States government undertook these repatriation measures in an attempt to alleviate the social and economic woes of the country during the Depression. And, unlike other ethnic and racial groups, Mexicans were an "easy target" for such a program.

Perhaps of even greater significance is the role deportations have played in Chicano history. Beginning in 1929, the Department of Labor launched an all-out effort to apprehend and deport Mexican laborers (without papers) who were "taking jobs away" from U.S. citizens. Los Angeles county was the focus of what amounted to a purge. All Mexicans in the area, U.S. citizens and non-citizens alike, were subject to federal harassment. In many cases, Mexican Americans who did not have proof of citizenship in their possession, and who could not speak English, were deported as well.[33]

Whereas the need to control the flow of labor provided the justification for the deportations, a political purpose was evident as well. Local and federal authorities used both the threat of deportation and its actual enforcement to undermine organizational activity among Mexicans. For example, during the mid-thirties, Mexican labor unions were most effective at laying the groundwork for organizing in the fields. Yet, "with scarcely an exception, every strike in which Mexicans participated in the [Southwest] ... was broken by the use of violence and was followed by deportations."[34]

Approximately two decades later, with the wartime labor shortage having passed, deportations struck the Mexican areas of the country once again. Organizational efforts suffered immeasurable losses as their leaders were deported, this time with the fervor of "anticommunism" so prevalent in the 1950s. One such leader, Luisa Moreno, had been involved in labor union activity and in attempts to maintain a regional organization called *El Congreso de Pueblos que Hablan Español* (Congress of Spanish-Speaking People).[35] In total, deportations of Mexicans numbered around two and a half million for the years 1950–53. The sheer magnitude of the deportations in this "Red Scare" period no doubt led some organizations, like the Community Service Organization (CSO) in Los Angeles, to temper their activities, lest they be judged "un-American."[36]

THE NATURE OF MEXICAN WORK EXPERIENCE

The nature of Mexican work experience is the third major factor that has set the basic parameters within which Chicano political development evolves. Both the nature of Mexican immigration and the nature of Mexican labor have been intimately intertwined throughout history. With this in mind, the focus now turns to the major occupations Mexicans have historically filled and those employment patterns and policies that have generated problems for organization.

As indicated previously, Chicanos overall do not figure very high in the present-day occupational structure of the country. Not surprisingly, this situation evolves from a history of restriction to a subordinated labor status in the economic order of the United States. It is this aspect of Chicano history that most clearly draws distinctions between white immigrant groups, on the one hand, and Mexicans on the other.

The restrictive uses of Mexican labor emerged early in the formation of a new class structure in the Southwest, shortly after the conquest of Mexican land. In his study of the development of capitalist agriculture in California in the latter part of the nineteenth century, Tomás Almaguer discusses the role racial minorities played in that economic order. During the period from 1870 to 1900, racial minorities primarily constituted contract labor. On the other hand, white immigrants during this period found employment in a variety of skilled and semiskilled occupations. In addition, it was largely this group who benefited from the sale of rancho lands, which created their small farms. As Almaguer notes, largely due to the economic alternatives accorded Anglo Americans, they were able to "avoid the type of labor status that befell racial minorities in California." As he explains, "with white labor largely unavailable, it was first the Chinese, then later the Japanese and Mexican who were relied upon to meet the seasonal labor needs of capitalist agriculture."[37]

The basic nineteenth-century employment practice of contracted Mexican labor continued into the twentieth century as well. The restrictive nature of contract labor becomes apparent when one notes that Mexican labor was sought "by particular employers, for employment in particular industries at particular tasks." From approximately 1900 to 1940, Mexican labor was confined primarily to three major sectors: agriculture, mining, and the railroad industry. A further observation emphasizes that "with few exceptions, only a *particular class* of employers has employed Mexican labor in the Southwest," that class represented by large-scale industrial enterprises.[38] One scholar offers the following literary summary of Mexican occupational history from the late nineteenth to the mid-twentieth century:

> Rounded up in small villages on both sides of the border and herded to ever larger railway centers, Mexicanos were then bunched into boxcars and dispatched to man the section crews and extra gangs of the Southern Pacific and Santa Fe, formerly the job of the despised Chinese, to pick the cattle-displacing cotton of middle and west Texas, a task abandoned by northward-moving Blacks; to do the risky, dirty-digging in the Gila Hills of southern Arizona, a job disdained by Anglo miners; to harvest the crops of the Great Western Sugar Beet Co. [and from there] to develop the empires of California's agri-businessmen ultimately to replace the Filipinos, who had before replaced the Japanese, who previously

tion was evident across industries as well as within certain enterprises. In California in 1930 within certain plants, Mexicans were used "exclusively in specific types of employment rather than being scattered through the plant."[42]

The resultant consequence for organization is that divisions among workers developed along racial lines. "Skilled labor groups regarded Mexicans as *group* competitors rather than as individual employees." Trade unions shunned the incorporation of Mexican workers. When Mexicans did manage to organize themselves and go out on strike, organized labor in many cases did not support them. Their organizations, for the most part, were not affiliated with either the CIO or the AFL.[43]

The third major aspect of the nature of Mexican labor is its use as an integral part of the nation's "reserve army of labor." In periods of intense labor needs, Mexicans were actively recruited into the industries of the Southwest.[44] A major portion of this Mexican work force came from Mexico as "imported" or migrant labor. Because of its mobility and availability, Mexican labor provided U.S. business and corporate interest with a manipulatable pool of reserve labor. As such, Mexican labor served political purposes as well.

The importation of Mexican labor often served two strategically important functions: to depress wages and to break strikes. With cheap labor readily and seemingly inexhaustibly available, large corporate interests were able to drive small farmers and tenants (predominantly Anglo) from agricultural land in west Texas. Divisions along racial lines "naturally" increased in what essentially was a clash of economic interests.[45] Labor conflict in the fields is replete with examples of the use of imported Mexican labor to break strikes. In more recent history, the development of the Bracero Program in 1942 added the full backing of the U.S. government to the economic game of supplying large amounts of labor at depressed wages (and miserable working conditions).[46] The use of Mexican immigrant labor in such exploitative situations has resulted in the creation of deep divisions among workers and internal splits within the Mexican community in the United States. The bottom line is that the focus of "blame" for these exploitative conditions has been directed toward the Mexican laborer and not on those economic interests and processes from which these conditions emerge. The nature of Mexican labor thus provides insight into how certain patterns and practices, structured over time, act as constraints on Mexican political development.

ORGANIZATIONAL EXPERIENCE IN THE "IMMIGRANT TRADITION" — SIMILARITIES AND DIFFERENCES

A fourth factor that has influenced the overall political development of Mexicans in the United States is the overall organizational experience acquired as

had replaced the Chinese, all of whom had become less manageable and the fore less desirable.[39]

In whichever major sector Mexicans held jobs (from the late 1800s approximately 1940), three aspects of their labor bore implications for org nization. These aspects are (1) the predominant characteristics of their wor (2) their employment as a group; and (3) their use as a "reserve army labor." The basic characteristics their jobs shared were the migratory and trai sient nature of the work, extremely limited opportunities for advancement, an conditions of social isolation.

Mexican labor was migratory and transient in several respects. For example work in the field and on the railroads entailed travel over vast distances as crop were picked and tracks were laid. Employment for most was either seasonal or casual. In addition, the migratory nature of the work encompassed the flow of the labor force itself. In response to the heavy recruitment efforts conducted on both sides of the border, Mexicans provided a constant flow of labor to various industrial sectors. What resulted was an occupational history riddled with instability and inconsistency—inherent obstacles to organization.

Few opportunities for advancement existed in those economic sectors that employed Mexicans. Mexican labor was largely unskilled, to begin with, and Mexicans worked in industries that were highly organized by big business interests and dominated by big capitalist investments.[40] Few opportunities for advancement lay ahead for field and packing-house employees in the farming industry or for those working in crews in the nation's smelters and refineries.

Employment as section-hands on the rail lines or as diggers in the mines often meant living and working in the physically remote desert areas of the Southwest. Social isolation also meant limited interaction with others outside of the work environment. The situation for many involved "traveling over a wide territory, usually in the company of other Spanish-speaking workers, bossed by a Mexican foreman, [and] living in a Mexican labor camp or shack-town."[41] Both the limited opportunity for advancement and the condition of social isolation imposed upon Mexican workers a certain degree of confinement. Combined with the migratory and transient aspects of the work, these characteristics promoted a general condition of "permanent" instability and inconsistency for Mexican workers. Thus, formidable obstacles were indeed laid for the development of political organization in Mexican areas of the United States.

Identified as a second major aspect of the nature of Mexican labor is the pattern of group employment imposed upon it. Industries employed Mexicans en masse, as a group and not on an individual basis. Families, including men, women, and children, worked the "factories in the fields." Mexicans worked in the mines, smelters, and railroads in gangs and crews. Occupational segrega-

an ethnic group in this country. The two organizational structures that scholars define as significant in the social and political history of ethnic or immigrant groups are the mutual aid society and the political machine. The way in which these organizations have penetrated Mexican communities in the United States thus becomes an important subject for analysis.

The significance of the mutual aid society was that it represented one of the first organizational efforts launched by newly arrived immigrants to help themselves as a group. By pooling meager resources together, mutual aid was offered in the provision of low cost funeral and insurance benefits, low interest loans, and other economic benefits. Although historians are apt to emphasize the social cohesion and organization that mutual aid societies lent to immigrant life, their contribution is political as well. Mutual aid societies provided a basis for the later development of trade unions and associations among the immigrant groups. And, of course, as immigrants maintained their societies, they picked up organizing skills along the way. As Oscar Handlin notes,

> The first encounter with the practice of governing came in their local associational activities. In time each society acquired a constitution and by-laws, no doubt printed from stock forms ... and no doubt frequently honored in the breach. Still, here they elected officers, and conducted debates, and made rules. If these affairs had little effect upon the world outside, they nevertheless gave the members a taste of what politics involved.[47]

Evidence shows that the mutual aid organization was also part of the Mexican experience as well. In Mexican communities, as early as the 1890s, *mutualistas* emerged to perform functions similar to their earlier counterparts on the east coast. *Mutualistas* in their initial stage of development in the Southwest directed their efforts toward the Mexican working class and, in some cases, proved to be very nationalistic. One historian notes that some *mutualistas* excluded non-Mexican nationals from their organizations.[48] The total extent to which *mutualistas* developed in Mexican communities is not known; however, it does appear that there were many indeed. In the 1920s one study on Mexican immigrants uncovered the existence of many Mexican mutual aid societies in various parts of the country. In Los Angeles alone there were forty-four in the late 1920s. Others appeared in areas such as Albuquerque, San Antonio, Chicago, Kansas City, and Michigan.[49]

Some societies did develop into explicitly political organizations. The anthropologist Manuel Gamio notes that a *mutualista* founded in Tucson in 1894 took on a political purpose. *La Alianza Hispano Americana* launched a campaign to replace those in power in Tucson politics with native Tucson residents of Mexican descent.[50] Shortly after World War I, in Los Angeles, members of the Lázaro Cárdenas Society held meetings to discuss community grievances. In Kansas City, La Liga Protectora Mexicana organized in a defensive posture to protect the rights of legal immigrants in the area.[51]

The development and evolutionary paths of *mutualistas* replicate in many ways those of the white immigrant societies on the east coast. The Mexican experience with the political machine, however, does not appear to follow as closely.

The vast amount of scholarly research on the political machine attests to the impact the machine had on the political development of white ethnic groups on the east coast and to a lesser extent on blacks in the north. In stark contrast, very little is known about the mere *existence* of political machines (much less about their overall impact and significance) in Mexican areas of the country. I will generate a tentative argument of how machine politics has figured in the political development of Mexicans in the United States.

In its most basic form, a political machine is a hierarchical party organization that distributes patronage and other inducements to win votes and thereby to control elections and government. It functions in a situation where mass suffrage exists. In its perhaps "classic" form, it existed in large urban areas (such as New York and Chicago) and drew its massive support from the immigrant voters. Its game was politics, its inducements were for the most part specific and tangible, and its overall effects were varied and multiple. A relationship of exchange existed between the political machine and its immigrant supporters. It was an exchange with economic, social, and political features.

The machine offered the immigrant voter certain economic benefits in exchange for a vote. Tangible benefits provided were jobs in the public and sometimes in the private sector, emergency aid, occasional monetary gifts, and the like. Political favors came in the form of personal help in dealing with the public bureaucracies, the police, and other representatives of officialdom. Social rewards came from having someone to turn to in time of need, for the precinct captain was on familiar terms with the voters in the local ward.[52]

In their critique of the political machine, Norman and Susan Fainstein note that while the machine "undoubtedly provided services to many proletarians," it did so by reaching out to them as individuals and not as a collectivity. For example, unlike trade unions, the machine "had no direct interest in increasing wages, or in opposing employers."[53] Several scholars also argue that because of the individualized and particularized nature of the reward extended them (plus other factors), immigrants were conservatively socialized in ways that prevented them from perceiving themselves as a class with common interests.

In spite of the individualized rewards, however, it seems apparent that the immigrants reaped some benefits as a group as a result of machine politics. Perhaps like no other mechanism, the machine furthered a process of *integration* into the political and social fabric of U.S. society for immigrant groups. Incorporation into the party organization provided some groups with an avenue for social mobility. The Irish, of course, are a case in point. "Many municipalities in the generation after the Civil War knew only Irish names among politicians." Irish domination in large cities extended to fire and police departments.[54] The fact that representatives of ethnic groups were brought into the party organization in itself meant that general recognition was given them as a group.[55]

In addition to those who moved up the ranks of the party organization, the general immigrant population enjoyed the benefits of political incorporation that the machine had to offer. In fulfilling its part of the bargain in the exchange for voters, the political machine set in motion the process of political acculturation for the ethnic minorities. As Cornwell indicates:

> The mere seeking out of the immigrants in quest of their support, the assistance rendered in getting them naturalized (when it was necessary to observe these legal niceties), and so forth were of considerable importance in laying the foundation for their more meaningful political participation later.[56]

In inducing electoral participation and turning immigrants into citizens, the machine furthered the political education of the ethnic minorities. Michael Parenti notes that campaigns, voting, and contacts with the local political clubs "gave the ethnic some small sense of participation and practice as an American, some tenuous feeling that his voice counted with the powers that be, and some claim to legitimacy and equal status." In the end, the political system became "an arena for the maximization of ethnic interests."[57] Thus, machine politics facilitated the incorporation and integration of ethnic immigrant groups into city government and the political system.

Political machines also made their appearance in such predominantly Mexican areas as Laredo, El Paso, and the rural counties of south Texas in the late 1800s. Historian Mario García documents the emergence of machine politics in El Paso, Texas, as early as 1860. It was not until the 1880s, however, that one particular party organization, known as "the Ring," assumed control and remained in power until around 1915.[58] In south Texas, one man, Jim Wells, bossed the border counties from 1880 until his death in 1920. Another by the name of Manuel Guerra bossed Starr County in Texas until 1915.[59] The evidence points to the existence of political machines in some areas with large Mexican populations.

Questions remain, however, regarding the similarities between the "classic" form of machine politics and that occurring in the Southwest. In its "classic" form, the machine provided jobs, most of which were "unskilled governmental or private-sector which the machine did not create, but only distributed." Outside of creating jobs within its own structure, the machine primarily allocated jobs within the working class. Business interests reaped these benefits and more, as they were awarded government contracts and the like.[60] Thus, there was a symbiotic relationship between political and economic interests. There was a good deal but not total overlap between the two spheres.

In the case of south Texas, for a time the overlap was complete. Politics revolved around a ranching economy. The political boss was also the economic king of the area. In the case of the cattle barons such as Jim Wells, they voted *their* tenants and their laborers on election day.[61] The *patrón-peón* relationship carried the bosses' role to the extreme.

Machine politics in El Paso approximated the "classic" form more closely. Machine politicians, representing El Paso's business and professional class, provided supporters with public jobs in return for their support. However, a significant difference of degree emerges. García explains that patronage was awarded to certain Mexican-American políticos "in return for their ability to organize and deliver Mexican voters."[62] The patronage extended to Mexicans in El Paso was to a select few and apparently did not approximate the degree to which jobs were distributed among the white ethnic populations. This is important to note since "the most significant, tangible return which the *largest* number of [white] immigrants received from the machine was a job."[63]

A further observation is that those patronage jobs awarded Mexican-American políticos brought them only into certain county positions and did not incorporate them into city government. The Ring supported Mexican-American candidates and offered patronage jobs in the sanitation and police departments. The majority of Mexican-American officeholders, however, served in "minor county positions." They represented the county commissioners, justices of the peace, local precinct chairmen, and officials from the outlying rural areas of El Paso. García comments on this pattern in the following manner:

> While the Ring did not hesitate to endorse Mexican Americans for certain county offices where the selection of a Mexican would be practical and beneficial, it apparently refused to nominate them for city positions for fear of offending American voters.[64]

While the political integration of Mexican-American políticos seemed somewhat limited and controlled, it appeared totally absent for the larger Mexican population. Some sort of exchange relationship existed between the machine and white ethnic groups. In the solicitation or "buying" of their votes, the machine provided certain services and benefits to the immigrant voters. In El Paso machine politics, an "exchange relationship" is difficult to find. The "buying" of votes did not translate figuratively but literally. And the "payment" in exchange hardly constituted a "service." García provided the following account:

> Both Democrats and Republicans in the 1889 city election . . . openly purchased Mexican votes not only in El Paso, but in Ciudad Juárez [Mexico] as well. Besides money, the politicians offered free beer and entertainment. According to one account, the festivities began on the day before the election and continued

all night. On election morning, the Mexicans discovered to their surprise that the doors of the dance hall had been locked and that they could not leave until the polls opened and their votes registered. At seven in the morning, therefore, the politicians assembled the Mexicans and under guard conducted them to the voting precincts where they were handed a prepared ballot and paid three dollars.[65]

The large property owners of south Texas followed similar practices. In addition to "voting their Mexicans," they imported "droves of Mexicans across the border [and] held them under guard in corrals and stockades" until election day.[66]

The corrupt practices of these machines did not stop with their buying votes, registering Mexican nationals, and "imprisoning" the voters. In El Paso, the Ring fraudulently purchased poll taxes (required as of 1902) for their Mexican supporters. Later an investigation showed that "in many cases Mexicans acquired these illegal receipts with the understanding they could also be used to secure employment with the city or county governments."[67]

While the type of individual rewards granted to white ethnics in the form of personal favors and the like may have been extended to Mexicans by the machine bosses, it appears that the economic inducements were limited. The group benefits provided to the white immigrants, such as social mobility and integration into city government and the political system, do not apply to the Mexican case in Texas. Mexican immigrants gained little or nothing as a result of machine politics. They were not incorporated into the political arena; rather they were herded like cattle from one polling place to another and "rewarded" in liquor and small change. The political education they received most likely "proved" to them the sham of American government in action. As García concludes, "it was not the Mexican immigrants who experienced acculturation into American life out of their political ties with the [machines], but rather the Mexican Americans."[68] It was from their ranks that a select few found social mobility and were reinforced in their belief in the efficacy of American politics.

The information presented here comes from two case studies on political machines in Texas. There is good reason to suspect, however, that these cases might be representative of how the machine functioned at its height in Mexican immigrant communities.[69] For one thing, Texas was the major funnel for early Mexican immigration to the United States. Texas cities, especially El Paso and Laredo, were the chief points of entry for Mexican immigrants in the early 1900s. In addition, this period, from 1910 to 1930, represented the first massive waves of immigration from Mexico.

When one compares the overall time frame for the massive immigrations from Europe and Mexico, the argument (drawn from the Texas case) that the machine did not offer to Mexicans what it did for European immigrants is strengthened. European immigration occurred much earlier than Mexican immigration. As many scholars agree, the massive waves of European immigration from the mid-nineteenth century to the early 1900s contributed greatly to the machine's emergence and longevity. Mexican immigration did not follow this time line. Its first peak years were from 1900 to 1930. This difference is significant when one notes that machine politics was on the *decline* in the 1920s. The urban reforms of the Progressives, the nationalization and bureaucratization of welfare services, and the virtual stop of European immigration in the 1920s robbed the machine of much of its power.[70]

The ascendancy of machine politics began as early as the mid-1800s, while such powerful machines as Tammany Hall in New York City reigned in the 1890s.[71] An urban, highly industrialized, densely populated region of the country set the basis for machine politics in the nineteenth century. In the Southwest, allowing for some regional variations, economic growth and transformation of the area "took off" from 1910 to 1929. The urbanization process for Chicanos in the Southwest unfolded relatively recently, from 1900 to 1930. With the exception of Los Angeles and San Francisco, the Southwest in 1920 had no cities with a population of over 100,000. As machines "peaked" in their power in the last decade of the nineteenth century, "urban growth in the Southwestern states had reached only 50 percent of the level found in the eastern and midwestern regions of the country."[72]

In general, the timing of Mexican immigration and the particular development of the Southwest created conditions for machine politics that differed significantly from those of the east coast. Political machines in the Southwest had less to offer, less resources at their disposal with which to "buy off" the Mexican population. Patronage jobs were few, and reform governments were taking over the cities. The first era of Mexican immigration coincided with the decline of the political machine. Mexican immigrants were not extended the benefits other ethnic groups gained from machine politics. As such, the organizational experience accorded white ethnic groups as a result of machine politics did not carry over to the same extent in the Mexican experience.

SUMMARY

Several historical factors, identified here, created the antecedent conditions to Chicano organizational development. The original "entrance" of Mexicans in the United States, the nature of Mexican immigration and labor history, plus their organizational experience as an "immigrant" group have set the parameters for Chicano political development. This listing, however, is by no means exhaustive; other factors, such as the role of the Catholic and Protestant churches, perhaps carry equal weight.[73] The contribution this study seeks to make is to provide a preliminary analysis of the structural preconditions to

Chicano organizational development. As more research is undertaken, of course, the picture will become more complete.

NOTES

1. Robert Blauner, *Racial Oppression in America* (New York: Harper and Row, 1972), ch. 2, pp. 51–81. Other defining characteristics include the nature of a group's labor history and its geographical location.

2. Carey McWilliams, *North from Mexico* (New York: Greenwood Press, 1968), p. 207. He attributes this observation to Dr. Carolyn Zeleny.

3. Ibid., p. 98. McWilliams refers to the "malignant conflict of cultures."

4. Ibid.

5. Rodolfo Acuña, *Occupied America: The Chicano's Struggle Toward Liberation* (San Francisco: Canfield Press, 1972), p. 28.

6. McWilliams, *North from Mexico,* p. 59.

7. Armando Navarro, "The Evolution of Chicano Politics," *Aztlán,* vol. 5, nos. 1 and 2 (Spring and Fall 1974), pp. 57–84.

8. McWilliams, *North from Mexico,* p. 51.

9. Alberto Camarillo, lecture at Stanford University, January 13, 1976.

10. Arturo Madrid-Barela, "Towards an Understanding of the Chicano Experience," *Aztlán,* vol. 4, no. 1 (Spring 1973), pp. 189–90.

11. McWilliams, *North from Mexico,* p. 110.

12. See Ibid., pp. 99–100. He argues that there was no tradition of self-government in the borderlands. He cites Texas, far removed from its capital of Mexico City, as a case in point.

13. Ricardo Romo, "The Urbanization of Southwestern Chicanos in the Early Twentieth Century," *New Scholar,* vol. 6 (1977), p. 183.

14. McWilliams, *North from Mexico,* pp. 51, 102. See also Acuña, *Occupied America,* pp. 29–30, for further elaboration of explicit provisions in the Treaty of Guadalupe Hidalgo.

15. Madrid-Barela, "Towards an Understanding," McWilliams, *North from Mexico,* and Navarro, "The Evolution of Chicano Politics," all address the issue of racial conflict between Anglos and Mexicans in the Southwest.

16. Rodolfo Alvarez, "The Psycho-Historical and Socioeconomic Development of the Chicano Community in the United States," *Social Science Quarterly,* vol. 53, no. 4 (March 1973), pp. 927–28.

17. Ibid., p. 928.

18. LULAC restricted its membership to American citizens. English was used exclusively at meetings. Its motto was, "All for one and one for all."

19. McWilliams, *North from Mexico,* p. 208.

20. Ibid., p. 58.

21. See Oscar Handlin, *The Uprooted* (Boston: Little, Brown, 1973) for a vivid account of the difficulties and conditions of crossing the Atlantic.

22. McWilliams, *North from Mexico,* p. 58.

23. Ibid., p. 59.

24. Alvarez, "The Psycho-Historical," p. 930.

25. Leonard Dinnerstein et al., *Natives and Strangers: Ethnic Groups and the Building of America* (New York: Oxford University Press, 1979), pp. 134–35 and following.

26. Alberto Carmarillo, lecture at Stanford University, January 13, 1976.

27. Félix Gutiérrez and Ramón Chacón, papers presented at the Annual Conference of the National Association for Chicano Studies, The Claremont Colleges, Claremont, California, March 1978.

28. For example, Mexican social clubs in the United States engaged in political debates, dividing into factions supporting either Porfirio Díaz or Francisco I. Madero.

29. Juan Gómez-Quiñones, *Sembradores: Ricardo Flores Magón y El Partido Liberal Mexicano: A Eulogy and Critique* (Los Angeles: Aztlán Publications, University of California, Los Angeles, 1973).

30. See José Limón, "El Primer Congreso Mexicanista de 1911: A Precursor to Contemporary Chicanismo," *Aztlán*, vol. 5, nos. 1 and 2 (Spring and Fall 1974), pp. 85–117.

31. The Carter Administration in January 1980 announced the appointment of Mexican-American educator Julián Nava to the post of ambassador to Mexico.

32. See Abraham Hoffman, *Unwanted Mexican Americans in the Great Depression: Repatriation Pressures, 1929–1939* (Tucson: University of Arizona Press, 1974).

33. Hoffman, *Unwanted Mexican Americans,* and Alberto Camarillo, lecture at Stanford University, February 10, 1976.

34. McWilliams, *North from Mexico,* p. 194.

35. Two historians at Stanford University, Alberto Camarillo and Vicki Ruiz, are compiling oral interviews with Luisa Moreno, who still lives outside the United States under another name.

36. Alberto Camarillo, lecture at Stanford University, February 12, 1976. He stated that because of the "Red Scare" during the years 1950–1953, the CSO had to lessen its intensive activity in obtaining rulings against abuses committed by law enforcement officers in Los Angeles.

37. Tomás Almaguer, "Class, Race, and Capitalist Development: The Social Transformation of a Southern California County, 1848–1903," Ph.D. dissertation, Department of Sociology, University of California at Berkeley, 1979.

38. McWilliams, *North from Mexico,* p. 215.

39. Madrid-Barela, "Towards an Understanding," pp. 191–92.

40. See McWilliams, *North from Mexico,* p. 215.

41. Ibid., p. 213.

42. Ibid., p. 215.

43. Ibid., pp. 194, 216. Mexican workers did receive considerable support from the IWW, for example, in their organization in the California fields in the 1930s. However, both the AFL and the CIO were slow to respond to the needs of Mexican workers. For further insights into the history of Mexican workers and organized labor see Devra Ann Weber, *The Organizing of Mexicano Agricultural Workers: Imperial Valley and Los Angeles, 1928–34, An Oral History Approach,* reprint from *Aztlán,* vol. 3, no. 2 (Fall 1972), pp. 307–50; Luis Arroyo, "The CIO and the Mexican Worker,"

Ph.D. dissertation, Department of History, University of California, Los Angeles, 1979; and Emilio Zamora, "The American Federation of Labor and the Mexican Worker in Texas During the Early 1900s," chapter of Ph.D. dissertation, The University of Texas at Austin, 1979.

44. Almaguer, "Class, Race, and Capitalist Development," p. 86.

45. McWilliams, *North from Mexico,* p. 216.

46. See the work of Ernesto Galarza for a lucid explication of the Bracero Program: *Merchants of Labor: The Mexican Bracero Story* (Santa Barbara: McNally & Loftin, 1964).

47. Oscar Handlin, *The Uprooted* (Boston: Little, Brown, 1973), p. 185.

48. Alberto Camarillo, lecture at Stanford University, January 13, 1976.

49. Manuel Gamio, *Mexican Immigration to the United States* (New York: Arno Press and *The New York Times,* 1969), appendix VIII, pp. 242–45.

50. Ibid., p. 133.

51. See Miguel Tirado, "Mexican American Community Political Organization," *Aztlán,* vol. no. 1 (Spring 1970), p. 55.

52. Elmer E. Cornwell, Jr., "Bosses, Machines, and Ethnic Groups," *The Annals of the American Academy of Political and Social Science,* vol. 353 (May 1964), p. 31.

53. Norman Fainstein and Susan Fainstein, *Urban Political Movements* (Englewood Cliffs, N.J.: Prentice-Hall, 1974), p. 18.

54. Michael Kraus, *Immigration and the American Mosaic* (Princeton, N.J.: D. Van Nostrand Company, 1966), p. 61.

55. Cornwell, "Bosses, Machines, and the Ethnic Groups," p. 27.

56. Ibid., p. 31.

57. Michael Parenti, "Immigration and Political Life," in Frederic Cople Jaher, ed., *The Age of Industrialism in America* (New York: Free Press, 1968), pp. 90–91, 95.

58. See Mario García, *Desert Immigrants: Mexicans of El Paso, 1880–1920* (New Haven: Yale University Press, 1980), ch. 7.

59. McWilliams, *North from Mexico,* p. 86. He refers to Manuel Guerra as Manuel Gerra.

60. Fainstein and Fainstein, *Urban Political Movements,* pp. 17–18.

61. O. Douglas Weeks, "The Texas-Mexican and the Politics of South Texas," *American Political Science Review,* vol. 24, no. 3 (August 1930), pp. 610–11.

62. García, *Desert Immigrants,* ch. 7, p. 155.

63. Fainstein and Fainstein, *Urban Political Movements,* p. 18, footnote 52, my emphasis.

64. García, *Desert Immigrants,* ch. 7, p. 160.

65. Ibid., p. 4.

66. McWilliams, *North from Mexico,* p. 86.

67. García, *Desert Immigrants,* ch. 7, p. 164.

68. Ibid., p. 21.

69. The case of New Mexico would probably be a major exception. Due to the large "native" Mexican population at the time of the conquest, plus other factors, Mexicans have continued to remain a large and visible part of New Mexican politics.

70. See Cornwell, Jr., "Bosses, Machines, and the Ethnic Groups," pp. 27–39; J.

David Greenstone and Paul E. Peterson, "Machines, Reformers and the War on Poverty," in James Q. Wilson, ed., *City Politics and Public Policy* (New York: Wiley, 1968), pp. 267–92.

71. Martin Shefter, "The Emergence of the Political Machines," in Willis Hawley and Michael Lipsky, eds., *Theoretical Perspectives on Urban Politics* (Englewood Cliffs, N.J.: Prentice-Hall, 1976), pp. 14–44.

72. Romo, "The Urbanization of Southwestern Chicanos," pp. 184–87.

73. There is a paucity of systematic research on this question. Generalization is virtually impossible concerning this important point.

III | Literature and Folklore

Overview

Chicano literature represents an intimate as well as a vital part of the contemporary Chicano experience. After all, it was a form of literature—theater—that sparked a whole new meaning for our existence and place in society in the mid-1960s. By then we had become so accustomed to being portrayed by others that El Teatro Campesino's innovative depiction in 1965 of our immediate social plight became a revolutionary act. Literature answered the need to manifest ourselves and it also nurtured the participants in an intimation of historical resurgence. Somehow, and almost inexplicably, these events gained greater significance when both literature and social unrest converged into one social movement commonly termed the Chicano Movement. From this emerged a revelation that we had, in effect, lost contact with the basic notion of our creative abilities. We had reached the critical crossroads of having to question the degree of assimilation, whether it was mental, physical, or social. Literature, then, provided the road to recovery, as a type of spiritual reconquest of our ethos from which a fuller appreciation of our cultural heritage was regained. The first issue at hand was to establish an operational identity of personal dignity to serve as a rallying point. The burning desire to create a liberated spirit demanded a better world where results were expected and promises challenged.

Literature has played an active role in this socialization process while trying to provide a stronger sense of community. In other words, it is the one thin string of cultural continuity we still have at our disposal to avoid being absorbed into foreign forms. Literary expression helps maintain contact with a part of ourselves that is in constant danger of becoming extinct. For this reason we find it purifying, for it keeps alive that special affinity we feel with our past as it relates to our present.

From the beginnings of the Chicano Movement in the 1960s and 1970s, our literature has exhibited a categorical engagement in creating images of our life experience as opposed to what is found in American literature. Such authors as John Steinbeck, Harvey Fergusson, Charles Lummis, Jack London, and many others have generally not managed to perceive the Mexican beyond the limited realms of caricatures or beings of unidimensional qualities. They failed to see our people as complex human beings with both strengths and frailties, due mainly to predetermined concepts of social classification. Chicano literature, therefore, embodies a viable alternative to previous failures in this area by advocating a less judgmental outlook toward Chicano realities and characters. The intention is not to idealize what is Chicano, but rather to project a fairer portrayal of a people that has been historically relegated to a secondary status, even in literature. Its purpose is not necessarily to compensate for the despicable treatment of anything Chicano in past American literature, although a clear motivator appears to be the avoidance of the "Frito Bandido" syndrome that used to be so prevalent. Our writers as image-makers are creators of a new sort who propose to document artistically the Chicano experience in all its facets.

The papers contained in the present section respond to these many issues as they relate to Chicano literature. The range forms a diverse cross section of topics, some general and others specific; at the same time the papers provide five variegated approaches in this field of study. As contributions to Chicano scholarship, each represents an original study covering a specific topic related to the larger body of creative literary expression.

In the first study, "An Overview of Chicano Letters: From Origins to Resurgence," which serves as the "framing" article, Francisco A. Lomelí traces the historical development of Chicano literature from its early Southwest beginnings to its contemporary status. He establishes the general groundwork for its historical context and conflicting classification and he also provides a brief summary of the contributions from each genre. Carmen Salazar-Parr surveys the topic "La Chicana in Literature" by first discussing the portrayal of Chicana women in Anglo-American literature. She concentrates on the work *The Day of the Swallows* by Estela Portillo Trambley to demonstrate how the woman character is treated in a subtle form according to the complexity of the story and surrealist literary tradition. The third article, "Contemporary Chicano Theater" by Jorge A. Huerta, provides a panoramic view of this unique form of theater, from its antecedents to its present evolution. He also summarizes the contributions of the different theater groups that have helped create TENAZ (Teatro Nacional de Aztlán). María Herrera-Sobek then amply deals with "Chicano Literary Folklore" in referring to a wide variety of subgenres in folklore. Her comprehensive overview covers the many manifestations in this area of study, including the scholarship accomplished in the field. Finally, Gary Keller, in "How Chicano Authors Use Bilingual Techniques for Literary Effect," proposes a linguistic cross-analysis of literary texts to demonstrate how bilingual techniques are effective tools with which to create new breakthroughs in literary expression.

The individual studies aim to provide a representative summary of each topic, thus, the contributions complement each other. The difference in scope and subject matter presents the diversity of this field of study.

6 | An Overview of Chicano Letters: From Origins to Resurgence

FRANCISCO A. LOMELÍ

A myth has persisted that the body of literary expression known as Chicano literature only parallels the popular usage of the word "Chicano," implying that its origins should be explained in terms of the mid-1960s. True, most scholars emphasize its recent development, what Juan Rodríguez calls "florecimiento" and Philip Ortego calls a "Chicano Renaissance,"[1] but the media in general reinforce the myth that our people—and, thus our literature—are strictly a recent contemporary invention. Though conveniently descriptive for an uninformed mass media, such attitudes are to a degree detrimental because they perpetuate, sometimes unconsciously, the portrayal of our people as a "sleeping giant" on the verge of waking up, thereby assuming there has been a dormant stage. The truth of the matter is that our literature has been perceived with as much confusion as have our people, the extreme case being that traditional literary circles do not admit its existence nor do they acknowledge its birthright. Though viewed as an invisible minority, Mexicans have always been a strong force in the Southwest, particularly in the areas of custom, architecture, foods, geographical names, agriculture, and the arts.

Our literary expression has remained vigorous through oral tradition and folklore, but unfortunately the language barrier has not permitted it to transcend cultural lines. It has never made an impact on Anglo-American literature, subsisting marginally as if it were not a part of the overall American experience. However, the rebellious and militant 1960s left an imprint on us as Chicanos. We came to the full realization of the capabilities we had at our disposal through the written word. If in the past literature represented a means with which to express a passing moment of beauty, in the sixties it became a concrete mechanism with which to convey images of our particular experience. In a sense, we had to undo a long history of misconceptions, distortions, and caricatures that misrepresented our way of being. The Chicano Movement provided a context in which we could function, thrive, and finally declare our artistic independence and demand self-determination—the right to define our art in its own terms.[2] The literary movement in the sixties advocated a cultural identity that previously had been stigmatized by the nebulous notion of a supposedly ahistorical people. From this affirmation of Chicano identity emerged the need to confront ourselves as a living paradox—as foreigners in our native land. We took serious note of economic defeats in our history, but at the same time we recognized our triumph of cultural survival.[3] Literary activity forms part of our cultural presence in the Southwest, even though it has been ignored by dominant society.[4]

Before developing a panoramic view of Chicano literature, we should first know some of the workings of literature. The creative art of using language reflects collective conditions when an individual chooses to write down a real or imagined experience.[5] From another perspective, literature is a medium for imagination, not limited to seeing reality for what it is, but including what it might be. Francisco Jiménez states: "By the term 'literature' we mean the imaginative use of language to interpret human experience."[6] In fact, it may well go beyond a given time and space, though these elements influence the writer's fancied construct of the world. The protagonist in the novel *Pocho* alludes to this idea when he tells his mother:

> Mama, do you know what happens to me when I read? All those hours that I sit, as you sometimes say, "ruining my eyes"? I travel, Mama. I travel all over the world, and sometimes out of this whole universe, and I go back in time and again forward. I do not know I am here, and I do not care. I am always thinking of you and my father except when I read. Nothing is important to me then, and I even forget that I am going to die sometimes. I know that I have so much to learn and so much to see that I cannot possibly have enough time to do it all, for the Mexican people are right when they say that life is only a breath.[7]

The authors of *Chicano Perspectives in Literature* see the question of literary expression in still other terms when they add:

> Literature mirrors the multiple personalities and motivations, the small victories and the quiet suffering, the outcries and the anguish—existence in its many phases. Literature assimilates all possible experience in order to recreate an original reality. . . . For these reasons, literature is history, economics, psychology, philosophy, politics and sociology molded by the acts of inspiration and creativity into a literary form which aims to produce an *effect that transcends the limits of merely informing.*[8]

Explicitly stated, its purpose does not have to be practical, nor its dividends immediate. Its objective is generally long-range, preferring to elicit a more intense or wiser life-awareness.

Chicano literature fulfills all the criteria above, and it underlines an ideology of *Chicanismo,* a social-artistic awareness within the bounds of our culture. It is imperative to discuss the origins of this literature in terms of an old phenomenon as well as in terms of a new one. It was not part of an overnight revelation. Chicano writings became noticeable in the mid-sixties, but further research

soon verified a continuous literary tradition that had survived almost sub-
merged in anonymity, marginal to what was accepted by Anglo-American
standards. Our literature is characterized by two distinct beginnings. The year
1848 marks its *historical beginning* because the Mexican-American confrontation determined that Mexicans in the United States automatically became
Chicano (circumstantially, at least, since the term was in very limited use at
the time). The more contemporary date of 1965 is significant as a *symbolic
spiritual rebirth* or resurgence. That year the Teatro Campesino joined the
social struggle of La Causa with César Chávez. Literature and social reality
converged in an inseparable entity.[9] Like the tip of an iceberg, the year 1965
represents a larger and unknown body of artistic activity that had been
ignored—one of the best kept secrets of the Southwest for 120 years. This
period of Chicano literary history has been accurately described by Philip
Ortego as the "Dark Ages" in American letters. It was not until the beginning
of a new era in 1965 that the Chicano boom began in all the arts—literature,
painting, murals, music. The arts became modes of expression for the Chicano
Movement as its members established a close relationship, each nurturing the
other.

One issue that consistently arises is whether Chicano literature deserves to
be called an entity in itself or whether it fits within American, Mexican, or
Latin-American literatures.[10] There are those who make the distinction according to linguistic differences: if written in English it is supposed to indicate its
American ties; if written in Spanish then it is associated with Mexican or
Latin-American literatures. If we use this scheme, however, how do we account
for its interlingual blending, its binary nature, and its bisensitivity,[11] the Chicano's access to diverse avenues and shades of expression? We are led to many
answers. Philip Ortego classifies it as an integral part of the Hispanic period
that constitutes a segment of the overall American experience. If this is true,
why has American literature refused to accept it? Certainly other factors
besides physical borders have to be taken into account, for example, actual
interaction or *convivencia* with Anglo Americans, and the issue of acceptance.
The fact that we have been categorically excluded and alienated from any significant participation at the decision-making level means that we are perceived
as nonentities, a people without a voice. Such institutional ostracism and
estrangement means that, for all practical purposes, Chicanos have never been
seen as part of American history. Luis Leal observes: "To consider Chicano
literature as part of American literature is an object too idealistic, at least for
the time being, for socially Chicanos are considered a group apart."[12]

Others suggest that our literature should be embraced under Mexican letters
when Spanish is the principal language used.[13] The general notion here is that
Chicanos represent a lost orphan overtaken by a dominant culture, who never
relinquished the Mexican heritage completely. Though partly true, such an

attitude fails to measure Chicano creativity on its own terms. It does not take into account linguistic uniqueness, distinctive shades of meaning, and historical purpose. Also, it implies that Chicano writing must form a part of Latin-American literature, since a larger number of Chicano and Chicana writers (including critics) have received their formal training in Spanish Departments. Admitting the influence of certain Latin-American authors such as Carlos Fuentes, Gabriel García Márquez, and Juan Rulfo is not enough proof to claim this literature for the literary tradition of Latin America.[14] Most writers "bor-row" or look elsewhere for inspiration: all writing is a human attempt to find the meaning of the world; Chicano expression is no different, except that here Chicanos are carrying out the activity in a Chicano context of historical cir-cumstance and social conditions.

We find the definitive answer to the original question of what is Chicano literature in the authors themselves. But what is Chicano? Usually nationality resolves any doubts, but a cultural identity based on ethnic background deserves special consideration in view of the fact that Chicanos perceive their creative efforts apart from, though much related to, American and Mexican traditions. The Basques in Spain, the French in Canada, and the Irish in Northern Ireland all face a parallel problem of identity. We are dealing with a literature within a dominant culture, whose posture is to make a stand against what the latter dictates, and to reach for "poetic autonomy" by resorting to two languages (and their variants) at will, and to their respective emotional substances. Both language and feeling contribute to this unique stance. *Bless Me, Ultima* is clearly a Chicano work, not simply because the author, Rudolfo Anaya, meets the definition of a Chicano (an American of Mexican descent), but also because his novel was imagined in Spanish but written in English. His worldview is culturally based, that is, Chicano based.

Many critics insist on defining Chicano literature by the product instead of by the producer. They demand a picture of social reality that is based on a clear-cut political theme, accompanied by unmistakable local color. They wish literature to serve as an instrument for combatting oppression, a social docu-ment or manifesto, narrow in scope. To establish a priori guidelines, to define the literary space[15] in which Chicanos should write is to impose preconceptions and curtail creativity. Literature requires a free spirit if it is to nurture the idea of liberation. Moreover, writing according to restricted subjects harms Chica-nos' ability to produce literature. Then the myth that our scope is confined to narrow horizons is really fulfilled. No one questions Kurt Vonnegut's right to fantasize, yet some are suspicious of Ron Arias's (in *The Road to Tamazun-chale*) apparent lack of realism. Literature cannot be expected to satisfy only our need for representative images. Lesser forms of it merely imitate; higher forms succeed in recreating.

Our literature needs to be judged according to universal literary criteria, but its own particular modes of expression and motifs should not be sacrificed in the process. Its origin already implies distinctive features, such as the motif of the barrio, codes of meaning through interlingualism, and the relationship between Anglo and Mexican histories. Our cultural roots are embedded in the Mexican heritage. However, our contact with Anglo culture has created a new protagonist—the Chicano—who is markedly different from his two main influences.

Chicano literature has its essential beginnings in the Southwest, though many migrated to the Midwest and Northwest during this century. According to Luis Leal, "we can say that Chicano literature had its origins when the Southwest was settled by the inhabitants of Mexico during Colonial times and continues uninterrupted to the present."[16] It began as an extension of Mexican letters because the Southwest was a part of Mexico, however distant it was from the cultural center of Mexico City. Due to its location in the extreme northern frontier, this region was pictured as a territory that both belonged and did not belong to mainstream Mexico. A strong sense of geographical isolation contributed to this state of limbo, between two worlds, and not within any particular one, as if it were destined to become a sort of "buffer zone" between the two cultures. The concept of Aztlán, a spiritual identification with the land of the Southwest as a homeland rightfully ours, embodied our Indo-Hispanic origins.

If the literature is an expression native to this geographical area, it should be possible to point out examples of antecedents that demonstrate a degree of originality. Somehow from the Southwest emanated an aura of mystery and curiosity, attracting a long series of expeditions. One explorer, Fray Marcos de Niza (1539), wrote an important account titled *Relación del Descubrimiento de las Siete Ciudades.* Francisco Vásquez de Coronado followed suit in 1540. He believed the legend of the Seven Cities of Cíbola, the Gran Quivira, and that belief motivated his explorations. After nine years of wandering alone in what is today the Southwest, Alvar Núñez Cabeza de Vaca wrote a significant work, *Relaciones* (1542), relating his encounters with numerous Indian tribes, with details about the flora and the fauna. His writing demonstrates the region's constant influence and omnipresence. Later in 1610, Gaspar Pérez de Villagrá published a poetic chronicle about New Mexico called *Historia de la Nueva México,* based on actual history he experienced during Juan de Oñate's conquest of that area in the 1590s. Other written material of this period documents the colonial enterprise, usually containing elements of literature, for example, Don Pedro Baptista Pino's *Exposición sucinta y sencilla de la provincia del Nuevo México* (1812).

The majority of literary expression prior to the conclusion of the Hispanic Period in 1821[17] is in the form of folklore, a popular literature in the oral tradition. Usually, invented stories were combined with actual history, the speaker retelling it from one generation to another. This style of transmission is particularly appropriate to our Hispanic heritage as well as to our Indian background, both rich sources of oral tradition whose literatures sometimes depended on it almost totally. Capitán Farfán, a soldier in Juan de Oñate's expedition, presented a play, perhaps the first one in the Southwest, on April 30, 1598, near the present site of El Paso, Texas.[18] Besides this and a few other known examples, literature consisted of an almost infinite number of *romances* (narrative fragments), *corridos* (ballads), *cuentos* (folktales), *alabados* (religious hymns), *décimas* (poems composed of ten-verse stanzas), and other forms.[19] The folk literature established a solid foundation for future creative endeavors in written forms by individual authors. This oral tradition remains an active source of inspiration to the present time.

During the Mexican Period from 1821 to 1848, the literature adopts a more Mexican base using most of the same models and in a sense nationalizing these forms by emphasizing the local region and subject matter. In this period numerous printing presses were founded. The first was set up in Texas in 1813, but most of the early presses began to have an impact in the 1830s and 1840s. Newspapers were the main source of sharing creative writings until the Anglo and Mexican conflict became the dominant subject of essays and editorials. Oral tradition remained relatively unchanged except that it acquired more of a local flavor, referring more and more to history, instead of alluding only to anecdotes from Europe.

Between the years 1849 to 1910, sometimes called the Transition Period, written literature reflected the linguistic and cultural contact with Anglo settlers and accentuated the identity crisis. For the most part the oral tradition continued with as much vigor as ever. It became one way to overcome the stigma of being a conquered people. Newspapers of that period reveal an active, literature-oriented people. These presses were gradually taken over and filled with Anglo views as the economic structure was infiltrated by Anglo-American entrepreneurs. Some *Mexicanos* chose to mix with the new settlers while keeping their identities, others tried to assimilate completely. Still others resisted strongly. They created newspapers with alternative views, social clubs (actually clubs for cultural resistance), and literary societies in which to cultivate *"la lengua de Cervantes."* This cultural self-defense was particularly evident in northern New Mexico and southern Colorado where isolation allowed a degree of autonomy and freedom of expression. The Spanish language's dominance gave the area a distinct advantage—a real link to our Hispanic and Mexican heritage. This was truly a case of a country within a country, something not possible in places like Texas and California because the Anglo presence dominated virtually every area of cultural life. The literature of this period of transition is extremely diverse: much of it is in search of regional identity; some of it attempts to associate itself with our Hispanic background through a jump back in time (a fact that explains, in part, the term "Spanish-American"); another portion incorporates elements of the English language. Anselmo Arellano, in *Los pobladores nuevo mexicanos y su poesía, 1889–1950,*[20] verifies such a variety. There we find poetry commemorating family events (such as weddings or deaths), lyrical outbursts of love or nostalgia, and also poetry addressing social concerns, issues of land and language. While most of the poetry speaks of social rituals, a considerable portion demonstrates that there indeed existed a cultural clash and friction. The Chicanos of the period were not silent and docile; they consistently set claims to the rights they had enjoyed prior to the Anglo occupation. One example is a poem by Jesús María Alarid written in 1889 ("El Idioma"), in which he advocates the acceptance of both English and Spanish as two equal, official languages of the Southwest.[21] Perhaps the first novelist of the region, Eusebio Chacón published two short novels completely in Spanish in 1892. The fact that his works build on storylines and characters from such classics as *Don Quixote* demonstrates some isolation from his literary contemporaries, but his inclusion of local color marks him as firmly rooted in social reality.[22]

The Interaction Period between 1910 and 1942 is characterized by two basic factors: first, the adjustment by Chicanos to having to share the Southwest with Anglos; and, secondly, an increased influx of Mexican immigrants. There was a general realization of having lost a power base which had formerly provided a sense of dignity. Economic alienation became a real threat as cheap labor became plentiful; there arose an institutionalized system of exploiting Chicanos and *Mexicanos* alike. Literary expression remained rich in the oral traditions, but any efforts to create publishing houses usually were aborted or they confronted insurmountable obstacles. Newspapers continued to voice contemporary issues, to print literary excerpts from local people, and to include translations of numerous works from Mexico, Spain, and Latin America. Much effort was made to maintain cultural contacts with other Hispanic countries. Small literary societies endured, whose members depended on newspaper presses to publish isolated works, most of which have been lost due to lack of interest on the part of monolingually oriented libraries. World War I, the Great Depression and other historical events limited participation in aesthetic activities. Survival demanded more attention. As Luis Leal points out, the diffusion of literature was reduced to publications by such associations as LULAC, Alianza, and other societies whose function became political in the struggle for equal rights,[23] combatting systematic propaganda against the Mexican. We find isolated cases of published works during this period, but none of them appear to have caused other writers to follow their lead toward a self-sustaining tradition of writing. Vicente Bernal, a New Mexican, died in 1915 before his book, *Las Primicias* (1916), was published. Today his work is cherished by surviving family and friends, and by a few interested critics. Felipe M. Chacón introduced his own *Poesía y Prosa* in 1924, written in both English and Spanish but mainly Spanish. José Inés García used the *El Faro* newspaper facilities to print his numerous books of poetry in Trinidad, Colorado, between the late 1920s and early 1930s. Fray Angélico Chávez, another New Mexican, wrote poetry and prose from a mystical and spiritual tradition in *New Mexico Triptych* (1940), *Clothed With the Sun* (1939), and other books. No one followed up what these writers began, but their work does demonstrate that not all literature was limited to newspapers. More significant is that while we do not notice much influence by contemporary Mexican writers in their work, we hear clear echoes of the Mexican literary past. Isolation is a factor here too. A more positive way of looking at our Southwest literature is as an expression in its own right, often retaining a Mexican flavor due to our Indo-Hispanic heritage, even when English is used.

The Pre-Chicano Period between 1943 and 1964[24] was a time for many Chicanos to make small breakthroughs in the publishing world in isolated cases, despite the latter's generally unreceptive attitude. Acceptance of Chicano manuscripts was truly a rare event, although a few managed to penetrate this field, controlled as it was by Anglo-American standards and tastes. The Zoot-Suit Riots of 1943 in East Los Angeles left a permanent mark, a harsh lesson in history for Chicanos: these incidents of persecution underscored our position vis-à-vis American society. Our small gains in material progress were clouded by major obstacles to other social changes we sought. A turning point in our history, these events brought to the surface the dark side of becoming an "American." Among many Chicanos there emerged hints of a new awareness of differences in style and language that set us apart from Anglo culture. Coming to grips with our circumstances, many writers tried to provide self-portraits of our people to show us as we are, countering the negative depiction of the Mexican in American literature and mass media. There were four principal reasons why Chicanos did not write more literature during the Pre-Chicano Period: (1) a negative social stigma that Mexicans could not write, (2) the emphasis given to English at the expense of Spanish expression, (3) the false illusion of equality after World War II and the Korean War, and (4) our systematic exclusion from any significant educational mobility by a society that needed a ready-made unskilled labor force and labelled our people as such. Despite these conditions, some writers do stand out for their important contributions: Arthur Campa for documenting the oral tradition in *Spanish Folk Poetry in New Mexico* (1943); Mario Suárez for providing one of the first developed complex Chicano characters in his short story "Señor Garza" (1947); and José Antonio Villarreal for publishing the forerunner to the contemporary Chicano novel, *Pocho* (1959), through a major Eastern publishing house. Many of the writings produced during this period, though sporadic and usually unrelated to each other, foreshadow the crucial crossroads Chicanos met later in the mid-1960s, when we would look more clearly at the choices we faced: to assimilate, to rebel, or to create other alternatives.

The year 1965 marks the beginning of the Contemporary Chicano Period or Renaissance of Chicano letters, an explosion or general boom in every literary genre. For the first time, our literature made concentrated effort to put forward and foster images and characters from our experiences. There was a keen emphasis on a search for authentic ways to express our society, our language, our reality. The adequacy of conventional and traditional literary modes was questioned. With renewed awareness, Chicanos rallied around the issue of identity, choosing the term "Chicano" voluntarily. It became the term of pride to replace other less adequate labels such as "Spanish American," "Latin American," and to some extent "Mexican American." If a rebellious spirit emerged at this time, it was one of cultural affirmation and historical reevaluation, while demanding a sense of dignity. Chicano literature of that time fulfilled a social role as an instrument or vehicle for change. The most obvious example is the Teatro Campesino directed by Luis Valdez, which promoted a type of literary expression that would reflect Chicano problems and themes. Initially, its primary purpose was to function as a didactic device for farmworkers; it set out to mirror the *campesino's* plight, to lead them into action and thus support the *huelga* in César Chávez's labor struggle. The Teatro Campesino not only created an interest in such modes of creative expression, but it also sparked our imaginations toward more ways to present our reality, and new ways to understand it. The Teatro Campesino presented situations on stage that pertained directly to the audiences for which it was intended, portraying, for example, *campesinos,* students, *vendidos* (sell-out), and current issues like the Vietnam conflict and mythology in Mexican history. In the introduction to *Actos,* Luis Valdez states:

> The nature of Chicanismo calls for a revolutionary turn in the arts as well as in society. Chicano theatre must be revolutionary in techniques as well as content. It must be popular, subject to no other critics except the pueblo itself; but it must also educate the pueblo toward an appreciation of *social change,* on and off the stage.[25]

The Teatro Campesino led the vanguard of one strong Chicano literary tendency, bringing social consciousness into all forms of literature. The political fervor of this period of civil rights demands generated an insatiable idealism, which, for Chicanos, became translated into early Movement poetry, that is, into instigative poetry with strong political overtones. Aesthetic qualities were often sacrificed in favor of social awareness. The main concern was a Chicano-style cultural nationalism stressing barrio themes, a historical uniqueness and our Indian heritage, particularly Aztec. Rodolfo "Corky" Gonzales was instrumental in promoting this focus through poetry in *Yo Soy Joaquín* (1967). His book established a precedent that has attracted many followers up to the present time. He resurrects a forgotten mythology from our Mexican-Indian past, and he traces Mexican history through its principal figures to show our turbulent search for justice and freedom. The poetry is intended to educate a Chicano audience about our roots and history, which are viewed as an extension of Mexico. It is a historical manifesto, universalizing our people's struggles for cultural survival. The name Joaquín was chosen as a symbol of resistance because it brings to mind the nineteenth-century rebel, Joaquín Murrieta. *Yo Soy Joaquín* is still considered by many to be a sort of poetic Bible for the Chicano Movement due to its oratorical tone of protest and its inspiring effects. Joaquin admits to feeling lost in the midst of an Anglo milieu while experiencing a sense of cultural alienation in contemporary society. The poetic spokesman confesses his people's loss of the economic battle but takes pride in being victorious in terms of cultural survival.[26]

Other early works such as *Los cuatro* (1968) by four authors (Abelardo Delgado, Ricardo Sánchez, Raymundo Pérez, and Juan Valdez) were combative and critical of American society in bursts of anger, inciting political activity and social change. Another example of early Movement poetry, Ricardo Sánchez's work *Canto y grito mi liberación* (1971) defiantly challenges dehumanizing elements such as technology and commercialism for their negative effects on the barrios. His graffiti-like language—original, irreverent, aggressive, and inventive—filters strong emotions to the reader/listener, at times becoming an ideological chant to shock us:

> with all that we fight   and we are sickened time after time
> fighting what we view   destroyed, at times, by an
>   unyielding society
>   demanding that we conform
>   to death
>   in sick hues.
> anger   angustia   angst   verboten monstrosities
> INCULCATORS   FORNICATORS   DOMESTICATORS
>   MAD*EEE*SON AVENUE
>   WALL STREET
>   PENN*SYL*VA*NIA AVENUE[27]

After the early Movement poetry, a second wave of poetry quickly emerged that can be classified as cultural nationalist, whose objective is not only critical but also constructive of a cultural base, combining the Indian past with symbols of contemporary barrios. This poetry seeks a refuge in the past, to understand our origins at the same time that it tries to confront the present. Poets like Angela de Hoyos, Alurista, Sergio Elizondo, and José Montoya reevaluate what is uniquely Chicano and what has been imposed by the dominant society. For example, Alurista makes a conscious effort to revive Amerindian cultural values while rediscovering the Aztec world of symbols:

> mis ojos hinchados
>> flooded with lágrimas
> de bronze
> melting on the cheek bones
> of my concern
>> rasgos indígenas
> the scars of history of my face
>> and the veins of my body
> that aches
>> vomita sangre
> y lloro libertad
>> i do not ask for freedom
> i am freedom[28]

While Sergio Elizondo recreates the detours and contradictions of the making of self-identity in his epic poem *Perros y antiperros* (1972), other poets such as Angela de Hoyos in *Chicano Poems for the Barrio* (1975) and José Montoya in his classic poem "El Louie" examine the barrio as victim and as a place where a distinct code of experience reigns.

A third kind of poet makes a symbolic-philosophical contribution, demonstrating that some writers are not limited to one trend. Nevertheless, we can point to a substantial group that tends to go beyond easily identifiable Chicano themes or situations. The earliest one to accomplish this is Ricardo García in *Selected Poetry* (1973). He writes surrealistic poems with dreamlike passages through conflicting spheres of the mind, both unconscious and conscious. Although Tino Villanueva's versatile *Hay Otra Voz Poems* (1972) deals with Chicano characters, his main concern is the transformation of the "I" into the "we" in a realm of infinite time. Juan Bruce-Novoa in *Inocencia Perversa/Perverse Innocence* (1977) is intrigued by metaphysical and philosophical questions about sex as it pertains to the "self" and "otherness" of a person. In *The Elements of San Joaquín* (1977) and *The Tale of Sunlight* (1978) Gary Soto seeks a description of the world through the precision of the poetic word, while allowing humble experience to become the main thrust as the poetic voice.

A fourth category of poetry is composed of women who draw on the above tendencies from the perspective of uniquely Chicana forms of feminism. With diversity and purpose, they explore all areas of human existence: politics, cultural affirmation, women's issues, barrios, poetics, and philosophy. Angela de Hoyos is highly regarded for transforming social topics into poetry, for captur-

ing an ethnic ideology in humanistic terms. She writes: "I was born too late/
in a land/that no longer belongs to me/(so it says, right here in this Texas
History)."[29] In *Restless Serpents* (1976) Bernice Zamora uses memory-flashes
of key incidents in her formation as a woman to show how the past forms a
living part of the present. The poet taps many dimensions of her experience in
order to confront her own shadows and to relive moments of peace. Her rest-
lessness coils and uncoils, eliciting feelings that have been repressed through
time and soothing them. Lorna Dee Cervantes uses concrete images of personal
anecdotes; and she probes her Mexicanness as an element of her identity with
which she is not fully acquainted:

> Sometimes she is my mirror:
> la mexicana who emerges con flores,
> con palabras perdidas,
> con besos de los antepasados.
>
> Somewhere in a desert of memories
> there is a dream in another language.
> Some day I will awaken
> and remember every line.[30]

   Another literary genre, the essay, is a distinct mode that serves as a platform
for issues to be raised, theories to be expounded, and concepts to be proposed.
In the early stages of our literary renaissance, the Chicano essay manufactured
ideas that later were taken into other forms of literature. For example, *El Grito*
in early 1967 and *Aztlán* in 1970 began to publish essays that set out to dis-
prove such notions as cultural determinism, stereotypes, and historical classi-
fications. These essays were unprecedented and helped determine intellectual
efforts to document Chicano forms of thought and culture through interpre-
tative and analytic approaches. Authors assimilated ideas such as cultural pluralism, social heterogeneity, historical vision, and cultural nationalism; they
transformed these concepts into more realistic, fairer portraits of the Chicano
people than those done by non-Chicanos. Essays such as those by Octavio
Romano, Francisco A. Ríos, and later Rudy Acuña and Juan Gómez-Quiñones
have all expanded *Chicanismo* as a philosophical basis in their respective
essays.[31] Their writings are inspirational to Chicanos who wish to express themselves creatively through literature.
   Still another literary genre, the short story or cuento has flourished in folklore, and still continues to be a main source of imagination and creativity. It is
relatively easy to find short stories transcribed from the oral tradition, for
example Juan Rael's *Cuentos españoles de Colorado y Nuevo México* (1957);
but rarely was this early short fiction created by one author. Oftentimes

authorship is attributed to a collective participation of shared experience. Most of this area is still open to further considerations and findings. Mario Suárez's "Señor Garza" (1947) is generally regarded as the first well-known cuento. It portrays an amiable character who lives his life by a nonmaterialistic philosophy. In "The Week in the Life of Manuel Hernández," Nick C. Vaca reveals an existentialist, rather pessimistic attitude toward life in contemporary society with all of its problems. Vaca, in a sense, views the Chicano as a nonfolkloric being. He does not believe those who depict him as a "noble savage." This attitude becomes more apparent in some of the cuentos in *". . . y no se lo tragó la tierra"* by Tomás Rivera, who achieves an important synthesis: his work is rooted in folklore, in the inner dimension of psychologically based drives that struggle with mental obstacles, and the tragedies of farmworkers who experience social exploitation. Sabine Ulibarrí, on the other hand, in *Tierra Amarilla: Stories of New Mexico* relies on folklore at times, but his main concern is to recollect and reconstruct memories of humor's part in the life of a small town in northern Mexico.

After poetry, the novel receives perhaps the most attention and dissemination. Its dramatic structure and its depth of characterization mark it as an advanced form of literary development among a people. It takes time and effort for authors to reconstruct the world as they perceive it. The novel functions as an *extended* metaphor of life, which represents complex human relationships, encapsulating what otherwise would take many approaches and disciplines to explain. Although there were early novelists such as Eusebio Chacón who published novels as early as 1892, José Antonio Villarreal is the initiator of our modern novel. His *Pocho,* published in 1959, was ignored and virtually unknown until the Chicano literary renaissance was well-established around the year 1969.[32] Tomás Rivera with his *". . . y no se lo tragó la tierra"* (1971) made the first impact, winning the Quinto Sol National Literary Award in 1970. Other works occurred first, however: for example, *City of Night* (1963) by John Rechy, *The Plum Plum Pickers* (1969) by Raymond Barrio, *Tattoo the Wicked Cross* (1967) by Floyd Salas, and *Chicano* (1970) by Richard Vásquez. Rivera developed a complex and fragmented narration from various perspectives that converges in one character at the end. He found complex elements in the apparently simple lives of migrant workers. Rudolfo A. Anaya in *Bless Me, Ultima* (1972) introduced the best-known character in the Chicano novel—Ultima, a *curandera* or folk healer, who teaches the young protagonist about the cosmic forces of Good and Evil. Oscar Zeta Acosta presented an irreverent macho protagonist in such daring and harsh novels as *The Autobiography of a Brown Buffalo* (1972) and *The Revolt of the Cockroach People* (1973). In 1974 Miguel Méndez made public his controversial work *Peregrinos de Aztlán,* which experiments seriously with different variants of the Spanish language, from standard to "Spanglish" to *caló.* During the same year, Isabella

Ríos, the first Chicana novelist, copyrighted *Victuum,* her novel about a psychic woman who has visions of knowledge; however, this work remained relatively unknown until 1979. Ron Arias revolutionized Chicano novel writing in 1975 with *The Road to Tamazunchale* by combining fantasy and reality into the unified story of an old man making every effort to live imaginatively in his last moments of life. Also in 1975, Alejandro Morales brought out *Caras viejas y vino nuevo,* dealing with the hard-core barrio life of drug addicts. Other significant novels are *Estampas del Valle y otras obras* (1973) by Rolando Hinojosa-Smith, who recreates the life of a valley through short sketches of a wide range of characters; and *El diablo en Texas* (1976) by Aristeo Brito, who also tells about a region, a demoniac and humorous one in this case. In the last decade, the Chicano novel has expanded greatly our store of self-images, the multiple forms we must have in order to conceive our diversity of experience.

The last genre of this discussion, the theatre, is generally thought to be most fully represented by the Teatro Campesino, but there are other important types of Chicano theatre. The Teatro Campesino established the *acto* as the main vehicle of theatrical representation, with its emphasis on immediacy; the *acto* was conceived as the product of a collective effort to present a social issue. Estela Portillo de Trambley was one of the first to deviate from this style: she created a symbolic work, more subtle in its theme of spiritual liberation. Her work *The Day of the Swallows* universalizes human reactions, their contrasts and hidden motivations. Doña Josefa, the protagonist, chooses to keep her lesbianism secret because the townspeople imagine her to be saintly; in the end, she is forced to commit suicide and therefore she becomes a martyr for the possibility of creating a new order. El Teatro de la Esperanza from Santa Bárbara also presents actos, but its contributions have more variety of topics and approaches to depicting Chicano reality. On the other hand, Nephtalí De León stands out for writing theatre of the absurd that deals with characters and situations that are not necessarily identifiable as Chicano. Although the Teatro Campesino remains the principal promoter of Chicano theatre, especially with the famous *Zoot Suit,* there is evidence of new trends and of experimentation with new techniques.

Chicano literature has undergone many phases and changes, depending on the historical period, on how the Mexicans have been perceived, and on how they have been projected. It has kept its integrity despite the odds and setbacks. It should be pointed out that this literature has developed apart from *literatura chicanesca,*[33] that is, writings about Chicanos from a non-Chicano point of view, which have tended either to romanticize or to denigrate our people historically. Chicano literature has become a medium in which we may tell our own stories and feelings without relying on others to tell them for us; it is an assertion of our place, exploring themes that are pertinent to our situation in dominant society. Just as *Zoot Suit* by Luis Valdez is talked about as a "new"

American play, Chicano literature deserves more attention as a phenomenon in its own right. It reflects our people and our realities through our own creativity.

NOTES

1. Philip Ortego has coined this expression in a number of publications, but the one we wish to cite is "The Chicano Renaissance" from *Introduction to Chicano Studies,* edited by Livie Isauro Durán and H. Russel Bernard (New York: Macmillan, 1973), pp. 331–50. Juan Rodríguez presents his concept in "El florecimiento de la literatura chicana" in Carlos Monsiváis' *La otra cara de México: el pueblo chicano* (México, D.F.: Ediciones "El Caballito," 1977).

2. This became particularly evident in Denver, Colorado, when the famous "El Plan Espiritual de Aztlán" was formulated in 1969 by Alurista in a national conference where it was symbolically stated: "We are free and sovereign to determine those tasks which we are justly called for by our house, our land, the sweat of our brows and by our hearts. Aztlán belongs to those that plant the seeds, water the fields, and gather the crops, and not to the foreign Europeans. We do not recognize capricious frontiers on the bronze continent." Quoted from Ernie Barrio, ed., *Bibliografía de Aztlán* (San Diego: Centro de Estudios Chicanos, San Diego State, 1971), p.v.

3. Though commonly known today, these ideas are found amply developed in David Weber's *Foreigners in Their Native Land* (Albuquerque: University of New Mexico Press, 1973). At the same time, they appear in a poetic form in the classic poem titled *Yo soy Joaquín* by Corky Gonzales, published originally in 1967.

4. Octavio Romano was one of the first essayists to expound on these ideas in his essay "The Historical and Intellectual Presence of Mexican Americans," *El Grito,* vol. 2, no. 2 (Winter 1969), pp. 32–46.

5. To fully understand the meaning of the term "literature," we might recall its etymology from Latin "letra," meaning letter, or as French popularized the idea of "littera," meaning writing.

6. Francisco Jiménez, "Chicano Literature: Sources and Themes," *The Bilingual Review/La Revista Bilingüe,* vol. 1, no. 1 (1964), pp. 4–15.

7. José Antonio Villarreal, *Pocho* (New York: Doubleday, pp. 1959), p. 64.

8. Francisco A. Lomelí and Donald W. Urioste, *Chicano Perspectives in Literature: A Critical and Annotated Bibliography* (Albuquerque: Pajarito Publications, 1976), p. 9. Beyond the first word, the rest of the underlining is done for further emphasis and is not in the original text.

9. Luis Valdez, the founder of the Teatro Campesino, indeed set out to utilize this popular theatrical form to create a consciousness among the exploited farmworkers, which fulfilled his concept of beginning a social revolution from the "grass roots" level. His objectives were clear: to educate and to entertain.

10. Luis Leal discusses the present issue in great detail in his well-researched study "Mexican American Literature: A Historical Perspective," which appears expanded in *Modern Chicano Authors,* edited by Joseph Sommers and Tomás Ybarra-Frausto (Englewood Cliffs, N.J.: Prentice-Hall, 1979), pp. 18–30.

11. The three concepts referring to an intrinsic duality are attributed to the following critics, respectively: Juan Bruce-Novoa, Philip Ortego, and Tino Villanueva, who have contributed much to the development of the theory of Chicano aesthetics and literary history.

12. Leal, "Mexican American Literature," p. 19.

13. One particular proponent of this idea is Salvador Rodríguez del Pino in *La novela chicana escrita en español: Cinco autores comprometidos* (Ypsilanti, Mich.: Bilingual Press/Editorial Bilingüe, 1982).

14. The question of autonomy is further clouded by publications like *PMLA* that list Chicano literature under the contemporary Latin-American section while other major publications prefer to include it within American literature.

15. Juan Bruce-Novoa develops a similar line of reasoning in his controversial article "The Space of Chicano Literature" in *De Colores,* vol. I, no. 4 (1975), pp. 22–42.

16. Leal, "Mexican American Literature," p. 22.

17. See Luis Leal's article, in which he establishes a parallelism with Latin-American literature and how it also had to struggle for recognition and autonomy separate from Spanish literature during the Colonial Period. Our study is based on the historical divisions he proposes, except where we deviate in the more contemporary period.

18. Note that the year 1598 is extremely early compared to the first English-speaking play presented between 1699 and 1702 in New England. Soon after the play by Farfán was presented, it has also been documented that another well-known play, which was historically based and motivated, was introduced: "Los moros y los cristianos" on September 8, 1598.

19. For further information, consult the collection by Juan B. Rael called *Cuentos españoles de Colorado y Nuevo México,* 2 volumes (Stanford, Calif.: Stanford University Press, 1957); also, Arthur L. Campa's master's thesis, "New Mexican Spanish Folk-Tales," from the University of New Mexico, 1930. Besides, some authors make a big distinction between creative literature and folk literature by the manner in which each is transmitted and also who is responsible for its creation.

20. It represents an important book of reference with regard to what was written in New Mexico newspapers, plus it provides possible sources for further research in this area.

21. See Anselmo Arellano, *Los pobladores nuevo mexicanos y su poesía, 1889–1950* (Albuquerque: Pajarito Publications, 1976), pp. 37–38.

22. The first ones to cite his short novels (*Hijo de la tempestad* and *Tras la tormenta la calma*) are Lomelí and Urioste in *Chicano Perspectives in Literature.*

23. Leal, "Mexican American Literature," p. 27.

24. Here Luis Leal calls it the Chicano Period, whereas some historians refer to it as the Mexican-American Period.

25. Luis Valdez, *Actos* (San Juan Bautista, Calif.: Cucaracha Press, 1971), p. 2.

26. Rodolfo "Corky" Gonzales, *Yo Soy Joaquín* (New York: Bantam Books, 1972), p. 6.

27. Ricardo Sánchez, *Canto y grito mi liberación* (Garden City, N.Y.: Doubleday, 1973), p. 87.

28. Alurista, *Floricanto en Aztlán* (Los Angeles: Chicano Cultural Center, UCLA, 1971), poem #40.

29. Angela de Hoyos, *Chicano Poems For the Barrio* (Bloomington, Ind.: Backstage Books, 1975), p. 12.

30. Lorna Dee Cervantes in "El sueño de las flores" in *Mango,* vol. 1, no. 1 (Fall 1976), p. 31.

31. See the landmark essays in order of the mentioned authors: "Goodbye Revolution: Hello Slum," *El Grito,* vol. 1, no. 2 (Winter 1968), pp. 8–14; "The Mexican in Fact, Fiction and Folklore," *El Grito,* vol. 2, no. 4 (Summer 1969), pp. 14–28; *Occupied America* (New York: Harper & Row, 1981); and "On Culture," *Revista Chicano-Riqueña,* vol. 5, no. 2 (Spring 1977), pp. 29–47.

32. It is interesting to note that this novel is not cited in *Bibliografía de Aztlán* (1970) done in San Diego State, but was actually "rediscovered" shortly after that.

33. See Lomelí and Urioste's discussion of such a concept in *Chicano Perspectives in Literature,* p. 12.

7 | La Chicana in Literature

CARMEN SALAZAR-PARR

INTRODUCTION

In the prologue to *The Female Imagination* Patricia Meyer Spacks states that "changing social conditions increase or diminish the opportunities for women's action and expression, but a special female self-awareness emerges through literature in every period."[1] She examines literature written in English during the past three hundred years to see if there are patterns in the female experience that are persistent ways of feeling, patterns that survive despite change. Although her investigation refers to the Anglo tradition, it identifies some elements characteristic of the "special female self-awareness" that are universal and that apply to other literary traditions as well.

If we were to examine literature written by women within the Hispanic tradition in a project as ambitious as the one undertaken by Spacks, we would recognize that throughout history women writers have voiced the same concerns from their female experience. It is this female perspective that makes a woman writer share common allusions with women writers of another period rather than with a male writer of her own period, as Spacks indicates.

A study of literature written by Chicanas would consider as its cultural antecedents the traditions of both Spain and Mexico. From sixteenth-century Spain, the writings of the mystic Santa Teresa de Jesús and of the *cancionero* poetess Florencia Pinar would serve as a point of departure for a discussion of the contemporary Chicana experience. From Mexico, with its dual Indian/Spanish heritage, the poetry of Macuilxochitzín,[2] and that of the seventeenth-century poet Sor Juana Inés de la Cruz would provide a relevant backdrop. It is the latter's work, particularly her "Respuesta a Sor Filotea" and her often-quoted *redondillas* "Hombres necios . . ." that most eloquently expresses a defense of women's rights, thus making Sor Juana one of the first feminist writers.

According to Spacks, "women have written books only during the eras of their social subordination" (p. 3). This bears further interpretation. It is not to be inferred that women do not write books at other times; rather, there are certain periods in the sociohistorical process that culminate for women in a stronger sense of awareness of their subordinate position in society. In contem-

120

porary times, such a period corresponds to the Women's Liberation Movement of the seventies which, in turn, had its precedent in the Suffragette Movement of the 1800s. In Chicana/Mexicana history, the period of awareness coincides with the National Women's Movement as well as with the Chicano Movement; its precedent is in Mexico with the Revolution of 1910, when women were forced to share responsibilities and assume active roles side by side with men.

As woman becomes aware of her strength and value, her desire to participate in an effective national life is intensified. Literature becomes one of the vehicles through which she can express a new consciousness of societal problems: poverty, racial injustice, corruption, oppression. This consciousness is reflected in contemporary Chicana writing; however, it echoes the concerns already voiced by Chicanas of past generations. Recent investigations on little-known Chicana authors of the past have uncovered several literary pieces with a sociopolitical thrust, thus giving a sense of history to Chicana literature. An example is the poetry of Sara Estela Ramírez, published in the South Texas newspaper *La Crónica* in 1910–11, verification of the affinity that exists between the Chicana writer of today and the Chicana whose political consciousness was awakened during the Mexican Revolution of 1910.[3] But, in addition to this political consciousness, and, perhaps more important in her contribution as a writer, is the challenge of male value systems that define the images and roles of women in society. The female perspective, then, offsets the imbalance created by a predominantly male-authored interpretation.

The Chicana became most prolific as a writer after 1975, International Women's Year. As Marcela Trujillo indicates, "the impetus of the woman's movement together with the Chicano Movement contributed to the Chicana's latent potential and so she began to focus in on her particular feminist experience through the arts."[4] From a feminist perspective, notes Trujillo, the Chicana examines the socioeconomic and political factors that affect her individuality. At times, she moves into the past in search of a lost paradise, in search of folklore and legends and traditions that seem to afford a saner world. In an attempt to attain total liberation, the Chicana has also explored the relationships between the Chicana and the dominant Anglo-American culture, but most importantly, she has reexamined the male/female relationships within the Chicano world of *machismo*.

Perhaps the most significant aspect of Chicana literature is the depiction of the female characters, for there is no question that Chicana authors write about women. The three novels written to date, Berta Ornelas' *Come Down from the Mound,* Isabella Ríos' *Victuum,* and Estela Portillo Trambley's *Woman of the Earth,* focus on a female protagonist. Similarly, Portillo Trambley's collection of short stories, *Rain of Scorpions,* deals mainly with women, as does her play *The Day of the Swallows.* Other examples are the short stories by Guadalupe Valdés-Fallis, Lucha Corpi, and Rosaura Sánchez.

The main emphasis in this essay will concentrate on the portrayal of female characters. The images of Chicana/Mexicana women in contemporary Chicano and Chicana literature will be compared and contrasted with those in traditional American fiction.[5] Finally, our focus will turn to the female characters in the works of one Chicana writer, Estela Portillo Trambley, as an example of how Chicanas view the changing role of women in society.

The Chicana in American Literature

In Anglo-American literature, as Cecil Robinson notes in his comprehensive study *Mexico and the Southwest in American Literature,* the early portraits of Mexicans stressed a degenerate and corrupt culture in contrast to the refinement of Anglo-American models with their prevalent Puritanical standards. These stereotypical depictions, for the most part, portray the Mexican woman as a colorful figure whose mode of dress and physical appearance were judged inappropriate by Anglo-American standards. She is criticized for behavior that the writers associated with sexual promiscuity. Harvey Fergusson is perhaps the writer who devotes the greatest attention to the presumed sexual practices of women. In *Wolf Song,* for example, a male character cautions another about serious involvement with Mexicans: "them women breed like prairie dogs and jest as careless. They look good when they're young but after they've calved a time or two they swell up like a cow in a truck patch an' you need a wagon to move 'em."[6] It is in *The Conquest of Don Pedro* where Fergusson presents the widest spectrum of female figures. By using a central character who is in contact with several women, the author creates a means of analyzing the sexual mores among women of different social categories, from the outcast to the aristocratic matron, all of whom maintain "the talent for sexual intrigue" regardless of status or convention.

In the second half of the nineteenth century, it was Spanish California that became a focal point in the literature of the Southwest. The Mexican romances focused on love affairs between Anglo-American soldiers and Spanish *señoritas* whose dazzling beauty, gentleness, and charm were exalted. The Castilian woman was romanticized in the novels of Justin Jones and Bret Harte and depicted as a socially prominent and proud woman. On the other hand, the Mexican woman or mestiza appeared as a passionate, promiscuous woman.

In works subsequent to Bret Harte's, there is an effort to present a more compassionate portrayal of the Spanish/Indian society; however, the emphasis remains on an idealized noble savage in a picturesque environment, as in Helen Hunt Jackson's *Ramona.* The twentieth-century Southwestern fiction of John Steinbeck and Katherine Ann Porter reveals an attempt to be more realistic; thus, the Spanish is replaced as a focal figure by the Mexican. Porter was outspoken in denouncing American authors who saw in the Mexican culture an opportunity to embrace a primitive alternative. That critical attitude is reflected in her own fiction in which characters are credible individuals presented without exaggeration, distortion, or judgment. Her women figures, like María Concepción in the collection *Flowering Judas,* are strong and sincere in following their basic emotional instincts. Steinbeck's women characters, though portrayed sympathetically, are naive and childlike. In *The Pastures of Heaven,* María and Rosa appear simple-minded and unsophisticated, while the principal female character of *Tortilla Flat,* Teresina Cortez, is a woman happy in her ignorance of biological processes:

> The regularity with which she became a mother always astonished Teresina. It occurred sometimes that she could not remember who the father of the impending baby was; and occasionally she almost grew convinced that no lover was necessary. In the time when she had been under quarantine as a diphtheria carrier she conceived just the same. However, when a question became too complicated for her mind to unravel, she usually laid the problem in the arms of the Mother of Jesus, who, she knew, had more knowledge of, interest in, and time for such things than she.[7]

Despite the sympathetic intentions of both authors, the image of the Mexican woman remained primitive, unsophisticated, and promiscuous, thus perpetuating several features of the stereotypical characterization offered by earlier writers.

The Chicana in Chicano Literature

Contemporary Chicano literature has sought a more faithful presentation of characters, although, for the most part, these have remained stereotypes rather than multidimensional beings. There are few memorable characters—except for Josefa in *The Day of the Swallows*—because there is only limited psychological analysis. In general, characterization depends on the social framework portrayed within the piece. The early literary works of the Chicano "renaissance" attempted to trace the historical and cultural roots of the Mexican American; hence, one finds an emphasis on the family and on traditional roles assigned to men and women by Mexican society.

In an effort to combat the negative stereotypes of Anglo-American literature, Chicanos have created numerous portraits of the idealized woman: pure, understanding, passive, long-suffering. This idealized role is assumed by mothers, wives, or *abuelitas* who are depicted as hardworking women who endure hardships and make sacrifices for their families. An example is the uncomplaining mother who works both within the home and in the fields in José Montoya's poem "La jefita:"

> Me la rayo ese! Mi jefita never slept
> Y en el fil, pulling her cien
> libras de algoda, se sonreía
> Mi jefe y decía
>   That woman—she only
>   complains in her sleep[8]

Female characters, unlike their male counterparts, are often defined by explicit archetypal references. One of the most frequently used archetypes is that of the virgin-mother who synthesizes the two most highly idealized feminine images. Although many virgin-mothers are of general reference, because of the prominence of Mexican history as a literary and cultural font, the most frequent allusions are to the Virgin of Guadalupe. In Rudolfo Anaya's *Bless Me, Ultima* there are references to both the image of the Virgin and to the maternal qualities she embodies—forgiveness, love, peace, beauty, and kindness—which endear her to the young narrator, Antonio. The boy associates the visual representation of the Virgin with his mother's maiden name, Luna, through the universal symbol of the moon, and eventually completes the fusion of the two women in one of his dreams when the empathetic Virgin of Guadalupe assumes María Luna's mourning.

In addition to the virgin-mother archetype, Chicano literature also casts the woman as Eve, sometimes in her Mexican historical role as La Malinche. For example, in Richard Vásquez' *Chicano,* the character Rosa is associated with the exploitation of undocumented workers, a modern activity analogous to La Malinche's historical betrayal of her people. Most often, however, the Eve figure appears in the role of temptress, as a mistress, or as a prostitute. In this role she is responsible for bringing tragedy to the man. Nina, in Estela Portillo Trambley's "The Trees," is identified with each of the symbols of temptation in the Garden of Eden: She is Eve, with her coquettish smile; the snake, in seducing her brother-in-law and destroying him; and the apple, "soft, with that special sweetness." But, unlike the negative stereotypes rendered in Anglo-American literature, Nina is a complex person whose actions derive from her childhood experiences.

It should be noted, therefore, that mistresses and prostitutes do not necessarily symbolize "bad" women in Chicano literature. Furthermore, prostitution is not censured when it becomes a means of support in the light of socioeconomic hardships. In Rolando Hinojosa's *Estampas del Valle* there is no moral condemnation for Fira the Blonde whose good and bad qualities are simply human qualities that have nothing to do with her profession. She is recognized for her forthrightness and sincerity and we sympathize with her struggle for survival: "Fira is a serious woman who carries her whoredom like schoolgirls carry their books: naturally."[9] We find the same nonjudgmental portrayal in

Viola Barragán, the twice-widowed mistress of Pioquinto Reyes. Although she flaunts her relationship with a married man, the narrator accepts the fact that she truly loves him.

Chicano literature also seeks to redefine *machismo* and female assertiveness as role changes are influenced by the Anglo culture and a different economic system. Hence, there is a new treatment of women, an attempt to portray women in a more realistic role, as neither all good nor all bad. Angelina Sandoval in the novel *Chicano* is a strong figure who represents the anglicized woman in contrast to the suffering *mujer abnegada*.[10] Rather than accept the traditional role of subjugation to a dominant husband, Angelina asserts her rights: " 'O.K., lover boy,' she said taking off her dark gloves. 'You've knocked me around for the last time. Got that straight? This brings us to number two. You toe the mark at the taco stand or it's out on your ear' " (p. 117). Angelina Sandoval, however, is one of the few examples in male-authored works in which a female character assumes a major role and dares to rebel against male domination. Other figures of this type are Consuelo Rubio in José Antonio Villarreal's *Pocho* and Esperanza García in Edmund Villaseñor's *Macho*.

It is in the works of women writers that portraits of women in overt rejection of traditional roles have become more consistent and significant. These works focus on the development of female protagonists confronting the problems of male/female relationships, physical abuse, and psychological and economic exploitation. Chicanas examine their situation within the social and economic circumstances that place them in subservient roles. At times these roles are identified within the Chicano culture and the traditional attitudes of machismo; at times, within the complex environment that admits influences from the Anglo culture. In so doing, Chicanas express an awareness of the need for changing the roles of women in contemporary society.

Women writers often initiate self-examination by looking to previous generations for which they express admiration and a nostalgia for the times spent in the company of mothers, grandmothers, and older women friends. At the same time, however, they acknowledge a sense of alienation from a generation whose experience differs markedly from theirs. Lorna Dee Cervantes's "Grandma" presents the coexistence of love/respect with a lack of understanding:

> I am a mystery to her
> I eat her *tortillas*
> We are friends,
> but to her I am a puzzlement.
>
> . . .
>
>   *"¿Por qué no te quieres casar?"*
> *Abuelita.* You don't understand.[11]

Like Cervantes, other authors have explored the philosophical aspects of generational identity. The majority of Chicanas, however, address themselves to the realities of everyday experience. They denounce sexual abuse, especially rape, both literally and metaphorically. Verónica Cunningham, in expressing a sense of solidarity with all women who have been violated, censures not only the rapist but the attitudes and legal system of a society that blames the victim:

> A woman
> was raped
> by her father
> yesterday
> and she was only thirteen
> . . .
> another woman
> was raped
> on her first date
> . . .
> they've suffered
> by the law
> with policemen
> in the courts
> in society
> inside themselves
> with guilt
> or shame.[12]

Similarly, in "Rape Report" Rita Mendoza censures physical rape but adds a metaphorical dimension to the literal sexual violence when she alludes to the historical and sociological rape of the Chicano culture:

> I am making this report in English, you see,
> I've been raped of my native tongue.[13]

Chicana writers have also addressed the questions of psychological and physical abuses within marriage. In "Las muñecas cuando se acuestan cierran los ojos," Guadalupe Valdés-Fallis examines the plight of a woman who discovers her husband's infidelity but is pressured by her mother to accept that situation uncomplainingly. Although the woman attempts to leave her husband and support herself and her family, she is overpowered by economic hardship and by the force of tradition, as expressed by her mother: " . . . uno tiene sus obligaciones. Primero son los hijos . . . Y uno se aguanta, uno se aguanta."[14] Valdés-Fallis creates a unique narrative by interweaving short rhymes that function as counterpoint and as an ironic device to illustrate woman's lot. Through this technique she shows how early training leaves a woman unprepared for a male-dominated society and in a submissive role:

Las niñas no juegan como los niños.	Girls don't play like boys
porque se ensucian	because they get dirty
porque son niñas	because they are girls
Las niñas no juegan como los niños. (p. 31)	Girls don't play like boys.

ESTELA PORTILLO TRAMBLEY

The broadest spectrum of female characters is found in the works of Estela Portillo Trambley, the most prolific of Chicana writers. Like Valdés-Fallis, she examines the questions of psychological and physical abuses within marriage. Valdés-Fallis portrays the woman in a traditional role from which she does not escape because social pressures overwhelm her. On the other hand, Portillo Trambley focuses on the woman who rebels against the social conditions that stifle her individuality. This social order to which the female protagonists react is summarized in the short story "If It Weren't for the Honeysuckle:"

> It had been decreed long ago by man-made laws that living things were not equal. It had been decreed that women should be possessions, slaves, pawns in the hands of men with ways of beasts. It had been decreed that women were to be walloped effigies to burn upon the altars of men. It had been decreed by the superiority of brute strength that women should be no more than durable spectacles to prove a fearful potency that was a shudder and a blow. It had been decreed . . . how long ago . . .? that women should approve of a manhood that simply wasn't there . . . the subservient female loneliness. . . . It had been decreed.[15]

In her drama *The Day of the Swallows* and in her collection of short stories *Rain of Scorpions and Other Writings* Portillo Trambley explores and protests the social conditions that relegate women to a subservient role. Kidnap and rape, physical and psychological abuse of women, matrimony as a result of social pressures—these are constants in Portillo Trambley's play and short stories.

The female protagonists are endowed with a "ferocity for life," a passion for living. This passion is subjugated by a male-dominated society that imposes an order and logic in the name of civilization. Portillo Trambley's female characters, however, are women who assert themselves; they rebel against the imposed order and emerge triumphant in their struggle for liberation. Josefa in *The Day of the Swallows,* Clotilde in "The Paris Gown," and Nina in "The Trees" symbolize the intuitive nature of humanity, the creative and imaginative expression that seeks to transcend the apparent rationality and logic of social convention. It is woman who is capable of understanding the world of fantasy and magic and the one who can lead man toward it. This idea parallels the surrealism of André Breton, which calls for reconciliation of opposites, for a resolving of the antagonism between dream and reality. The surrealists sought a new reality that would fuse all levels of experience: real and imaginary, natural and supernatural, external and internal. This new reality is an ineffable one that transcends this world. Love—passion—was a chief preoccupation, a source of hope, in attaining life's most meaningful goal: transcendence and unification.

In surrealism, as Gloria Orenstein observes, the role of woman, be it the *femme-enfant* of André Breton or the *femme-fatale* of Benjamin Péret, is a contradictory one in that woman is exalted for her feminine qualities and yet restricted by being stereotyped. In her positive aspect, the female surrealist protagonist is the *femme-enfant* who possesses grace, harmony with nature, intuition, reverie, irrationality, and child-like innocence, and is therefore the source of redemption for mankind. The *femme-enfant* represented by Breton's Melusine offers the possibility of the true act of love, the highest form of art. It is through this act of love that a couple can be united in an experience of totality. The physical act becomes the concrete form through which the opposites in the real world are unified. But, as Orenstein observes:

> ... the same femme-enfant that Breton exalted and that Benjamin Péret felt would attract only the totally virile man, who would reveal love to her, remains woman deprived of her human position in the world as long as her uniqueness is restricted by any stereotype.[16]

Female surrealist dramatists, however, have searched for a new definition of the role of the female surrealist protagonist. They have explored the symbolism related to the feminine archetypes of woman as goddess, as the Great Mother, as creator, as seer, in order to interpret woman's attributes. In contrast to the masculine definition of the surrealist woman, the feminine interpretation shows that a woman's individual autonomy is necessary for creation and that she must reject her traditionally subordinate position.[17]

Estela Portillo Trambley joins other female playwrights such as Elena Garro, Joyce Mansour, and Leonora Carrington in defining the new surrealist protagonist. Portillo Trambley's work is an especially daring contribution to Chicano letters mainly because of the controversial theme with which it deals: lesbianism. *The Day of the Swallows* is firmly grounded in surrealism, both in the imagery and symbolism and in the portrayal of the main character, Josefa. The symbol of virtue and perfection in the Mexican village of San Lorenzo, Josefa has created a world of her own in her house, exquisitely decorated with her own lace work and filled with a light that overwhelms anyone who enters. The room, as seen by others, is the product of love, the wonder of her magic. In her invented world, Josefa is guided by her "magicians" whom she discovered the night of the Festival of San Lorenzo, when the virgins bathe in the lake. Josefa has made the lake her lover and describes their union in very sensual terms:

> For me ... it came true! ... the wonder was my magicians. That night at the lake there was a different music ... the stillness sang inside me ... the moonlight grew in me ... it became my lover ... There by the lake, I felt the light finding its way among the pines ... to me ... It took me ... then ... perhaps it was my imagination ... it said to me "We are one ... make your beauty ... make your truth." Deep, I felt a burning spiral ... it soared in my ears ... in my heart ... It was too much to bear.[18]

The serenity and peace afforded her by her world of magic contrasts sharply with the violence of concrete reality. Josefa's lover is Alysea, a young woman whom she had saved from prostitution and who now lives with her. Josefa recognizes that her lesbianism is an act of nonconformity and becomes obsessed with concealing this from the village folk. When the young boy David sees the two women making love, Josefa cuts out the tongue of the little boy to prevent his divulging their secret. She confesses to the priest who forgives her for her sins, but she cannot forgive herself and she commits suicide by drowning herself in the lake.

The Day of the Swallows is rich in surrealist imagery and symbolism reminiscent of the plays of García Lorca. The moon, the light, the lake, and the birds symbolize a new dimension of reality beyond the boundaries of concrete time and space. They are symbols associated with the feminine and they are especially significant because they underline Josefa's psyche. The moon, for instance, is a symbol for variable and inconstant behavior. It evokes the ideas of fantasy and imagination. Josefa's fantasies make the "magicians" a reality for her. She despises men because they don't love; they simply take; and so she invents her own lovers; the moon and the lake. Josefa is called the "lady of light." This is significant, too, because light symbolizes knowledge and wisdom and the ability to see things in their true form. Josefa, in the symbolic act of weaving and in her obvious union with light is a creator and initiator for mankind. Ironically, others sense the presence of the light, but they do not participate in Josefa's world, neither in the real nor in the imaginary. Thus, the reality that she seeks is one that can be attained only in death. She knows that her lesbianism would not be understood by the village. Her final act of defiance is suicide by drowning. In giving herself to the lake, again a feminine symbol, Josefa has asserted her identity as a lesbian and liberated herself from established norms. As in most surrealist plays, death is not viewed as a tragic outcome. Josefa experiences a clarity and joy that is evident in her final monologue:

> My day . . . my day, but, oh, my people . . . it was not meant to be shared with you . . . my day was planned by my magicians . . . long before you planned this one for . . . me . . . I must get ready. (p. 191)

In this play, Portillo Trambley has portrayed Doña Josefa in traditional surrealist terms, as the *femme-enfant* described by Breton: graceful, virtuous, intuitive, charitable. Those who surround her see her as an angel, an avenging angel who helps others by warding off wickedness. Portillo Trambley, nevertheless, has redefined the surrealist protagonist by adding another dimension: the woman does not seek an androgynous union as the ultimate realization of totality. In addition, woman is seen in her dual aspect, as Judy Salinas observes:

> Portillo suggests that it is wrong for a woman or for anyone to be so pressured into a rigid role, not allowing for variations. That is, she implies that Doña Josefa was not totally bad as her acts condemned her nor was she totally good as her false image portrayed her to be.[19]

Transcendence is achieved also by Nina in the short story "The Trees." Like the village of San Lorenzo, the town of Cetna is also immersed in tradition. The lives of the people "were well patterned like the rows of apple trees and the trenches that fed them. Men and women had separate given images until Nina came" (p. 13). Like Alysea in *The Days of the Swallows,* Nina had been abused sexually as a young girl. She marries into the wealthy Ayala family—her chance to be a somebody. She rejects, however, the "lives of imitated rituals" of the high-born, comfortable women of the Ayala family. Her disdain for submissiveness is reflected in the coquettish smiles and the "easy ways" she displays with the Ayala men. Unlike Josefa, Nina is the *femme-fatale,* the seductress. She is the "Eve in the Garden of Eden."

Nina represents newness and innovation to the Ayala family and is compared to the Quinteca apple:

> It is said that experience is not merely physical, biological or even just human. There is a quality in experience that is very much like the Quinteca apple. The newness itself, nevertheless, be it creation or destruction, finds its way of changing people, apples, ways. Experience finds expansion in this newness, in this unknown. Even if it becomes the remnants of a dead paradise, it leaves another richness and creation for other men. It becomes a growth into understanding. (p. 12)

With the Ayala family, however, any change is seen as disruption. Their social patterns do not acknowledge growth or change, and for that reason Nina is rejected by the family. Nina, however, refuses to live within the boundaries of their ritualistic lives. She becomes obsessed with power and money to disguise the inhumanities from the past and plots a way of dishonoring the Ayala brothers so that her husband Ismael may inherit a larger portion of the estate. One by one the brothers die through the violence instigated by Nina, and the Ayala empire is destroyed.

Unable to attain the freedom she seeks, Nina turns to a violence that eventually brings self-destruction. She commits suicide by plunging from a hill. Like Josefa's suicide, Nina's is seen as a form of liberation:

> She leaned over simply to be caught by wind and the openness of things. A shower of rocks followed by the path of her falling body in full symphony. It sang the praises of something new in erosive change. Not a nothingness, but a coming desolation. When her body hit the bottom of the hill, the praises still followed like the lingering fullness of one note until her body was covered with debris. She was now a part of all . . . sooner or later. (p. 22)

Josefa's lesbianism and Nina's obsession with power represent a change from the traditional roles assigned to women in the society in which they live. They are punished in the literary sense because they have committed violent acts. Nevertheless, they triumph in death for they have dared to rebel against a static society. Their deaths are seen as a form of freedom.

Death is not always the final outcome for rebelliousness. In "The Paris Gown" Portillo Trambley suggests a more positive result. "The Paris Gown," the introductory story to the collection, is narrated mostly in dialogue form as Clotilde reminisces with her granddaughter Theresa. Through their conversation we learn that Clotilde Romero de Traske, now an art dealer in Paris, had outwitted her father in Mexico in order to free herself from a marriage arranged by her family. The marriage, thought of as a business venture that would join the two families' fortunes, was seen as a form of slavery by Clotilde. Unable to persuade her father to free her from this arrangement, Clotilde hits upon a plan. She pretends to go along with her father's wishes, asks for a lavish wedding gown from Paris, only to appear stark naked in front of the wedding guests. For all this, she is treated as an insane woman and is sent off to Paris, far away from the dishonored family. There she pursues a career in art, has several marriages, and through her "ferocity for life" becomes a "liberated form in civilized order."

As in many of her stories, Portillo's digressions from the narrative serve to philosophize on life's circumstances. In "The Paris Gown" these digressions focus on the dialectics of order and reason versus instinct. From a human viewpoint, says Clotilde, "barbarism is the subjugation of the instinctual for reason . . . Man's reason is a boxed-in circumstance that has proved itself more violent against human beings than instinct" (p. 13). Clotilde and Theresa recognize that women suffer the barbarism of men and the injustices of social convention. Clotilde, however, maintains a positive outlook and does not condemn men entirely: "Men have attempted fairness since the beginning of time; it's just that sometimes they are overwhelmed . . ." (p. 13). For Clotilde, men know and understand instinct as well as women, but "thousands of years of conditioning have made them blind to the equality of all life" (p. 3).

Clotilde is like Josefa and Nina, a daring woman who is still in the process of change, awakening the still-undefined passions. As an artist, she participates in the creative process that is instinctual, emotional, and subjective. The contrasts between Mexico and Paris, between the perfectly manicured garden of her father's home and the asymmetrical Parisian garden, underscore the confinement of traditional order and the freedom that characterize Clotilde's two phases of life.

Portillo Trambley seems to imply that there is hope for liberation. Although Theresa is still bound by tradition—she is traveling in France with a university group since that is the only way girls are allowed to travel away from home—she has seen Paris as her grandmother did many years before, and she will follow her footsteps in her struggle for liberation.

The dual aspects of women are explored in "If It Weren't for the Honeysuckle." In contrast to the three women mentioned above who seek escape from order, Beatriz "loved order above all things" (p. 98). This is symbolized by the manner in which she clips and trims the honeysuckle when it tends to grow profuse and chaotic:

> There was simply no nonsense in Beatriz's life. She knew not of passionate infatuations or long waitings for dreams to be realized by mere suppositions. She had no patience with the romanticizing of things. Things were what they were. One only had to give them order. She functioned on volition and a given routine. She was like the self-contained river-bed, dry in appearance, but with an underground network of seeming order that fed a green life. (p. 100)

At the age of fourteen Beatriz had run off with Robles in order to escape the slavery of her home where she had to care for her nine brothers. Although she knew Robles was no good, she felt that washing for one man was better than washing for nine. Besides, since he was already married, he had little time for her. Little by little, she scraped enough to build a little hut. One day Robles brings her a young woman, Sofa, who is to replace Beatriz. The physical abuses with Sofa begin, and Beatriz is forced to intercede for Sofa, who has become her good companion. It is Beatriz who brings order to the house when Robles comes. But the insatiable man continues his rampage. He brings fourteen year old Lucretia for the women to look after. "Beatriz knew it was up to her to find and keep an order as she had always done. She must add and subtract the reality of things" (p. 103). With Sofa, she plots to kill the evil Robles by serving him poison in his soup.

In this story, as in "The Trees" and "The Paris Gown," Portillo uses the paradise or garden motif as a means of illustrating the effects of unbalanced order. For Beatriz, there is a clash between a sense of order as she sees things and the established order from a man's point of view. Nevertheless, Beatriz replaces the latter with an equally violent and destructive order. Portillo suggests, once again, that there must be harmony and an ideal balance of opposites, otherwise the result is destructive. As Tomás Vallejos suggests, "the overbalance of one characteristic (masculinity, darkness, reason versus femininity, light, instinct) leads to overcompensation of the other, a catastrophic tipping of the scale in the opposite direction. In these cases, the ideal balance, the wholeness, the paradise Portillo Trambley envisions, is lost."[20]

Portillo Trambley portrays her female protagonists as strong, assertive women who take their destinies into their own hands. Although women commit violent acts, they are treated compassionately and sympathetically. There is a justification for their actions. For the most part, Portillo depicts her female characters as rebelling against an order that is oppressive. Finally, although these characters seem to perpetuate the myth that women are irrational, they must instead be seen as beings endowed with a sensitivity and imagination that must contend with a hostile environment. Women struggle to liberate themselves from the subservient roles to which they are relegated, and even death is not defeat.

NOTES

1. Patricia Meyer Spacks, *The Female Imagination* (1972; rpt. New York: Avon Books, 1976), p. 1.

2. Macuilxochitzín was the daughter of Moctezuma's adviser Tlacaelel.

3. Other precursors of Chicana feminism who published in Mexican and Texas newspapers as a result of their sociopolitical awakening were Juana Belén Gutiérrez de Mendoza, Elisa Acuña y Rossetti, and Dolores Jiménez y Muro. See "Chicana Feminism" in Alfredo Mirandé and Evangelina Enríquez, eds., *La Chicana: The Mexican-American Woman* (Chicago: University of Chicago Press, 1979), pp. 202–43. For research on Sara Estela Ramírez see Emilio Zamora, Jr., "Sara Estela Ramírez: una rosa en el movimiento," in Magdalena Mora and Adelaida del Castillo, eds., *Mexican Women in the United States* (Los Angeles: UCLA Chicano Studies Research Center, 1980), pp. 163–69.

4. Marcela Trujillo, "The Dilemma of the Modern Chicana Artist and Critic," *De Colores,* vol. 3, no. 3 (1977), pp. 38–48.

5. For a more comprehensive study of the images of the Chicana in literature see "Images in Literature" in Mirandé and Enríquez, *La Chicana,* and "The Image of the Chicana in Literature," by Carmen Salazar-Parr and Genevieve Ramírez, in Julio A. Martínez and Francisco A. Lomelí, eds., *Chicano Literature: A Reader's Encyclopedia* (Westport, Conn.: Greenwood Press, 1984).

6. Quoted by Cecil Robinson, *Mexico and the Hispanic Southwest in American Literature* (Tucson: University of Arizona Press, 1977), p. 79.

7. Quoted by Raymund Paredes, "The Image of the Mexican in American Literature," Ph.D. dissertation, University of Texas, 1973, p. 163.

8. *El Espejo–The Mirror: An Anthology of Selected Chicano Literature,* ed. Octavio Romano-V. and Herminio Ríos C. (Berkeley: Quinto Sol Publications, 1975), p. 233.

9. Rolando Hinojosa, *Estampas del Valle* (Berkeley: Quinto Sol Publications, 1973), p. 43.

10. Richard Vásquez, *Chicano* (1970, rpt. New York: Avon Books, 1972).

11. Lorna Dee Cervantes, "Grandma," *El Grito del Sol,* vol. 3, no. 3 (1978), p. 38.

12. Verónica Cunningham, unpublished.

13. Rita Mendoza, "Rape Report," in *Second Chicano Literary Prize* (Irvine: University of California, 1976), pp. 81–82.

14. Guadalupe Valdés-Fallis, "Las muñecas cuando se acuestan cierran los ojos," *Tejidos,* vol. 1, no. 3 (1974), p. 34.

15. Estela Portillo Trambley, "If It Weren't for the Honeysuckle," in *Rain of Scorpions and Other Writings* (Berkeley: Tonatiuh International, 1975).

16. Gloria Feman Orenstein, *The Theatre of the Marvelous* (New York: New York University Press, 1975), p. 109.

17. See Orenstein's study of "Surrealism and Women" in *The Theatre of the Marvelous,* pp. 99–147.

18. Estela Portillo Trambley, *The Day of the Swallows,* in *El Grito,* vol. 4, no. 3 (Spring 1971), pp. 4–47.

19. Judy Salinas, "The Image of Woman in Chicano Literature," *Revista Chicano-Riqueña,* vol. 4, no. 4 (Autumn 1976), p. 144.

20. Tomás Vallejos, "Estela Portillo Trambley's Fictive Search for Paradise," *Frontiers,* vol. 5, no. 2 (1980), p. 56.

8 | Contemporary Chicano Theater

JORGE A. HUERTA

When discussing Chicano theater, it is imperative to introduce the topic with the opening of a poem by Luis Valdez, the founder of El Teatro Campesino. In an effort to explain the emerging philosophy of his Teatro in 1973, Valdez wrote:

Teatro	Theater
eres el mundo	you are the world
y las paredes de los	and the walls
buildings más grandes	of the biggest buildings
son	are
nothing but scenery.[1]	nothing but scenery.

Chicano theater is a reflection of the world, first from the perspective of Chicanos, but ultimately, as a universal statement about what it is to be a Chicano in this society. By discussing the recent evolution of that which we call "Teatro Chicano," we can support the assertion that "Teatro es el mundo" ("Theater is the world").

When Luis Miguel Valdez went to Delano, California, in 1965 to see if he could start a farmworker's theater group, he took with him a desire to help the incipient farm labor union of César Chávez. Valdez had worked the fields since age six, and he knew well the struggles of the campesino. He had recently graduated from San Jose State College, where he had seen two of his plays produced, and he had just left the San Francisco Mime Troupe. Both his experience as a playwright and as an actor in a radical street theater were necessary elements in Valdez's basic training. His plays introduced the young playwright to the world of dramatic plots and character delineation, and his roles in the commedia dell'arte scenarios of the Mime Troupe were essential to the director's role in creating entertaining presentations.

The Italian commedia dell'arte is a strongly physical, farcical type of theater, noted for its use of masks, stock characters, and rambunctious presentations. When Valdez first saw the San Francisco group performing outdoors in the park, he knew that if any style of theater would have an impact on the farmworker, it was this one. The commedia scripts were never written down as

135

dialogue, but rather as outlines called scenarios, which have a basic situation and allowed the actors to improvise their characters. The scenario gave a beginning, middle, and end, but the actors had to use their imaginations and wit to fill in the dialogue. Valdez knew that there were no plays dealing with the plight of the farmworker, and that if he was going to create a farmworker's theater, the scripts would have to come from the participants themselves.

THE ACTO

When Valdez met with a group of striking farmworkers for the first time, he took signs and masks with him identifying the stock characters in the daily dramas in the fields. The protagonists were the Huelguistas, the striking campesinos; and the antagonists were the Esquiroles, or scabs; aided by the Coyote, the farm labor contractor, and the Patroncito. When Valdez asked for volunteers to demonstrate for the rest of the workers what had happened on the picket lines that day, he simply placed a sign on each of the "characters" identifying him or her immediately. This innovative young director knew that there was no time in the theater of the fields for deep psychological motivations or subtle character development. Instead, each of the figures in the improvisation had a clearly defined purpose or objective. When he places a pig-like mask on one of the workers, everybody knew that he could only be one person: "El Patroncito."

These first, simple improvisations were called *actos* by Valdez, for want of a better term. In retrospect, the name is significant, for it can mean an act in the theatrical sense as an act of a play, or it can have its base in the active verb, to act, to make a movement, or to *do* something. And that is what the newly formed Teatro Campesino was doing with its actos. These were not Hollywood actors performing on a stage in front of bright lights and well-dressed patrons of the arts; these were campesinos, fresh off the picket lines, demonstrating their own realities. Whether in the fields, on flatbed trucks, or on campuses or community auditoriums, the Teatro Campesino was entertaining and educating people about the problems and social plight of the farmworker.

The acto became the foundation of all that was to follow in Teatro Chicano. It was simple, direct, immediate, and relatively easy to create. All that is needed to create an acto are the people to improvise and the situation or conflict one wishes to resolve. In the early days of the Teatro Campesino, the actos all had one clearly defined solution: "Join the Union." But, as the Teatro left the fields and explored the many different problems of the Chicanada, the solutions became increasingly difficult to offer. When Valdez published the Teatro's first anthology of actos in 1971, he listed five goals of this genre: to (1) inspire the audience to social action; (2) illuminate specific points about social problems; (3) satirize the opposition; (4) show or hint at a solution; and (5) express what people are feeling.[2] What was so new? Political theater had already been doing that for centuries, and accomplishing it in various degrees. But what makes the acto unique is the fact that it deals specifically with the problems of the Chicano, created and performed by Chicanos and Chicanas who have lived the experiences they dramatize.

Actos emerge out of the need to dramatize or express through theater a given problem. As a basic rule, there is no drama without conflict, dilemma, or predicament. Besides, the slightest problem or situation can be put on stage, no matter how ridiculous or farfetched it might appear. The acto is really an extended commercial of sorts whose purpose is to educate as well as entertain. One of the earliest actos created by the Teatro Campesino is "La Quinta Temporada," first performed in 1966, while the Teatro was still aligned with the Farmworkers Union. This acto demonstrated the need for a union hiring hall rather than the common practice of getting work through the farm labor contractor, or coyote as he is unaffectionately termed by campesinos. The coyote is the grower's middleman, responsible for gathering workers and making his profits at their expense. Under this system, the campesinos have no rights, and certainly no benefits to which all workers should be entitled. "La Quinta Temporada" graphically demonstrates the collusion between the growers and the contractors at the expense of the humble workers.

In all actos, "La Quinta Temporada" opens with a character communicating directly to the audience. There is no setting, a minimum of props, and the lighting comes from the sun or car headlights if performed outdoors. The costume is the actor/campesino's own work clothes; nothing more is really necessary.

There is, of course, a sign hung around the character's neck which immediately identifies him or her. The first character we see is a campesino with a sign that says: "Esquirol." He walks onto the acting area and addresses the audience:

> Oh, hello—quihubole! My name is José . . . what else?. . . and I'm looking for a job. Do you have a job? I can do anything, any kind of field work. You see, I just got in from Texas this morning and I need to send money back to my familia. I can do whatever you want—pick cotton, grapes, melons.[3]

The character immediately identifies himself, his purpose, and even where he is from. He has, in theatrical terms, stated his objective or told us what it is he wants. In every acto, as in every drama, each character must want something, and it is the desire to get it that keeps the action rolling forward.

The moment José finishes his little introductory speech, Don Coyote appears on stage identified by his sign as well as his coyote howl. For those in the audience who do not know what a coyote is, he tells the campesino: "My friend! My name is Don Coyote and I am a farm labor contractor." The campesino is thrilled that he will have a job, and agrees to work for Don Coyote, who has promised him a "fat summer, covered with money." The Patroncito enters, calling for his summer crew. When he sees that the coyote has hired somebody, he calls: "Summer! Get in here." Summer is an actor dressed in ordinary work clothes, but whose shirt and hat are covered with fake money. Campesino audiences knowingly laugh at this sight for they recognize the metaphor and visual imagery. By presenting allegorical figures, such as Summer, the acto becomes a modern morality play in the tradition of the early Church dramas that presented mortals side-by-side with allegories such as Justice, Death, or Good Deeds. Allegorical figures are visual representations of ideas or conditions, or yes, even the seasons.

To illustrate in graphic terms what happens to the campesino's wages, the following occurs: as summer crosses the stage, the farmworker follows right behind him, picking-off the money and placing it in his back pockets; the coyote follows the campesino, taking the money out of the worker's pockets and placing it in his rear pockets; and finally, the grower takes the money out of the contractor's pockets. When summer has passed, each of the three characters stop to count their earnings. The grower has a large wad of bills in his hands, the coyote is counting his "take," but the campesino is left with empty pockets. "Where's my money?" he demands, but he is told by the coyote that fall has his money. "You're stupid," the coyote tells the campesino, "you don't know how to save." In order to persuade the worker to pick the fall crops, the coyote reminds him that winter is coming, with little or no work at all.

The campesino is thus forced to work the fall season, and once again the same thing happens with the money. When winter arrives, dressed in white and strewing snowflakes about the stage, we know that the campesino is in for a lean winter season. While the grower and contractor go off for cushy vacations in sunnier climates, the campesino is left to suffer the ravages of winter. After a period of physical abuse, once again metaphorically representing the suffering of the farmworkers during the winter, spring arrives, a young woman gaily dressed, tossing flowers instead of cold snow in her wake. Spring represents hope for the farmworker, indicative of the renewal of the vegetation, the crops, and the resurrection of Mother Nature. She kicks out winter and tells the farmworker to fight for his rights.

With the hope offered him by spring, the farmworker tells the coyote he is on strike, and refuses to pick the next summer's crops. Summer passes, as before, but this time there is no one to pull off the dollar bills, and the coyote and patrón are left enraged. Fall passes, and once again the farmworker holds firm, while the money remains on the actor's back. When winter comes, he lunges onstage with a vengeance, announcing "Llegó el lechero! And my name ain't Granny Goose, baby." He goes to the farmworker first, but is protected by actors wearing signs identifying them as The Churches, La Raza, and the Unions. Unable to get anything out of the worker, the harsh winter season then attacks the grower, who must finally submit to the campesino's demand for a union contract. The forces of good triumph over forces of evil, and the coyote is left onstage with winter eager to abuse him. Winter kicks the crooked contractor offstage, and turns the sign around his neck to read "Social Justice," proclaiming: "Si alguien pregunta qué pasó con ese contratista chueco, díganle que se lo llevó la quinta chin—LA QUINTA TEMPORADA!!!" (If someone asks what happened with that crooked contractor, tell him that the fifth chin— The Fifth Season—took him!!!) The "Fifth Season," he has told the coyote, is that social justice for which the Union is fighting so hard.

By mixing the real with the allegorical, the acto is reaching for a statement that is larger than life, and does not have to make excuses for its style. Events take place on different sides of the stage, and we are told that one side is the United States, while the other is on Asian soil. La Muerte walks on and announces that he is about to tell a story, as if it were quite natural for Death to make appearances on stage or off. There is no concern for the theatrical realism in the acto as it searches for the most expedient means of exposing a problem and reaching toward a solution. All of the Valdezian actos are extremely entertaining, and are also educational. But, above all, the Teatro Campesino's actos became the inspiration for other actos created by new teatros all over the country.

The Teatro Campesino began making tours of the Southwest soon after it was born, and by its second year had ventured as far as the East Coast. Everywhere this unique group of actors/singers/campesinos performed, it dropped seeds of creativity that soon sprouted into other teatros, eager to express what they were feeling. The problems dramatized by the Teatro Campesino's actos were universal to the Chicano, but they had not yet dealt with all of the concerns of La Raza, and these newer teatros began to improvise their own actos that illustrated regional concerns. Most of these young groups were formed on college and university campuses in the late sixties, and several of these teatros still exist. But whether they created original actos or based their improvisations on what the Teatro Campesino had performed, there was not a group among them that did not owe its inspiration and genesis to the original Chicano theater group.

THEATRICAL ANTECEDENTS

By original Chicano theater group, it is not meant that before 1965 the Chicano had no theatrical tradition. On the contrary, we can look as far back as the pre-Columbian ritual dramas for our theatrical and spiritual heritage. The ancient Azteca and Maya peoples had a developing tradition of ritual dramas, but of course, the Spanish colonizers destroyed all that they could of the records, leaving us with fragments of scripts and relatively little information about the theater before Cortez. One ritual dance-drama, the "Rabinal Achí," survived the ravages of the book-burning missionaries, and it is proof of at least one important Maya-Quiché drama. For the Chicano's longest lasting theatrical tradition, however, we must turn to the Spanish religious dramas of the colonization period.

When the Spaniards arrived in the so-called New World, they soon realized that theater would be an important tool in the educational process, Christianizing and attempting to erase any vestiges of the "pagan" way of life. By 1526, the first religious play was produced, and soon, the friars had the natives reciting and staging religious dramas in their own tongue. The plays were in the European tradition of dramatizing stories from the Bible, the lives of the saints, in a combination of styles created by the Spaniards, called *autos sacramentales*. The *autos* mixed allegorical figures and situations with human characters and generally attempted to uphold the teachings of the Church by dramatizing situations that would elaborate Christian theology for an illiterate audience. One drama made such an impression when it ended with the horrors of hell and damnation, depicted graphically with smoke, flames, and fireworks, that it sent thousands of natives to the baptismal fount.

Didactic religious theater followed the Spanish missionaries wherever they went, and became a tradition in the Southwest-language churches of Aztlán soon after the colonization of the Southwest. The two most popular religious dramas to date are *Los Pastores* and *Las Cuatro Apariciones de la Virgen de Guadalupe,* plays that can still be seen in barrio churches today. Following the example set by Valdez's troupe, some teatros are now presenting annual productions of *Las Cuatro Apariciones de la Virgen de Guadalupe* during the month of December, thus linking contemporary teatros with a tradition that dates back centuries. Of course, the teatros alter the script a bit to give a more contemporary view of Juan Diego's apparitions. The Teatro Campesino's version, retitled "La Virgen del Tepeyac," begins with the Spanish friars arguing over whether the Indians are worthy of baptism—a debate that most modern-day priests would rather forget. Of course, "La Virgen del Tepeyac" remains a staunchly reverent view of the Virgencita Morenita (the Little Brown Virgin), for the Teatro Campesino knows how far it can go with the devout.

Though published accounts of the Chicano's nonreligious theatrical activity are limited, we know that there have been periods of activity in both the Southwest and Midwest during the last half of the nineteenth century and up to the present. Many theater troupes from Mexico would tour the barrios of Aztlán, presenting plays in Spanish for culture-starved Raza. A vaudeville type of entertainment, called a *carpa* for the tent in which it was performed, became a popular attraction in the 1930s both in Mexico and on this side of the border. Sometimes, these carpas would include topical sketches that satirized the

Anglos, ridiculing their behavior and releasing the audience's possible resentment toward the "gringos."

Before the advent of the Teatro Campesino, political theater in the barrios was limited, if it existed at all. One Chicano scholar, Tomás Ybarra-Frausto, of Stanford University, has conducted interviews with a gentleman who belonged to a touring Spanish-language theater company in the late 1920s. The company, called El Cuadro México-España, dramatized the life of a Mexicano who was being falsely prosecuted for a crime which he had not committed. The immigrant, Aurelio Pompa, was attempting to organize the Mexicanos, and became an early political prisoner for his efforts. The Cuadro presented his story, followed by an appeal to the audience for moral and financial support. A petition was circulated after the presentation, in an effort to save Sr. Pompa from certain execution. Unfortunately, the accused met his death at the hands of Injustice, but the Cuadro México-España became an early twentieth-century teatro, a predecessor of the Teatro Campesino and all the groups that followed it.

DIVERSE THEMES

After the Teatro Campesino separated from the Farmworker's Union in 1967, it began to dramatize themes that were not strictly related to the rural campesino. *Los Vendidos* ridiculed the Chicano "sellout"; *No Saco Nada de la Escuela* commented upon the failure of the educational system to educate Chicanos; and *The Militants* poked a satirical finger at the so-called revolutionaries of the Chicano Movement. During the War in Vietnam, the Teatro created two antiwar statements: *Vietnam Campesino* and *Soldado Razo*. Each of these actos succinctly and simply gave their analysis of the situation and demonstrated the problems for its audience. As the themes became more complex, the solutions were not as easily defined, but the actos were at least exposing problems that had not been dramatized before.

While the actos were the products of a collective creative process, guided in improvisations by the director, Valdez was also writing plays that his Teatro group would perform. His first play was written while he was an undergraduate at San Jose State College, and dealt with a Chicano family struggling for economic and cultural survival. The play was titled *The Shrunken Head of Pancho Villa*, and was written in a surrealistic style, with *cucarachas* crawling on the walls, and one of the sons without a body. The bodiless head is possibly the stolen head of Pancho Villa, but we are never really told its true identity in this interesting statement, which was Valdez's first full-length play. Like each of the plays that followed it, *Shrunken Head* dealt with a family in crisis, though each succeeding work explored a different style.

Bernabé, written in 1970, explored the Chicano's indigenous heritage and myths, as it told the tale of a "loquito del pueblo" (the town's idiot) whose desire to "marry La Tierra" symbolically transforms him into a Natural Man. His marriage is presided over by La Tierra's father, El Sol, and her brother, La Luna, who is dressed as a 1940s zoot-suiter, smoking marijuana. The playwright's next work dealt with the War in Vietnam, and also attempted to link contemporary issues and characters with indigenous legend. It is called *Dark Root of a Scream,* and takes the audience to a wake for a dead Chicano soldier, revealing the young Chicano's unnecessary demise in a war nobody understood. While the mother, his girlfriend, and a priest discuss the soldier's past, three local *vatos* (dudes) carry on a conversation that parallels the discussion at the wake. The vatos are on the street which is actually the base of a pyramid which supports the setting for the wake. The pyramid setting recalls the Chicano's native ancestry, and also divides the action into distinct levels of reality. The soldier, whose given name was Quetzalcóatl, is a contemporary Chicano redeemer figure whose death reminds us that the time will come when all of mankind will live in harmony once again. In this play Valdez is investigating the indigenous myth of the redeemer Quetzalcóatl, who, like Christ, is supposed to return to calm the troubled waters of man's existence.

THE MITO AND CORRIDO

It is difficult to talk about Teatro Chicano without discussing the works of Luis Valdez and his Teatro Campesino because he and his group have been the leading force behind this contemporary renaissance of Chicano dramatic expression. Plays such as *Dark Root of a Scream* are important because they herald a new direction for the playwright and his group, exploring a form other than the acto, which he terms the mito (myth). In Valdez's analysis, the acto is the Chicano seen through the eyes of man, while the mito is the Chicano as seen through the eyes of God. The most elaborate and successful of the Teatro Campesino's mitos is *La Carpa de los Rasquachis,* first created in 1973. This full-length collective creation has been performed throughout the United States and has toured Europe twice. It is a combination of the acto, mito, and another form, the corrido (ballad), which employs music, song, movement, and action to tell the story of Jesús Pelado Rasquachi.

The term *rasquachi* is difficult to translate, but might be translated to "funky," "unsophisticated," or "humble." It is really a combination of all of these meanings for a Chicano; it describes his house, his car, his humble *anything.* It is an endearing term, not an insult, as it attempts to define an attitude as well as a social condition. When a family is described as "rasquachi," it is a signal to the audience that it can expect some daring and funny situations. *La Carpa* mingles the slapstick humor of the acto with musical narration of the corrido and the reverence of the mito, as it tells the story of "Jesús Pelado Rasquachi." It is an epic tale, beginning with a ritualistic crucifixion and procession that recalls the Spanish religious dramas, and then going into the story itself, culminating with the return of Quetzalcóatl hand-in-hand with the Virgen de Guadalupe. The bulk of the *Carpa* deals with the misadventures of the main character once he bribes his way across the border to look for the land of milk and honey. He finds, instead, poor wages and working conditions, a bride and children, and eventual death through humiliation at the welfare office. It is another Valdezian family in crisis, and the resolution becomes a return to the Maya philosophy: "In Lak 'Ech; tú eres mi otro yo; si te amo y te respeto a ti, me amo y me respeto yo; si te hago daño a ti, me hago daño a mí" ("In Lak 'Ech; you are my other I; if I love and respect you, I love and respect myself; if I hurt you, then I hurt myself").

"You are my other self," the saying goes, and like the Golden Rule, reminds us that whatever good or bad we do will surely come right back to us. It is a well-grounded philosophy, and one that caused a great deal of concern among those who felt that the leading Chicano theater artist and theorist had succumbed to ethereal philosophies rather than pragmatic truths. In response to his critics, Valdez wrote the poem referred to at the opening of this discussion, "Pensamiento Serpentino," in which he discussed the reasons for this emerging philosophy. "El Indio baila," he wrote; "he dances his way to truth in a way no intellectuals will understand."[4] And Valdez, the leader of a neo-Mayan Teatro persisted in his ideas, no matter what the critic thought. One thing remained certain in 1973: no other Teatro Chicano approached the vitality, the style, or the aura of the Teatro Campesino.

TENAZ

Looking back at what we call the Teatro Movement of 1979, we can safely say that it is second only to the Farmworker's Union in vitality and tenacity. As we look around us for Chicano leaders to step forward, we are unfortunately hard-pressed to find a person besides César Chávez who can rally thousands of Chicanos behind a cause. Yet all the while, during the student protest years, the Vietnam War years, and now the apathetic years, teatros have been working on campuses and in communities, expressing the problems of their barrios in particular, of the Chicano in general. Many of these teatros are members of a national coalition of Chicano theater groups whose very name reflects endurance: TENAZ, El Teatro Nacional de Aztlán.

TENAZ was formed in 1971, after the second annual Chicano theater festival in Santa Cruz, California. The idea of a national organization of Chicano theater groups had interested Luis Valdez since the days when groups began to form throughout the country. These incipient teatros were usually the products of political necessity rather than artistic endeavors, and the early members had little or no formal training in theater. When these groups would seek advice and guidance from the Teatro Campesino, it became apparent to Valdez that a national coalition was imperative. It was time to get organized, and time to share experiences and materials with one another.

The first festival had been hosted by the Teatro Campesino in the spring of 1970, and witnessed the gathering of fifteen groups from all parts of the country. These teatros all shared one thing in common: a desire to create good theater—a politically aware theater that effectively educated and entertained La Raza. The yearly festivals became an important time of learning and working together, helping each other with music, movement, makeup, acting, and all the other areas of theater necessary to a successful production. Since few of the participants had formal training in theater, workshop leaders such as Ron Davis, former director of the San Francisco Mime Troupe, were brought in for workshops in their respective areas of expertise. The festivals were a time to get together, like a family reunion, and grow together. They were never competitive, but rather, supportive in nature, each group attempting to help the other. There were differences, of course, but these were mainly political rather than aesthetic, and the organization never attempted to define one political direction for its members.

Each of the annual festivals revealed the same major problem: a lack of plays or actos that approached the work of the Teatro Campesino. The Teatro Campesino was the only full-time teatro, remunerating its members enough to survive without having to study or work full- or even part-time. None of the other teatros were sufficiently organized to allow their members to do only teatro, and thus suffered the inevitable amateurism such involvement can often generate. Actos presented at the festival were often poor imitations of the Teatro Campesino style, and usually lacked a clear sense of direction and discipline. For many, teatro became an occasional activity, an avocation rather than the vocation it had become for Valdez's troup. For others, however, teatro became a way of life, a meaningful search for creative expression of the Chicano condition.

It is difficult to discuss the leading teatros in this country without leaving some groups out. To list all of the active teatros in TENAZ, it would read like a catalogue, leaving insufficient information on any of the groups to satisfy an interested reader or listener. Rather, it would be best to discuss a few of the many, choosing them for their uniqueness, location, or works. At the "Fourth Annual Chicano Theater Festival" in 1973, we listed 55 known teatros, and the number has grown rather than diminished, one indication of the scope of this ever-evolving movement. Many of the groups listed in 1973 no longer exist in name, but their members have gone on to create or work with other teatros, thus keeping a constant line of communication and evolution. Some groups are formed for a particular political rally, and then fade away, to be brought together for the next cause. Some of the New Mexico teatros in the late 1970s banded together in what they termed an "all-star teatro," to improvise and perform anti-nuclear actos around Las Cruces. After the rally, the members returned to their respective groups, working in their own communities.

RECENT TRENDS

There are very few full-time teatros today; some by choice, others by necessity. People who first got involved in a teatro in the late sixties as university students are now in their early thirties, have families, and cannot live the insecure existence that theater of any kind offers. Aside from the Teatro Campesino, there are only two other groups that approach full-time work: El Teatro de la Gente, of San Jose, and Santa Barbara's Teatro de la Esperanza. Teatro Libertad of Tucson, Arizona, chooses to remain a community-based teatro whose members are workers or students involved in other political activities along with their teatro. Teatro Bilingüe, of Texas A & I University in Kingsville, is a student group that performs its works in either Spanish or English, choosing its repertoire from Latin America, Spain, or the United States. Some of its members have graduated to seek work in the professional theater, or joined other teatros, such as the Santa Barbara Troupe. Teatro Desengaño del Pueblo, of Gary, Indiana, is one of the few multiracial teatros, its membership composed of children and adults expressing the problems of urban residents of "Steel City."

All of the teatros have one goal in common, whether they perform actos, corridos, traditional plays, or original scripts: to educate as well as entertain. Anyone who has had the experience of performing for La Raza knows that our people are anxious to see themselves reflected onstage, particularly when that reflection is presented with the honesty and sincerity a teatro can offer. Our audiences are still unaccustomed to teatro Chicano, and sometimes are rather patronizing, jumping to their feet with appreciation, even if the production was not of high quality. They sometimes respond to the fact that they are seeing people like themselves on that platform, speaking to them in their own language on their level.

When Teatro Libertad performs *Los Pelados,* an acto about a Chicano who works for the sanitation department, and is a garbage collector, the man who plays that role *is* a garbage collector. The teatro is presenting a situation that one of its own members lives daily, not a play that takes place in some remote time or place. The familial relationships in the acto are based on personal experiences and are also embellished with the humor that arises from barrio life. Only a garbage collector can laugh at himself and comment upon his daily struggles with personal knowledge. When that experience is presented for an audience in the barrios of Tucson, the audience knows intuitively that those "actors" have first-hand knowledge of what they are dramatizing. There is a certain "rasquachiness" about *Los Pelados* that cannot be pretended. When you perform in parks, community halls, gyms, and all the other situations a teatro finds itself in, you cannot pretend to be the "Ice Follies."

Teatro Bilingüe, on the other hand, is dedicated to training its actors, most of whom are drama majors, preparing them for the professional stage or screen. This group has been responsible for bringing Spanish-language productions to communities in this country and in Mexico. Though the director, Joe Rosenberg, does not choose to call his troupe a "Teatro Chicano," because they produce mainly non-Chicano plays, this group should be considered a Chicano theater group because its members are mostly Chicanos and Mexicanos and they perform for La Raza as well as non-Hispanics. The troupe has recently begun to adapt Chicano short stories and poems, and has revised positive reactions from the community. The director prefers to produce scripts that have been successfully produced in their own countries, and as we have too few plays in either Spanish or English, the Teatro Bilingüe is training its actors to excel in two languages rather than only one.

By selecting its repertoire from Latin-American plays, the Teatro Bilingüe is introducing important playwrights and themes to its bilingual audience. When they perform *Historias para ser contadas* by Argentine playwright Osvaldo Dragún, they demonstrate to both the English and Spanish-speaking public the variety and importance of Latin-American theater. When the group tours Mexico, it is a living example of what Chicanos can create and present with confidence, in a language that has often been denied them. When the same group performed at the John F. Kennedy Center in Washington, D.C., it made its audience take note: Chicanos can act too!

One of the oldest California teatros, Teatro de la Gente, first began as the urban counterpart to Luis Valdez's troupe, El Teatro Urbano, directed by Luis's younger brother, Daniel. Daniel returned to work with the Teatro Campesino, and the group then changed its name to Gente under the guidance of students at San Jose State College. Adrián Vargas originally saw the student teatro at a campus rally and decided to become a part of the group. He eventually became a codirector. Today, Vargas is the director of the Teatro de la Gente, and the Organizational Coordinator of TENAZ. One of the most effective works this teatro has performed was *El Corrido de Juan Endrogado*. As the title implies, this is a corrido about a drug addict named Juan, but it is more than just a ballad in the popular tradition. The corrido style was first created during a TENAZ summer workshop hosted by the Teatro Campesino in 1971. The form is basically a dramatization of a popular corrido; actors moving to the music, recreating the action of the song while a singer narrates the tale in song. *El Corrido de Juan Endrogado* maintained a constant musical undertone to highlight and accentuate the action as we learned about this barrio victim of drugs. The music changed to fit the mood, always present, always commenting upon the action.

Currently, Teatro de la Gente is evolving an original play written by Vargas, entitled *El Quetzal*. It is the story of another barrio youth who, like the quetzal bird, cannot survive a caged existence. The play attempts to describe the main character's struggles to maintain his individuality and dignity in the face of societal pressures and conflicts. He has just returned from prison, and is on his way to organizing the barrio youths against the drug traffic when he gives up and orders a "friend" to give him an overdose of heroin. It is a disturbing comment, but one that attempts to create real people whose lives we can get involved in. *El Quetzal* goes beyond the acto in the playwright's search for another form, a form that can also speak to La Raza.

El Teatro de la Esperanza has been hailed by some observers as the leading Chicano teatro of the 1980s. This group, which began as a student teatro on the University of California, Santa Barbara campus, has become the leading example of disciplined acting and playwriting, collectively creating three outstanding examples of teatro Chicano: *Guadalupe, La Víctima,* and then, *Hijos; Once a Family.* In its search for a form to call its own, this group has evolved from the strictly docudrama fiction of *La Víctima,* to the current fictional creation, *Hijos.* Each work reflects distinct issues and a tendency to experiment.

Guadalupe was based on a report to the U.S. Commission on Civil Rights entitled "The Schools of Guadalupe: A Legacy of Oppression." Mexicano parents in the little town of Guadalupe, sixty miles north of Santa Barbara, attempted to organize against oppressive school officials and political leaders, but were thwarted by the overpowering forces that maintain a feudal economy in that agricultural empire. Members of the teatro conducted interviews with residents, visited the schools and the church, and then improvised situations based on the documents and interviews, dramatizing what had happened. The teatro members discovered that this little town was a microcosm of any barrio, rural or urban, and attempted to expose the town of Guadalupe as only one of many similar situations.

The group's next piece, *La Víctima,* was based on documentation about the mass deportations that have been conducted by the government whenever there is a financial crisis, effectively blaming the ills of the economy on the so-called illegal alien problem. The play traced a fictional family from their entry to this country during the Mexican Revolution, to the present, following the young "Amparo" as she grows up in this country, marries, has a family, and is then deported, losing her oldest son at the railroad station. Sammy, the son, is adopted by another family and grows up to become an Immigration Officer. Meanwhile, "Amparo's" other children have crossed back to this country to work, and smuggle her across when her father dies. When Sam conducts a raid on striking factory workers, his mother is among them, and he finds himself deporting her, not wanting to admit that she is who she is. The play closes with Sam screaming at the vision of his mother "I hate you!" as he searches for a rationalization for what he does to earn a living.

Audiences enjoyed the emotion of *La Víctima,* mingled with the humor brought about by typical barrio conflicts and personalities. Each of the fifteen scenes was introduced by a quote giving factual information behind the fictional situation. Placards were displayed in both English and Spanish, introducing the theme of each scene, urging the audience to think about what was happening as it evolved. Critics praised the playwriting, the acting, and the discipline demonstrated by this teatro, and the group became the second Chicano theater group to travel to Europe during summer and fall of 1978. They performed *La Víctima* for audiences in Poland, Yugoslavia, and Sweden, dramatizing a problem that few people are even aware of.

Teatro de la Esperanza's other collective creation, *Hijos,* traces the dissolution of a typical lower-income Chicano family. The alcoholic father, with his dreams of "un ranchito en Tejas"; the mother, struggling to make ends meet; one son a *vato loco;* an anglicized daughter; and the youngest son who becomes the only hope for the future—all reflect a family in crisis. This creation has left the realm of the document, and is completely fictional, yet strikes home with its audiences for the truth of the representation. It is presented with a minimum of props and a simple backdrop, as it focuses on the actors and the different characters they bring to life. It is a masterpiece of character delineation, as each of the six actors portrays more than one person. At the close of the play, we expected more than the six actors to take a bow, looking for all the other people who had appeared before us so ingeniously.

Another development in the growing realm of teatro Chicano is the university drama department production, directed by a Chicano faculty member. Though few drama departments have yet developed an interest in hiring Chicano directors, there are a few we must recognize for their vision and support. Rubén Sierra at the University of Washington in Seattle directed the Teatro Quetzalcóatl in a production of his script *Manolo,* and also directed Luis Valdez's first full-length play, *The Shrunken Head of Pancho Villa.* This last play was a drama department-sponsored production, and received positive responses from the community. Some members of Teatro Quetzalcóatl participated, along with other actors from the department. It was significant because it demonstrated the importance of producing Chicano plays, and the need for dramatic expression relevant to La Raza.

Rómulus Zamora has taught in the Drama Department at California State University at Sacramento and has directed his own works as well as Chicano adaptations of Mexican or even Spanish plays. His productions of Emilio Carballido's *Yo También Hablo de la Rosa,* and Alfonso Sastre's *Muerte en el Barrio,* received excellent press and positive support from the community. He has also directed a work of his own, *La Creación del Mundo,* and actos by other teatros.

In the 1970s, the University of Texas at El Paso began a program in bilingual theater in its Drama Department, and the department at Texas A & I has strongly supported the Teatro Bilingüe for several years. Jorge Huerta has directed a student group, Teatro Mil Caras, at UC San Diego along with a Drama Department-sponsored production of Carlos Morton's *El Jardín,* and a Chicano adaptation of Arthur Miller's *A View from the Bridge.* There is an increasing awareness of the importance of reaching the Spanish-speaking community, and university drama departments are finally taking note of teatro Chicano and looking for qualified faculty members.

Once again, we must turn to Luis Valdez for his inspiration and example; for just as his Teatro Campesino made Chicano theater what it is today, one of his greatest triumphs, *Zoot Suit,* altered the course of teatro Chicano. When the creative genius behind the world-famous Teatro Campesino made the decision to "go to Hollywood," it was because the time had come to expose the public at large to the Chicano experience. Teatro audiences had become the already initiated people who had the same political background, and whose minds did not need to be altered. But by producing his statement about Chicanos in Los Angeles from the 1940s, now transposed into the 1970s, at the Mark Taper Forum in that same city, Valdez was saying "Chicanos are professionals, too." What happened is now history. The initial work-in-progress sold out in record time for its fourteen performances; the season opener a few months later again sold out in record time at the large Aquarius Theatre in Hollywood. The original cast went to Broadway in March 1979 and the play lasted four weeks after devastating reviews persuaded audiences to stay away.

But whether *Zoot Suit* survived on Broadway or not, Luis Valdez is still the undisputed leader of the Chicano Theater Movement. It is not an accident that *Zoot Suit* became a sell-out in Los Angeles. La Raza went to see that spectacular production over and over again, because it spoke to their history, their people, and their concerns. The discrimination that is dramatized in Valdez's play is still a reality, whether in Los Angeles, Detroit, or Houston, and Chicanos know this. But beyond the reality of the presentation, other teatros must look at the professionalism displayed on that stage, and learn that Chicanos like well-written and superbly performed productions just as well as any other group. Audiences have not only been composed of Chicanos, but have included Anglos, blacks, and members of every culture in this society. Perhaps that is the most important achievement of Valdez and his production: people who would otherwise never have seen a play about Chicanos went to the Aquarius

Theatre, witnessing history in the making, and returning to their homes a little wiser. *Zoot Suit* educates as it entertains, and that is the least a teatro Chicano must attempt to do.

NOTES

1. Luis Valdez, *Pensamiento Serpentino* (San Juan Bautista: Cucaracha Publications, 1973), p. 1.

2. Luis Valdez, *Actos* (San Juan Bautista: Cucaracha Publications, 1971), p. 6.

3. Ibid., p. 22.

4. Valdez, *Pensamiento Serpentino,* p. 7.

9 | Chicano Literary Folklore

MARÍA HERRERA-SOBEK

Up to the present the formulation of an exact definition for the term "folklore" has been a difficult and elusive goal. The *Standard Dictionary of Folklore, Mythology and Legend* incorporates no less than twenty-one separate definitions submitted by experts in the field. A cursory examination of these definitions, however, does show a certain consistency in the general framework of their constructs. We note, for example, that certain key words are repeatedly utilized in the descriptions of this cultural phenomenon. Scholars generally agree that folklore encompasses the *oral traditions* (as opposed to the written traditions) of a people that have been handed down from generation to generation. Traditions considered under the field of folkloristics include: (1) prose narratives (myths, folktales, legends, memorates, *casos,* jests); (2) folksongs (ballads, *canciones, décimas, coplas*); (3) folk speech; (4) proverbs and proverbial expressions; (5) folk drama; (6) children's songs and games; (7) riddles; (8) beliefs and folk medicine; (9) folk festivals; (10) folk arts and crafts; (11) folk dance; and (12) folk gestures. In this study we focus on the first eight genres subsumed under the category of literary folklore.

We define Chicano folklore as that folklore belonging to the group of people of Mexican-American descent residing in the United States; the majority living mainly in the American Southwest: Texas, California, Arizona, New Mexico, and Colorado. Interest in Chicano folklore scholarship began early in the twentieth century with the efforts of Aurelio M. Espinosa (from New Mexico) who collected, analyzed, and published articles and books related to Hispanic folklore. Espinosa contributed serious articles and books on New Mexican-Spanish romances, folktales, children's songs and games, and other related areas. Generally regarded as an "Españolista," Espinosa was principally concerned with demonstrating that the folklore evidenced in New Mexico was a direct descendant of the folklore the original Spanish settlers introduced in the area and that it had not been "contaminated" by Mexican influences. This thesis was of course debunked by later scholars, but his collections and studies nevertheless first pointed out the richness of oral traditions extant in the Southwest. Espinosa is particularly remembered for his studies on the New Mexican romance. In his collections are included such famous romances as "La aparición," "Gerineldo," "Estaba señor don Gato," "El piojo y la liendre," and others. The following is a short version of "La esposa infiel":

Andándome yo paseando	While I was travelling
por las orillas del mar	along the seashore
me encontré una chaparrita	I met a petite woman
y me puse a platicar	and we started to talk.
"¡Mi marido, mi marido!	"My husband, my husband!
¡Válgame Dios! ¿Qué haré yo?"	Oh my God! What shall I do?"
"Siéntese aquí en ese catre.	"Sit down on this cot.
Déjeme ir a conversar yo."	I will talk to him."
"¿De quién es ese caballo	"Whose horse is that
que en mi corral relinchó?"	which hee-hawed in my corral?"
"Ese es de un hermano tuyo	"It belongs to your brother.
que tu padre te lo mandó	Your father sent it to you,
pa que vayas al casorio	so you could attend the wedding
de un hermano que se casó."	of one of your brothers."
"Ya me puedes ir diciendo	"You can tell me now
que caballos tengo yo."	which horses belong to me."
La mujer murió a la una	The wife died at one o'clock,
y el hombre murió a las dos.[1]	the man died at two.

Other scholars from New Mexico, such as Arthur León Campa and Aurora Lucero-White Lea, continued to collect and analyze the folklore of New Mexico in the decades that followed. Succeeding authors, however, began to acknowledge the great influence Mexican folklore has had on Chicano folklore. Research activity also flourished in Texas with such publications as J. Frank Dobie's *Puro Mexicano* and Mody C. Boatright's *Mexican Border Ballads and Other Lore* in the 1930s and 1940s.

The foremost Chicano folklore scholar, however, is no doubt Américo Paredes from Texas, who has been at the forefront of folklore scholarship in general and Mexican-American folklore research in particular since the publication in 1958 of his book *With His Pistol in His Hand: A Border Ballad and Its Hero*. In the three decades since then, Paredes has published close to one hundred articles and books dealing specifically with Mexican-American folklore. His expertise and intimate knowledge of the Chicano experience led him to examine such wide ranging topics as the *corrido,* the *décima,* folk speech, folk medicine, the jest, the proverb, as well as other Chicano-related issues. His clarity of thought, perceptiveness, and incisive logic provided him with the proper tools to make serious, original contributions to the field in general and to Chicano studies in particular.

In recent years the turbulent 1960s and 1970s initiated a new awareness of the Chicano experience. The social upheavals and confrontations of this era were no doubt directly responsible for stimulating research related to and dealing specifically with Mexican-American issues. Chicano folklore benefited directly from this upsurge in interest; the numerous books and articles published since the 1960s in various genres of folklore attest to this fact. In an issue of *Aztlán* dedicated to Mexican-American folklore and art, Américo Paredes elaborates in no uncertain terms that:

> folklore is of particular importance to minority groups such as the Mexican Americans because their basic sense of identity is expressed in a language with an "unofficial" status, different from the one used by the official culture. We can say, then, that while in Mexico the Mexican may well seek lo mexicano in art, literature, philosophy, or history—as well as in folklore—the Mexican American would do well to seek his identity in his folklore.[2]

No doubt Chicano folkloristics will continue to prosper in the future and will prove profitable in the understanding and elucidation of the Chicano character and experience.

PROSE NARRATIVE

The categories subsumed under the broad umbrella of "prose narratives" include myths, folktales, legends, *casos,* memorates, and jests. There are no "true" Chicano myth narratives as such; myths evidenced in Chicano literature derived mainly from Aztec and Mayan sources. These myths proved vitally important in the Chicano's quest for self-definition and identity in the past twenty years. It should not be surprising that Aztec myths found fertile ground in the creative thought processes of Chicanos, who, having been denied their Indian heritage in previous decades, suddenly felt a renovated affiliation with that heritage. Thus, a new political meaning was grafted into the old myth of Aztlán, the land of the Chicanos' mythic Aztec ancestors who dwelled in the American Southwest before migrating south, to Tenochtitlán (Mexico City). Early Chicano political activists and creative writers renovated these Aztec myths in their groping for a reaffirmation of their centuries-old roots in America, for a sense of identity which they perceived to be not wholly Mexican, not wholly American, but Chicano. *Lo indio, lo azteca, lo maya* was no longer a source of embarrassment or something to be ashamed of, but a source of pride. Through the breathtakingly beautiful myths of the Ancients, one could perceive that brown was indeed beautiful. Alurista, one of the most prominent poets of the Chicano literary renaissance, liberally sprinkles his verses with the themes of Quetzalcóatl, priest-god of the Toltecs; Kukulcán, Mayan god; Coatlicue, an Aztec mother goddess; and many other Aztec and Mayan deities to effectively convey this new-found pride.

The folktale, on the other hand, bears the stamp of both an Indian and Spanish heritage and is a rich source of Chicano folklore. The European-Spanish heritage surfaces in the fairytale or märchentype of narratives. *María Cenicienta, Caperucita Roja, Blancanieves, The Little Horse of Seven Colors, Juan y las habichuelas,* and others of this type are obviously of European origin, having migrated with the Spaniards to the New World. It was inevitable, however, that contact with a large Indian population would eventually produce a syncretism of European tales with Native American ones. In addition, a significant number of Meso-American Indian tales integrated themselves into the general Mexican and Mexican-American folktale repertoire. Thus an important number of animal tales such as those pertaining to the coyote cycle originate from Native American stock.

A similar statement can be formulated for the legends. Although many came from Europe, particularly the religious legends, a good number derive from Meso-American Indian lore. Others demonstrate a decided syncretism in the type of motifs found in the structural framework. A good example of this process is evident in the *La Llorona* legend. Two strands exist and intermingle in this legend: one Mexican and one Aztec. According to the former version, *La Llorona* was originally a beautiful young mestizo woman madly in love with a wealthy Spanish caballero. The fruit of this love resulted in various children (one to nine, the number varies) out of wedlock; the Spaniard having promised to eventually marry her. It came to pass that one night the young mestizo mother was informed of her caballero's impending wedding. On the night of her lover's wedding, after peeking through the window of her lover's house and witnessing the wedding scene, she returns to her own home intensely distraught. There, in a fit of rage and/or insanity, she kills all her children. Having realized her deed, she madly rushes out of her house screaming "¡Ayyyy, mis hijos!" As punishment for this barbaric deed, she roams the waterways, any dark street or road screeching, "¡Ayyyyy, mis hijos!" forever in search of her lost children. According to the Aztec version, on the other hand, *La Llorona* was a woman who, before the conquest, predicted the fall of the Aztec empire and was seen in the streets of the Aztec capital in a white dress, long hair in disarray and screaming in anguish, "¡Ayyyy, mis hijos!" in anticipated pain of the loss to come.

Some excellent work has been done on the Mexican/Chicano legend and folktale. Juan Rael published a large collection of tales from Colorado. Stanley L. Robe from UCLA has done extensive research on tales and legends from various parts of Mexico and the Southwest. Elaine Miller published a collection of folktales from the Los Angeles area called *Mexican Folk Narrative from the Los Angeles Area* (1973). Her collection includes religious narratives such as La Virgen de Talpa and El Santo Niño de Atocha, devil narratives, the return of the dead—that is, legends depicting the apparition of dead persons, another very popular type being the dead person that returns to pay a *manda* (promise) to some saint—buried treasure, *duendes,* as well as traditional tales (animal tales, tales of magic, stupid ogre tales, and others).

Américo Paredes amply explains the usefulness of legends in exploring the character of Mexicans and Mexican Americans. In an incisive article entitled "Mexican Legendry and the Rise of the Mestizo" published in 1971,[3] Paredes proposes that the "rise of the mestizo as representative of the Mexican nationality may be illuminated by the study of Mexican legendry" (p. 98). According to the author, before the "rise of the mestizo" (prenineteenth-century Mexico), legends dealt generally with supernatural, miraculous events such as the apparition of saints. As the mestizo seized power, legend content leaned toward the recounting of the deeds of flesh and blood heroes such as Heraclio Bernal, Gregorio Cortez and later, during the Mexican Revolution of 1910, the deeds and actions of the revolutionary heroes such as Pancho Villa, Emiliano Zapata, Francisco I. Madero, and others.

Recently, scholars are grappling with the new concepts of caso and memorate. These new terms are designed to meet the ever-increasing problem of defining in more precise terms the large corpus of prose narrative present in all cultures. More and more scholars are realizing that the old terminology (folktale, legend, märchen) is inadequate and too broadly based to meet the needs of rigorous scientific analysis. The terms caso, memorate, and personal experience narrative are currently used to classify a large body of narratives extant in the Mexican/Chicano folklore. The above terms generally encompass narratives that happened to the informant or to someone the informant knows. Joe Graham provides the following definition:

> a relatively brief prose narrative, focusing upon a single event, supernatural or natural, in which the protagonist or observer is the narrator or someone the narrator knows and vouches for, and which is normally used as evidence or as an example to illustrate that "this kind of thing happens."[4]

Graham offers fourteen types of casos discernible by their theme and structure in Chicano folklore. The following is an example:

Caso Type I
A Mexican American becomes ill and is taken to a doctor, who either treats him, with no visible results, or says that the person is not ill. The person is taken to a *curandero* or folk practitioner, who provides the proper remedy, and the patient gets well. (p. 31)

These new areas of endeavor in folklore, such as the caso, memorate, and personal experience narrative, illustrate the richness and complexity of Mexican/Chicano culture.

An equally significant area of folklore is the *chiste* or jest. Again, Américo Paredes undertook seminal research in this genre and provided a theoretical construct for understanding the underlying basis of much of Chicano folklore in general, and Chicano jokes in particular. Paredes' basic thesis underscores the element of cultural conflict as the principal moving force generating Chicano folklore.

Much of Chicano humor derives from the confrontation of two cultures: one Mexican, Catholic, Spanish-speaking; the other Anglo, Protestant, English-speaking. A large corpus of jokes, for example, relies on Mexican-Anglo conflicts using the linguistic differences between the two cultures as points of departure. Notice the following:

> A gringo was travelling on a rural Mexican road in his cadillac when suddenly a man and his burro block his path. The gringo gets down from his car, takes off his glove, and slaps the Mexican in the face with the glove yelling, "Son-of-a-bitch!" Whereupon the Mexican takes off his huarache, slaps the gringo in the face and yells, "B.F. Goodrich!"[5]

Here, although the Mexican does not understand the insult, he manages to outsmart the Anglo by striking the hardest blow. It is typical of Chicano humor in general that the Mexican/Chicano protagonist comes out the best in the exchange.

There is a cycle of jokes, however, where the protagonist (a Mexican immigrant) is the butt of the joke. This cycle of jokes portrays the difficulties recently arrived Mexicans have due to the differences in language. A good example of this type of joke follows:

> A recently arrived Mexican immigrant who cannot read English wants to buy a coke. He sees a coke machine and takes the smallest coin he has which is a dime and inserts it in the slot. A red light flashes out reading *DIME*. The man reads it in Spanish with its equivalent meaning of "Tell me!" So the fellow looks around and whispers: "¡Dame una coca!" ("Give me a coke!")[6]

These jokes told by immigrants themselves to other immigrants serve the cathartic function of relieving the stress and anxiety concomitant with moving to a foreign country.

A second basic factor that characterizes many Chicano jokes is the bilingualism expressed within the jokes as evidenced in the two examples given above. Many Chicano jokes require an understanding of both Spanish and English due to the fact that the structure of the jokes utilizes the misunderstanding of one or both languages to deliver its intended humor and punch line.

FOLKSONGS

Two of the most researched genres of Chicano folksongs are corrido and the décima. Both Arthur L. Campa and Américo Paredes have contributed substantial scholarly articles and collections of these two types of folklore.

The corrido or ballad has been and continues to be an important means of self-expression for the Chicano community. In fact, the corrido, according to Américo Paredes' theory on the renaissance of this genre, experiences its rebirth as a result of the bloody conflict between Mexicans and Anglos in the Mexican-American War of 1848. A conquered people, having been denied access to the printing press of the dominant culture, seized the corrido as a valid form of self-expression, historical documentation, and information dissemination.[7]

Most scholars agree that the corrido originally derived from the Spanish romances. Imported to America during the fifteenth and sixteenth centuries, it languished in the area until the nineteenth century; at this point in time historical events propelled it to the center stage where it became the literary instrument of protest and revolt par excellence. Paredes posits that it was the clash of cultures in the Lower Río Grande Valley where men of Mexican descent were forced "defender su derecho con su pistola en la mano" (to defend their right with a pistol in their hand). The heroic deeds and actions of these valiant, fearless men were duly recorded in the oral history and expressive folklore of the people. Corridos were lustily and proudly sung from ranch to ranch and pueblo to pueblo, the lyrics of these depicting the exploits of Chicanos who resisted the encroachment and heavy hand of the Anglo settlers.

Paredes incisively analyzes one of these corridos in his seminal book *With His Pistol in His Hand: A Border Ballad and Its Hero.* The corrido examined in this work depicts the legend of Gregorio Cortez who, having been unjustly accused of killing a Texas sheriff, was hunted down through the state of Texas until he voluntarily surrendered to the Texas Rangers (after realizing his family had been imprisoned).

Another example of the Chicano/Anglo conflict-type corridos that vividly portrays this state of affairs is the "Corrido de Joaquín Murieta."

Yo no soy americano	I am not an American
pero comprendo el inglés.	but I understand English.
Yo lo aprendí con mi hermano	I learned it with my brother
al derecho y al revés.	forwards and backwards.
A cualquier americano	And any American
lo hago temblar a mis pies.	I make tremble at my feet.
Cuando apenas era un niño	When I was barely a child
huérfano a mí me dejaron.	I was left an orphan.
Nadie me hizo ni un cariño,	No one gave any love,
a mi hermano lo mataron.	they killed my brother,
Y a mi esposa Carmelita,	And my wife Carmelita,
cobardes la asesinaron.	the cowards assassinated her.

Yo me vine de Hermosillo
en busca de oro y riqueza.
Al indio pobre y sencillo
lo defendí con fiereza.
Y a buen precio los sherifes
pagaban por me cabeza.

A los ricos avarientos,
yo les quité su dinero.
Con los humildes y pobres
yo me quité mi sombrero.
Ay, que leyes tan injustas
fue llamarme bandolero.

A Murieta no le gusta
lo que hace no es desmentir.
Vengo a vengar a mi esposa,
y lo vuelvo a repetir,
Carmelita tan hermosa,
como la hicieron sufrir.

Por cantinas me metí,
castigando americanos.
"Tú serás el capitán
que mataste a mi hermano.
Lo agarraste indefenso,
orgulloso americano."

Mi carrera comenzó
por una escena terrible.
Cuando llegué a setecientos
ya mi nombre era temible.
Cuando llegué a mil doscientos
ya mi nombre era terrible.

Yo soy aquel que domina
hasta leones africanos.
Por eso salgo al camino
a matar americanos.
Ya no es otro mi destino
¡pon cuidado, parroquianos!

Las pistolas y las dagas
son juguetes para mí.

I came from Hermosillo
in search of gold and riches.
The Indian poor and simple
I defended with fierceness
And a good price the sheriffs
would pay for my head.

From the greedy rich,
I took away their money.
With the humble and poor
I took off my hat.
Oh, what laws so unjust
to call me a highwayman.

Murieta does not like
to be falsely accused.
I come to avenge my wife,
and again I repeat it,
Carmelita so lovely
how they made her suffer.

Through bars I went
punishing Americans.
"You must be the captain
who killed my brother.
You grabbed him defenseless
you stuck-up American."

My career began
because of a terrible scene.
When I got to seven hundred
[killed]
then my name was dreaded.
When I got to twelve hundred
Then my name was terrible.

I am the one who dominates
even African lions.
That's why I go out on the road
to kill Americans.
Now my destiny is no other,
watch out, you people!

Pistols and daggers
are playthings for me.

Balazos y puñaladas,	Bullets and stabbings
carcajadas para mí.	big laughs for me.
Ahora con medios cortados	With their means cut off
ya se asustan por aquí.	they're afraid around here.
No soy chileno ni extraño	I'm neither a Chilean nor a
en este suelo que piso.	stranger
De México es California,	on this soil which I tread.
porque Dios así lo quiso.	California is Mexico's
Y en mi sarape cosida	because God wanted it that way,
traigo mi fe de bautismo.	And in my stitched serape,
	I carry my baptismal certificate.
Que bonito es California	How pretty is California
con sus calles alineadas,	with her well-laid-out streets
donde paseaba Murieta	where Murieta passed by
con su tropa bien formada,	with his troops,
con su pistola repleta,	with his loaded pistol,
y su montura plateada.	and his silver-plated saddle.
Me he paseado en California	I've had a good time in
por el año del cincuenta.	California
Con mi montura plateada,	through the year of '50 [1850].
y mi pistola repleta.	With my silver-plated saddle
Y soy ese mexicano	and my pistol loaded
de nombre Joaquín Murieta.	I am that Mexican
	by the name of Joaquín Murieta.[8]

Early corridos from the Lower Río Grande Valley in Texas served as paradigms for the *guerrillero*, rebel corridos that surfaced in Mexico during Porfirio Díaz's repressive regime, one of the most famous of these corridos being "El corrido de Heraclio Bernal." The events of the Mexican Revolution of 1910 provided further material for corrido productions. The heroes of the revolution were immortalized in the lyrics of the corrido: Pancho Villa, Emiliano Zapata, Benjamín Argumedo, Francisco I. Madero, Venustiano Carranza, La Adelita, and many others.

The ever-present stream of Mexican immigrants to the United States in search of work continually replenishes the general repertoire of Chicano folksongs with Mexican corridos. Thus, literally thousands of corridos exist in the southwestern part of the United States with as varied themes as Mexican immigrant corridos ("El deportado," "Corrido de Pennsylvania," "Corrido de Texas"), corridos whose main subject is horses ("El potro lobo gatiado"), those depicting the exploits of drug and tequila smugglers ("El tequilero"), love-tragedy corridos ("Rosita Alvirez," "La 'Güera' Chavela," "Rafaelita"), those extolling the life and death of political figures such as the Kennedy corridos and those dealing with protest. During César Chávez's farmworkers' union movement of the 1960s and 1970s, numerous songs appeared depicting the hardships and aspirations of the farmworkers. These are frequently sung at protest rallies and serve as an effective means of uniting the people in a common cause. At present the corrido is very much a vital force in ethnic identification and in expressing through its lyrics the continuing struggle for achieving social justice in America.

La décima, on the other hand, experienced its apogee in the eighteenth and nineteenth century in both Mexico and the Southwest. Américo Paredes has several articles on the décima in Texas and Arthur L. Campa has a significant collection of décimas from New Mexico. Its rigid form, however (in contrast to the flexible form of the corrido), doomed it to be discarded in favor of the more flexible corrido.

FOLK SPEECH

Chicano Spanish has recently been the focus of intense study, particularly by linguists and those interested in bilingual education. The realization by American schools and by linguists that the Spanish spoken in the Southwest differed markedly from that spoken in Spain, Mexico, and other Latin-American countries, led to a flurry of research. The most comprehensive bibliography on Chicano speech is Richard V. Teschner, Garland D. Bills, and Jerry R. Craddock's *Spanish and English of United States Hispanos: A Critical, Annotated, Linguistic Bibliography* (1975), which cites 675 items. The most fruitful work undertaken is on the aspect of code-switching (switching in the middle of a phrase, sentence, or paragraph from English to Spanish or vice versa), but the most outstanding area of research from a folklorist's point of view has been neglected. Thus, little in-depth research is available on *caló* (the jargon of the underworld or the pachuco) or other areas of folk speech. A seminal work by George C. Baker "Pachuco: An American-Spanish Argot and Its Social Function in Tucson, Arizona" (1975)[9] is still one of the best works in the field. Baker studied the speech of *pachucos* from Tucson and related this speech to the social function it played within the in-group and the out-group. Some of these words include: *carnal* (brother), *jaina* (girlfriend), *chante* (house), *ruka* (girl), *birrea* (beer), *cantón* (house), *chale* (no), *lisa* (shirt), *simón* (yes), and *refinar* (to eat). The lack of studies in this genre is indeed deplorable. José Limón, a scholar on folklore, has amply demonstrated the importance of this area in his article "The Folk Performance of 'Chicano' and the Cultural Limits of Political Ideology." Limón analyzes the failure of the folk term *Chicano* to gain widespread acceptance in the community and posits the thesis that "*in part* this failure may be attributed to the unintentional violation of the community's rules about the socially appropriate use of the term—rules keyed on the community's definition of the performance of the term as belonging to the folklore genres of nicknaming and ethnic slurs."[10] It is fairly easy to deduce from this study that if political movements are to succeed, the leaders of these movements must have an intimate and working knowledge of the people they propose to represent. One way to accomplish this is through an in-depth understanding of the cultural vectors (such as folklore) operative in the community.

PROVERBS AND PROVERBIAL EXPRESSIONS

Proverbs and proverbial expressions, entities intimately related to folk speech, form an integral part of Chicano folklore. Although used most frequently by the older generation, a recent study undertaken by Shirley Arora[11] demonstrates that the younger generations of Chicanos are indeed aware of proverbs, having been raised by a mother, father, or other family member who interspersed their speech with these colorful expressions.

A proverb may be defined as a short, succinct expression that encompasses within its words a philosophical wisdom. Examples include:

1. Más vale pájaro en mano que ver un ciento volar. (Better a bird in hand than two in the bush.)
2. Dime con quién andas y te diré quién eres. (Tell me who your friends are and I'll tell you who you are.)
3. De tal palo tal astilla. (A chip off the old block.)
4. El que con lobos anda a aullar se enseña. (He who runs around with wolves will learn how to howl.)
5. En boca cerrada no entran moscas. (In a closed mouth no flies can enter.)
6. Todo cabe en un jarrito sabiéndolo acomodar. (All can be filled in a mug if you know how to place things right.)
7. Al que madruga Dios lo ayuda. (He who rises early God helps.)
8. Dios dice: "Ayúdate que yo te ayudaré." (God helps those who help themselves.)
9. El que con niños se acuesta mojado se levanta. (He who sleeps with children wakes up wet.)[12]

The proverb, as other folklore genres prove to be, is yet another important area in which the philosophy or worldview of a people can be profitably explored. Américo Paredes, however, advised extreme caution when attempting to analyze the character of a people and warns against literal interpretation of proverbs and/or deducing Mexican/Chicano traits when taken out of context. Analysis of proverbs must be undertaken in the context in which these expressions are uttered. Otherwise, the social scientist or folklorist may be, albeit unwittingly, misled to make totally false and harmful generalizations about the character of a people. Valuable information regarding the Chicano experience can be gleaned from careful research of these entities and their use in Chicano households as demonstrated by Shirley Arora's article "Proverbs in Mexican American Tradition." Her study provides key insights into status and usage of proverbs by Chicanos in Los Angeles. For example, Arora found that frequent use of proverbs is most noticeable in the area of child-rearing, "from the inculcation of table manner—El que come y canta loco se levanta, la mano larga nunca alcanza—to the regulation of social relationships and dating behavior" (p. 59). Arora also indicates that proverbs have a potential and may indeed be already employed for purposes of ethnic identification and group solidarity. Needless to say, more in-depth studies on proverb usage need to be undertaken to better comprehend this particular aspect of Chicano folklore.

Shirley Arora has also undertaken extensive research on proverbial comparisons in the Los Angeles area in her work *Proverbial Comparisons and Related Expressions in Spanish.*[13] The comparison may be defined as a phrase in which the following formulaic structures appear:

esta como . . .
tan . . . como
tan . . . que

The exaggeration likewise employs the formulaic structures of:

más . . . que

Arora interviewed 517 informants and collected thousands of entries. Some examples follow.

1. Más aburrido que un abogado (more boring than a lawyer) (p. 37).
2. Tan flaca que si se traga una aceituna parece que está preñada (so skinny that if she swallows an olive she looks pregnant) (p. 38).
3. Más alegre que un día de pago (as happy as payday) (p. 172).
4. Es tan avaro que no da ni los buenos días (he's so stingy that he doesn't even give a good morning) (p. 172).
5. Se repite como disco rayado (he repeats himself like a scratched record) (p. 179).

The humorous nature and originality of many of these proverbial expressions, together with the large number collected within a relatively small geographic area (greater Los Angeles), indicate the amazing creativity present in the speech of the Chicano community. It is evident in the large number of entries of both proverbs and proverbial expressions collected by Arora that a great premium is placed on language skills and language dexterity by Chicanos. Arora found in her study that more often than not people with a large repertoire of proverbial expressions elicited admiration and respect from the community.

Proverbs and proverbial expressions provide a strong affectivity factor toward the Spanish language and are no doubt one important reason for the high premium placed on preserving the Spanish language. The wealth of Spanish proverbs and the witticism inherent in proverbial expressions contribute to the widespread folk belief that Spanish is one of the most delightful languages in the world. This folk belief in turn brings us to closer understanding of why a conquered people, after one hundred years of political and cultural domination, tenaciously clings to one of their cultural manifestations—the Spanish language.

FOLK THEATRE

The folk theatre of the Chicano, like Mexican- and Latin-American theatre, traces its roots to the Spanish *conquistadores* and their religious plays. The early missionaries, interested in converting the Indians of the New World, discovered that, due to the differences in language representations of biblical and religious stories, drama provided an effective means of indoctrinating them into the Catholic faith. Thus, early theatrical works in the western hemisphere were religious plays in which the Indians themselves played major roles and which were extremely popular with the faithful. These plays generally took place in the church atrium and were presented to the populace on specific holy days such as Christmas or Easter Sunday. When New Mexico was settled in the seventeenth century, works that had been successful in Mexico migrated with the Spanish and Mexican settlers into what is now the American Southwest. Arthur Campa and Aurora Lucero-White Lea have both collected folk plays from this region. Among those collected is *Coloquio de los Pastores,* which, according to Lea, "represents that older type of traditional Nativity play which was presented in the village church on Christmas Eve in lieu of Midnight Mass when that village had no resident priest."[14]

Other popular plays collected include: *La aurora del nuevo día, Adán y Eva, Los tres reyes, El niño perdido, Las cuatro apariciones de Nuestra Señora de Guadalupe,* and *Los moros y cristianos.* One should also mention the pastorelas or shepherd's plays performed during the Christmas season and which are still being enacted today. Folk theatre influenced to some extent present-day Chicano theatre, particularly that of Luis Valdez. Like the corrido, present-day Chicano theatre is being effectively used as a vehicle to convey and express the injustices perpetuated on the Mexican/Chicano by Anglo society.

CHILDREN'S SONGS AND GAMES

As is true of most of the other genres of folklore, children's songs and games from the Chicano Southwest evidence basically the same categories and specimens as those from Spain. A rather flexible division of songs and games played or sung by or for children is attempted in the following major categories: (1) *canciones de cuna* (lullabyes) "Duérmete mi niño"; (2) *canciones de manos y dedos* "Tortillitas" (hand and finger games); (3) *rondas* "Naranja dulce"; (4) *retahilas* "El castillo de Chuchurumbel"; (5) *canciones* "La muñeca"; (6) *conjuros* "Sana, sana colita de rana"; and (7) miscellaneous "escondidas," "matatena," "los encantados," "rayuela."

Those of us who grew up in a Spanish-speaking environment can nostalgically remember songs and games of yore such as:

Duérmete mi niño
que tengo que hacer
lavar los pañales
ponerme a coser.

Go to sleep my child
I have work to do
wash the diapers
and some sewing too.

Tortillitas de manteca
pa mamá que está contenta.
Tortillitas de cebado
pa papá que está enojado.

Little tortillas made of lard
for mommy, for happy is she.
Little tortillas made of barley
for daddy, for angry is he.

Naranja dulce
limón partido
dame un abrazo
que yo te pido.

Sweet orange
lemon is cut
Give me a hug
I ask of you.

Doña Blanca está encerrada
en pilares de oro y plata
romperemos un pilar
para que salga Doña Blanca.

Doña Blanca is imprisoned
within pillars of gold and silver
let us break one of these pillars
so Doña Blanca can be free.[15]

Paredes made a revealing observation with regard to children's songs and games and cultural conflict—the basic thread that runs throughout Chicano folklore. As innocuous and free from anxiety and conflict as children's games may appear, the opposite state of affairs is discovered upon close analysis. Experts agree that children oftentimes express their fears and anxieties through play. Paredes pointed this out in a game played by Chicano children that exemplifies the point. The game is "la roña" also known as "la mancha" (tag). In this game children flee from the one that has "la roña" and the latter in turn tries to "touch" or "tag" the others. In Texas the game is known as "la correa," a name given to immigration officers. Thus, by implication, the Texas children enact the real-life situation of Immigration and Naturalization Services officers trying to capture undocumented workers.[16]

RIDDLES

Riddles comprise another area of Chicano folklore. Archer Taylor, a folklorist from Berkeley, provides us with the classic definition of a "true riddle": "questions that suggest an object foreign to the answer and confound the hearer by giving a solution that is obviously correct and entirely unexpected."[17]

More recently, Elli Kongas-Maranda has suggested that "the riddle is a structural unit, which necessarily consists of two parts: the riddle image and the riddle answer. In a riddling situation, these two parts are 'recited' by two different parties."[18] *La adivinanza,* as it is called in Spanish, is an integral part of the expressive culture of the Chicano. However, few studies have been undertaken on Chicano riddling habits. An exception is John M. McDowell's *Children's Riddling* (1979). McDowell's in-depth study offers extremely relevant conclusions as to the function of riddles in children's ludic activities. For McDowell,

> Riddles in the modern, industrial society serve as models of synthetic and analytic thinking. They encourage children to discover the archetypical set of commonalities binding diverse experiential realms into a single, coherent world view; and at the same time, they require children to confront the tentative status of conceptual systems, thereby fostering a flexibility of cognition evidently of some utility in a great many cultural settings.[19]

The following are some popular examples of riddles common throughout Mexico, Latin America, and the Southwest:[20]

Agua pasa por mi casa	Water passes through my house
cate de mi corazón.	my beloved.
Si no me adivinas ésta	If you do not answer this one
eres puro burro cabezón.	you are a thick-headed donkey.
(aguacate)	(avocado)
Adivíname esta adivinanza	Answer this riddle for me:
que se pela por la panza.	You peel it from the tummy.
(la naranja)	([navel] oranges)
Una vieja larga y seca	A tall, skinny old lady
que le escurre la manteca.	that drips lard.
(la vela)	(the candle)

Tito, Tito capotito	Tito, Tito, little cape
sube al cielo	fly up in the sky
y tira un grito.	and give out a scream.
(el cohete)	(the firecracker)

As is apparent, the adivinanza challenges the intellect and the reasoning processes by offering descriptions that are close enough to resemble the objects yet so hidden between the texture (metaphors, similes) of the words as to yield them difficult to answer. The riddle, a thoroughly social act in itself in that at least two people are required for it to function, provides the players with an excellent instrument to play with language. Different opportunities are offered: rhyming schemes (nos. 1–5); disconnecting and connecting various morphemes (nos. 1 and 5); deceiving metaphorical images (nos. 2 and 3) and alliterative, onomatopoetic sounds (no. 4).

McDowell perceived two different sets of riddles in the repertoire of the children interviewed (Chicano children from a barrio in Austin, Texas in 1972): (1) a collection of riddles learned at school, from Anglo children, from the media (television, radio) and (2) a set of more traditional ones learned at home from parents, relatives, and/or peers. One significant function deduced in this Texas study is the proposition that riddles serve enculturation purposes, (enculturation being defined as "the process of induction, wherein the individual acquires competency in his own culture, or the kinds of knowledge requisite to fulfillment of recognized social roles.")[21] In the acquisition of the riddling/habits of the dominant society one is also being acculturated into this dominant culture. The riddle, then, aside from serving the pleasure function manifest in all ludic play, equally serves other cognitive endeavors.

FOLK BELIEF AND FOLK MEDICINE

The folk-belief system of the Chicano community, particularly as it deals with folk medicine and curanderismo, is one of the most controversial areas of scholarship in Chicano folklore. In a revealing article by Beatrice A. Roeder, "Health Care Beliefs and Practices Among Mexican Americans: A Review of the Literature,"[22] the author identified four stages in the trajectory of folk belief scholarship vis-à-vis Mexican Americans. These stages include: (1) works dealing with the sources and historical development of Mexican folk medicine, (2) pioneer works of documentation—that is, collections done between 1894–1954, (3) the 1950–1960s—Lyle Saunders and his follower's era (who seek to understand Mexican American health practices by placing them in their cultural context), and (4) the 1970s—includes revisionist Chicano scholars who vigorously challenge previous research findings and take a socioeconomic approach to understanding Mexican medical practices as opposed to a "cultural context" approach.

The basic controversy between the last two major groups centers upon the question of whether the Mexican-American folk belief system is largely responsible for the Chicano's "inability" or reluctance to utilize and take advantage of modern "scientific" medical services. In other words, this perspective posits that it is the Chicanos' own cultural restraints that hamper them in obtaining adequate medical services. Chicano revisionists such as Nick C. Vaca, Miguel Montiel, and Armando Morales argue on the other hand that the culture-as-culprit thesis, or "cultural determinism" as they label it, is a "myth" propagated by and used as a rationalization tool by the Anglo-dominant society, which, through institutionalized racism (such as segregated schools, lack of bilingual personnel), prevents Chicanos from attaining proper medical care. A glaring example is found in Joe S. Graham's article "The Role of the *Curandero* in the Mexican American Folk Medicine System in West Texas." In his introductory remarks he states:

> In West Texas the term "scientific medicine" became almost synonymous with "Anglo medicine"—and still is. To my knowledge, there is not one licensed Mexican American doctor practicing in the whole rural region between Del Río and El Paso, separated by over four hundred miles—this in spite of the fact that over half of the population is Mexican American.[23]

What Graham failed to do in this otherwise sensitive article was to point out (1) that Texas has had a de facto segregated system (Chicano schools are generally much inferior to all white schools), (2) that medical schools in the United States previous to the 1970s had racial quotas and it was next to impossible for a black, Mexican American, or a woman to be admitted, and (3) that border-area residents in Texas did heavily utilize Spanish-speaking Mexican doctors from Mexico (who in addition tend to be less expensive than their American counterparts). The above issues were totally neglected in the article, which instead zeroed in on the culture-as-culprit theory.

As can be deduced from the expressed concerns of the above investigators, folk medicine has been largely studied from a social scientist's perspective and is very much the concern of the anthropologist and sociologist.

The inclusion of belief and folk medicine in this study, however, is due to their close proximity to the legend, the caso, the memorate, and personal-experience narrative. Folk beliefs cover a wide range of cosmological and human experiences and are perceived by some scholars as man's attempt at "scientific" explanation for an otherwise incomprehensible event. Beliefs are interconnected with prose narratives in the sense that for any given belief there may be a "story" explaining this belief. In addition to a narrative explicating the belief, additional narratives corroborating the truthfulness or efficacy of this belief may be present. These narratives may surface in (1) the form of a personal experience, (2) an experience that happened to a close relative or acquaintance, or (3) an experience that happened to some unknown person. For example, numerous folk beliefs are associated with the Catholic religion. A common belief is the following:

> A *manda* (promise) to a saint is sacred. One must always keep these promises or suffer the consequences.

Generally, when the above belief is stated, a narrative or series of narratives will illustrate this specific point. The *casos* described earlier are frequently corroborating stories of a belief. There are literally thousands of beliefs. The following are but a few examples:

1. belief in the existence of witches *(brujas)*
2. belief in *curanderas (os)* or folk healers
3. belief in the devil
4. belief in la Llorona
5. belief in ghosts, evil spirits, *duendes,* werewolves, vampires, headless riders, *espantos* (supernatural beings both good and bad), poltergeists, kobolds, bewitched areas or places *(lugares encantados)*
6. belief in buried treasures
7. belief in objects to put hexes or prevent bewitchment
8. belief in folk medicine and folk ailments such as *susto* (shock), *empacho, aire* (air), *caída de la mollera* (fallen fontenelle), *mal puesto* (bewitched)

For each of the above entities there are thousands of narratives in existence detailing how in fact such an event was witnessed by someone or how it actually happened to a specific individual. All of these narratives, of course, are jewels in the rough that when discovered by a literary genius can transform them into veritable gems. For example, the Colombian novelist Gabriel García Márquez utilized hundreds of folk beliefs in the process of constructing the magical-fantastic universe of his masterpiece *One Hundred Years of Solitude* (1967). One needs to mention only three well-known Chicano works—"... *y no se lo tragó la tierra"* by Tomás Rivera; *Bless Me, Ultima* by Rudolfo Anaya; and *El diablo en Texas* by Aristeo Brito—to realize the impact of folk beliefs on Chicano literature. Folk beliefs, then, are an integral and significant element in Chicano folklore (and of course in the folklore of all cultures) and certainly merit continued investigation.

This necessarily short introduction to Chicano folklore provides the reader with a greater appreciation of the cultural phenomenon called folklore and with a better understanding of the richness of Chicano culture.

NOTES

1. Aurelio M. Espinosa, *Romancero de Nuevo México* (Madrid: Consejo Superior de Investigaciones Científicas, 1953), p. 66.
2. Américo Paredes, "Folklore, Lo Mexicano and Proverbs," *Aztlán,* vol. 13, nos. 1 and 2 (Spring and Fall 1982), p. 1.
3. Américo Paredes, "Mexican Legendry and the Rise of the Mestizo," in Wayland D. Hand, ed., *American Folk Legend: A Symposium* (Los Angeles: Universtiy of California Press, 1971), pp. 97–107.
4. Joe Graham, "The *Caso:* An Emic Genre of Folk Narrative," in Richard Bauman and Roger D. Abrahams, eds., *"And Other Neighborly Names": Social Process and Cultural Image in Texas Folklore* (Austin: University of Texas Press, 1981), p. 19.
5. Collected from the personal repertoire of a student in my folklore class at the University of California at Irvine in 1980.
6. María Herrera-Sobek, "Verbal Play and Mexican Immigrant Jokes," *Southwest Folklore,* vol. 4 (Winter 1980), p. 16. *See also* María Herrera-Sobek, *The Bracero Experience: Elitelore Versus Folklore* (Los Angeles: UCLA Latin American Center Publications, 1979).
7. For further discussion on the topic, see Américo Paredes, "The Mexican Corrido, Its Rise and Fall," in Mody C. Boatright, Wilson M. Hudson, and Allen Maxwell, eds., *Folk Travelers* (Austin: Texas Folklore Society Publications, 1957), pp. 91–105.
8. "Corrido de Joaquín Murieta," collected by Philip Sonnichsen and printed in "Texas-Mexican Border Music," vols. 2 and 3, corridos 1 and 2, Arhollie Records, 1975.
9. This particular study appears in Eduardo Hernández-Chávez, A. D. Cohen, and A. F. Beltrano, eds. *El lenguaje de los chicanos* (Arlington: Center for Applied Linguistics, 1975).
10. José Limón, "The Folk Performance of 'Chicano' and the Cultural Limits of Political Ideology," in Bauman and Abrahams, eds., *"And Other Neighborly Names,"* p. 197.
11. Shirley Arora, "Proverbs in Mexican American Tradition," *Aztlán,* vol. 13, nos. 1 and 2 (Spring and Fall 1982), pp. 43–69.
12. Collected from my grandmother Susana Escamilla de Tarango.
13. Shirley Arora, *Proverbial Comparisons and Related Expressions in Spanish* (Berkeley: University of California Press, 1977).
14. See Aurora Lucero-White Lea, *Literary Folklore of the Hispanic Southwest* (San Antonio: Naylor Company, 1953), p. 5.
15. Collected from my grandmother Susana Escamilla de Tarango.
16. Américo Paredes, "El folklore de los grupos de origen mexicano," *Folklore Americano,* no. 14, año 16 (1966), p. 158.

17. As quoted in John Holmes McDowell, *Children's Riddling* (Bloomington: Indiana University Press, 1979), p. 18.

18. Elli Kongas-Maranda is quoted in McDowell, *Children's Riddling,* p. 20.

19. McDowell, *Children's Riddling,* p. 20.

20. Collected from my grandmother Susana Escamilla de Tarango.

21. McDowell, *Children's Riddling,* p. 222.

22. This article appears in *Aztlán,* vol. 13, nos. 1 and 2 (Spring and Fall 1982), pp. 223–56.

23. Joe S. Graham, "The Role of the *Curandero* in the Mexican American Folk Medicine System in West Texas," in Wayland D. Hand, ed., *American Folk Medicine* (Berkeley: University of California Press, 1976), p. 176.

10 | How Chicano Authors Use Bilingual Techniques for Literary Effect

GARY D. KELLER

One of the most unusual qualities of Chicano poetry and prose is its use of code-switching, which can be defined simply as the alternation of two (or more) languages in a single literary text. The two codes that Chicano writers most typically alternate are, of course, Spanish and English, although from time to time certain other languages are brought into play such as Nahuatl, the language of the Aztecs.

This paper will attempt to illustrate the rich variety of literary strategies available to bilingual Chicano writers. Bilingual writers, by their marshalling of both Spanish and English and their switching between the two, are able to depict characters, explore themes, express ideologies or messages, and fashion rhetorical devices in unique ways. Two orienting observations should be made about the examples of code-switching that are offered in this paper. One is that the reader may find it curious that certain well-known, excellent Chicano literary texts are not cited, while others, less-known, are mentioned. This is the case because the paper does not deal with Chicano literature per se, only *bilingual* Chicano literature. Contrary to the assumption of some critics who really do not know Chicano literature well, not all of our literature switches between Spanish and English. Many excellent Chicano works have been written either wholly in English or wholly in Spanish, but these will not be referred to here because the focus of this paper is exclusively on those works that are bilingual. The second observation is that most of the examples are taken from Chicano poetry. There are two reasons for this. The primary one is that code-switching in fact is far more evident in Chicano poetry than it is in prose, so that the examples reflect the preponderance of the phenomenon as it appears in literature. The second reason is that since poetry is more concise, more examples can be included.

This chapter is a revised version of "The Literary Stratagems Available to the Bilingual Chicano Writer," in Francisco Jiménez, ed., *The Identification and Analysis of Chicano Literature* (New York: Bilingual Press, 1979). Reprinted by permission.

171

Why do so many Chicano writers code-switch? To answer, we must realize that the recourse of code-switching is available to Chicano writers because it is so very common in Chicano society. Code-switching is not exclusive to Chicano society and Chicano literature. It appears in the literature of all societies that have utilized more than one code, to cite a few, Russian literature of the nineteenth century, reflecting Russian-French code-switching by the nobles during that period, Flemish literature throughout the ages, and the Dutch literature of the Lowlands. In all of these societies more than one language has been operative and the literature has reflected that fact.

We have answered the question why Chicano writers code-switch by pointing out that it is a recourse of Chicano society and thus a recourse of Chicano literature. However, its availability to the author as part of his or her culture doesn't fully answer the question. Broadly speaking, one group of Chicano code-switches are achieved in the interests of a fiction of mimesis, where literature aspires to become the microcosm and mirror of the social macrocosm. In these instances where the literary text embraces the aesthetic philosophy of realism or naturalism, the code-switch is fashioned to reflect, like a mirror, the phenomenon as it occurs in Chicano society. The second group of code-switches, while achieved with the assumption that the Chicano reader will understand them because the reader is familiar with the phenomenon in common speech, is intended to obey a more purely literary canon. These literary code-switches in a formal sense are instruments in the pursuit of such goals as irony, characterization, cross-cultural comparisons, rhetorical devices, double entendres, puns, and so on. Clearly the two groups of code-switches are not mutually exclusive. Indeed, they could be reduced to one group, for even the code-switch that is undertaken as a reflection of Chicano society obeys the literary purpose of being a realistic reflection of that society. However, it is useful to separate code-switches into these two groups because those that reflect social usage have been utilized to a significant extent by sociolinguists for the purpose of better understanding Chicano language as it is communicated in society, while the purely literary code-switches are not easily incorporated into a data base that is useful for Chicano sociolinguistics. Let us turn now to an analysis of three basic categories of code-switches in Chicano literature, those that have thematic purposes, those that function to characterize protagonists, and those that are used for formal stylistic effects, often as rhetorical devices.

THEMATIC CODE-SWITCHING

As certain sociolinguists have seen, such as Guadalupe Valdés,[1] much code-switching in Chicano literature serves the special function of highlighting the theme, message, ideology of the author. Moreover, the most common example of this sort of alternation also occurs frequently in social communication, reflecting a sharp division of domains signaled by the use of English and Spanish. The English language is used to represent the Anglo world, the Spanish language, the Chicano world. Here is a clear example from Ernesto Galarza's moving autobiography, *Barrio Boy*.

> Crowded as it was, the *colonia* found a place for these *chicanos,* the name by which we called an unskilled worker born in Mexico and just arrived in the United States. The *chicanos* were fond of identifying themselves by saying they had just arrived from *el macizo,* by which they mean the solid Mexican homeland, the good native earth. Although they spoke of *el macizo* like homesick persons, they didn't go back. They remained, as they said of themselves, *pura raza.* So it happened that José and Gustavo would bring home for a meal and for conversation workingmen who were *chicanos* fresh from *el macizo* and like ourselves, *pura raza.* Like us, they had come straight to the *barrio* where they could order a meal, buy a pair of overalls, and look for work in Spanish. They brought us vague news about the revolution, in which many of them had fought as *villistas, huertistas, maderistas,* or *zapatistas.* As an old *maderista,* I imagined our *chicano* guests as battle-tested revolutionaries, like myself. . . . Beds and meals, if the newcomers had no money at all, were provided—in one way or another—on trust, until the new *chicano* found a job. On trust and not on credit, for trust was something between people who had plenty of nothing, and credit was between people who had something of plenty. It was not charity or social welfare but something my mother called *asistencia,* a helping given and received on trust, to be repaid because those who had given it were themselves in need of what they had given. *Chicanos* who had found work on farms or in railroad camps came back to pay us a few dollars for *asistencia* we had provided weeks or months before.[2] (Italics are the author's.)

A second example of the use of English to represent the Anglo world and Spanish to represent the Hispanic world appears in Alurista's poem, "We've Played Cowboys." The two examples are rather different however. Galarza can be said to take a cross-cultural approach, while Alurista's poem is bicultural.

> We've played cowboys
> >not knowing
> nuestros charros
> >and their countenance
> con trajes de gala
> >silver embroidery
> on black wool
> >Zapata rode in white
> campesino white
> >and Villa in brown
> y nuestros charros
> >parade of sculptured gods

```
on horses
   —of flowing manes
proud
   erect
they galloped
and we've played cowboys
   —as opposed to indians
when ancestors of mis charros abuelos
indios fueron³
```

Alurista uses Spanish basically in order to signal where his ideals, politics, values, allegiances, etc., lie. There is nothing to suggest that the poet cannot think of the English equivalent of certain words or expressions and therefore uses Spanish. On the other hand, Galarza uses Spanish precisely when he is confronted with a concept or domain that is alien to Anglo culture. At this point Galarza uses the Spanish word or expression and then immediately elucidates it with an English definition. In this fashion, while Galarza is a Chicano writer, his procedure does not differ from authors writing for Anglo readers. John Steinbeck, for example, often uses a Spanish concept, and then, in "anthropological" fashion goes on to explain it for his monocultural reader. Alurista is bicultural in the sense that, even though the English language usually represents the adversary, he switches between the two languages with a bilingual's natural ease; Galarza's procedure is cross-cultural, taking his reader by the hand through the esoteric or unknown world of the Chicanos. Yet both have in common the same semantic field for their use of Spanish—it represents the Chicano domain. The same sort of characteristic can be seen when the base language is Spanish. In the poem by Pedro Ortiz Vásquez, "Quienes somos," English is the language consigned to express strangeness, alienation:

```
it's so strange in here
todo lo que pasa
is so strange
y nadie puede entender
que lo que pasa aquí
isn't any different
de lo que pasa allá⁴
```

A special category of thematic code-switching should be established for those expressions in literature that reflect what sociolinguists analyzing normal social discourse have termed "identity markers." As in communal language, literary "identity markers" such as the examples of *órale, ése, ésa* are used to establish rapport in Spanish between the author and his Chicano readers. In

Luis Valdez's classic *acto, Las dos caras del patroncito,* the farmworker manages to trick the *patrón.* The play ends this way:

> *Farmworker:* Bueno, so much for the patrón. I got his house, his land, his car—only I'm not going to keep 'em. He can have them. But I'm taking the cigar. Ay los watcho. (EXIT)[5]

"Ay los watcho" is the perfect ending for this sort of consciousness-raising and rapport-establishing exercise, a theater the avowed intention of which is to motivate the migrant worker to join the union. At the end of El Huitlacoche's poem, "Searching for La Real Cosa," after having debunked the conventional identifications of the Chicano, the poet asserts:

> Por fin, ¿eh? ¡Ya estuvo!
> ¿Quién es la real cosa?
> A dime, dime for the love of God!
> ¡Madre! Ese vato, ¡qué sé yo![6]

The identity markers ¡*Ya estuvo!* ¡*Madre!, Ese vato, ¡qué sé yo!* are all pressed into a plea for a vision of Chicanismo that transcends stereotyping.

Of course, not only English and Spanish need be involved in Chicano literary code-switching. We see particularly from time to time the incorporation of lexicon from pre-Columbian, Amerindian languages. For example, Alurista uses many such words as *Quetzalcóatl* and *Cihuacóatl.* He also makes up portmanteaus (words that are created by combining two languages, in these cases English and Nahuatl) such as *Pepsicóatl* and *Cocacóatl.* El Huitlacoche uses terms such as *esquintles, huaraches, Netzahualcóyotl,* and *Huitzilopochtli,* among others. Jesús Maldonado (el flaco) writes an "Oda al molcajete." In the poetry of Lorenza Calvillo Schmidt and Adaljiza Sosa Riddell the powerful figure *Malinche* is evoked. *La Malinche* can only stir up deep and ambivalent feelings, since in the Chicano mythos this "Eva mexicana,"[7] as Octavio Paz has termed her and José Clemente Orozco has painted her, represents at least three major motifs:

1. She is the "Indian woman" par excellence.
2. She is a "traitor" to the Indians since she joins with the Spaniards. Indeed, *Malinche* is commonly used as an antonomasia for traitor. But she is also the "romantic lover and rebel," inasmuch as she is enamoured of Hernán Cortés and becomes his mistress.
3. She is the "mother" of the mestizo—that is, the Chicano, José Vasconcelos's "raza cósmica"—since she bears out of wedlock the fruit of the sinful yet exalted sexual congress between herself, aristocratic Indian maiden, and Cortés, Spanish adventurer and conquistador.

Both of the women poets mentioned above refer to their *malinchismo,* the *malinchismo* of the Chicana woman. For Sosa Riddell it is part of Chicano transculturation (or perhaps, if we care to be more optimistic in the interpretation of the poem, merely biculturalism):

> Malinche, pinche
> forever with me
>
> . . . .
> Pinche, como duele ser Malinche
> Pero sabes, ése
> what keeps me from shattering
> into a million fragments?
> It's that sometimes,
> You are muy gringo, too.[8]

For Calvillo Schmidt this treachery is partly the result of the exploitation of the Chicano male, who has been sent to Korea, Vietnam, barber's school, anywhere far away from the more "docile" Chicana who is permitted to attend college but who is also coopted by the white male:

> A Chicano at Dartmouth?
> I was at Berkeley, where
> there were too few of us
> and even less of you.
> I'm not even sure
> that I really looked for you.
>
> I heard from many rucos
> that you
> would never make it.
> You would hold me back;
> From What?
> From what we are today?
> "Y QUE VIVA"
> Pinche, como duele ser Malinche.[9]

In the popular and anonymous folk poem "Los animales,"[10] collected by Américo Paredes, a number of pre-Columbian terms (in origin) for animals, plants, foods, etc., are referred to: *huacales, coyote, zopilote, tlacuache, jicote, mitote, pinacate, mayate, guajolote, mole, pozole, huitlacoche,* and so on. These Amerindian terms are essential to evoke the folkloric, Chicano themes of the poems in question. They serve as the mortar for the creation of a Chicano folklore with unique, distinguishable features.

The thematic purposes for expanding the variety and levels of register and for incorporating elements of additional languages such as Nahuatl are as varied as the thematic concerns of the authors themselves. For many Chicano writers, and specifically in the examples that I have cited from Alurista, Jesús Maldonado, Calvillo Schmidt, Sosa Riddell, El Huitlacoche, and the anonymous author(s) of "Los animales," the added Amerindian lexicon represents an effort to recuperate Chicano history and create or recreate a Chicano mythos based on the four essential ethnic progenitors of Chicanismo: the Indian, the Spaniard, the Mexican, and the Anglo. Whether in reference to a glorious past *(Quetzalcóatl)* or a painful one *(Malinche),* multilingualism is a way to give each ancestor his (or her) due.

Spanish Used to Express the Alien

As we have seen, when one aspect of the theme revolves around what is intimate and known versus what is alien, typically Spanish expresses the former and English, the latter. Yet this does not necessarily have to be the case. Occasionally, under special circumstances, the tables can be turned and Spanish can be used to express that which is alien. Take for example a passage from El Huitlacoche's "The Urban(e) Chicano's 76." The poet is criticizing a moment in John Steinbeck's famous screenplay, *¡Viva Zapata!,* which featured Marlon Brando in the main role. The scene in question has Brando-Zapata dressed in his pajama bottoms on his wedding night, lamenting to his bride that he can't read or write. The bride then offers to educate him. At this moment a group of Zapata's followers congregate below the nuptial balcony and Zapata comes out in pajamas to address them:

> Zapata comes out on the wedding night
> in pajama bottoms, he yearns to read and write
> I love you Johnny, the way you write
> but shit, you stink, babosísimo fool
> that's my boy up there in striped bottoms
> addressing armed campesinos in broad-rimmed sombreros
> from the balcony railing with Arabesques
> ¡el frito bandito![11]

The words, "campesinos," "sombreros," and "frito bandito" (instead of *bandido*) are all examples of Spanish lexicon that are well-known to English speakers and have actually been partially assimilated into English. What the poet

does is to show how these words have been used in the Anglo world to stereotype the Hispano. Thus they become "alien" to the Hispanic world to the
degree that they are used by the Anglo to characterize (and caricaturize) the
Hispano. In another poem by the same author the following lines appear:

> You turned el chile into preprocessed velveeta
> and Tiburcio Vásquez into el frito bandito
> You made Emiliano Zapata
> Marlon Brando who went to bed
> in his pajama bottoms on the wedding night.[12]

A similar example of this process of alienation, this time not in literary language but in communal language, is the term *caramba*. Having been stereo-
typically associated with Hispanics for several decades now in the English language, virtually no Hispanic ever uses it. A somewhat related example appears
in the passage of Sosa Riddell's poem which I have quoted earlier, "Malinche":

> It's that sometimes,
> You are muy gringo too.

Here the Spanish word, *gringo,* used to depict the sociocultural Other, is now
directed to what is (or perhaps was) alien in one's own cultural makeup. Thus
a special sort of tension, one that is highly productive from an artistic point of
view, is set up in the code-switch involving a Spanish designator for an Anglo
sort of otherness having established itself in a Hispanic persona.

Having described two polar and antithetical usages, the first where Spanish
is used for what is familiar, the second, in special circumstances, where Spanish
expresses that which is alien, namely, Anglo, we are obliged to round out the
dialectic and exemplify a code-switch depicting the creative synthesis between
the self and the Other. In Angela de Hoyos's poem, "Café con leche," the poet
ambivalently observes that she has seen a male Chicano friend coming out of
a motel with a *gringuita.* The final stanza encapsulates a stirring and subtle
irony:

> No te apenas, amigo:
> Homogenization
> is one good way
> to dissolve differences
> and besides
> > what's wrong
> with a beautiful race
> café con leche?[13]

The expression *café con leche* serves many functions, only two of which are to evoke the beauty of the prior *mestizaje,* the fruit of Spaniard and Indian, and second, to prefigure the potential new *mestizaje,* between Chicano and Anglo. In addition, the image lends itself admirably to the central conflict: we can think of *café* and *leche* as separate entities, and identify each with the skin color of each race (milk walking with coffee from the motel), or we can think of that cappuccino color that they make in the blending.

CODE-SWITCHING FOR CHARACTERIZATION

The one Chicano character that counts for much, with respect to code-switching, is the compound bilingual. The term compound bilingual in sociolinguistics is somewhat controversial. Here I define it merely as someone who is incapable (either chronically or temporarily, because of some specific, say, traumatizing, circumstance) of separating out the two codes. Thus the individual mixes languages (and/or registers) constantly, typically within phrases and sentences. The opposite, the coordinate bilingual, while certainly capable of producing compound structures, does so as a reflection of his or her conscious volition, is not involuntarily forced to alternate codes. The coordinate bilingual is not particularly worth investigating in this paper on bilingual literary strategies because when functioning coordinately such an individual will be speaking either in English or Spanish exclusively. Conversely, when functioning in a compound fashion, the coordinate bilingual's potential for language separation would be masked. Hence it is not possible to distinguish the coordinate bilingual from a compound bilingual as a literary character on the mere basis of a literary text.

The psycholinguistic nature of the compound bilingual has received attention from the Chicano writer, who, naturally, must use code-switches to reflect that phenomenon. Nick Vaca's story, "The Purchase," a prayer cum free associations, is intended to psychologically portray a compound bilingual episode.

> Ave María Purísima, I must make another pago hoy or else it'll be too late. Sí, too late, and then what would I do. Christmas is so close, and if I don't hurry con los pagos, I'll have nothing to give any of mis hijos. If that should happen, it would weigh muy pesado on my mind. Even now, con el pensamiento that I may not be able to give them anything, I have trouble durmiendo en la noche. And, Santo Niño de Atocha, if Christmas should come and catch me sin nada, I would never sleep well por el resto de mi vida.[14]

CODE-SWITCHING AS A FUNCTION OF STYLE

Let us begin by noting that much code-switching that occurs in the community reflects considerations that are basically stylistic. Identity markers, contextual switches, triggered switches (due to the preceding or following item), sequential responses (speaker uses language last used, thereby following suit), and so on[15] have clear stylistic purposes. Therefore, we can say, that there is much stylistic overlap between social and literary code-switches. At the same time we note that the stylistic possibilities available to literature far surpass those found in society.

Let me also state that I am convinced that bilingual literature in theory can display all of the stylistic features that have been unearthed in the literary analysis of monolingual literature at all levels, whether structure, the sound-stratum, imagery, rhetorical devices, diction, tone, or whatever, as well as some additional features not available to monolingual texts, as our analysis of certain cross-cultural and bicultural word plays has shown. This is not to say that in practice we shall find them all, for writers express themselves within a certain literary space, definitely subject to constraints, particularly cultural ones. In short, while allegorical verse plays exist in Chicano literature, I have yet to find a bilingual Chicano sonnet, although I'm sure one could be written.

Tone

Chicano themes revolve around a number of different loci, some of the major ones being social protest against Anglo, or more rarely, Mexican oppression, consciousness-raising of the "naive" Chicano, usually a migrant worker and/ or Mexican newly arrived in the United States, the recuperation of Chicano history (the Treaty of Guadalupe Hidalgo, the Mexican Revolution, the Zoot Suit incidents, etc.), the creation or recreation of a Chicano mythos (*Aztlán, La Raza,* Emiliano Zapata, etc.), the emancipation of the Chicana from both Anglo and Hispano male dominance, and the quest for a personal identity within the bicultural Mexican-American milieu. All of these thematic categories can be and usually are evoked by means of differing tones. Take for example the charge of Anglo oppression. The tone can run from the Ginsbergian *rant* or *howl,* as in Ricardo Sánchez's "smile out the revolú,"

> smile out the revolú,
> burn now your anguished hurt,
>
> crush now our desecrators,
> chingue su madre the u.s.a.
>
> burn cabrones enraviados,
> burn las calles de amerika[16]

or El Huitlacoche's, "From the Heights of Macho Bicho,"

> Tell US marines
> que aquí 'tamos nomás

> a las justas alturas
> de las circunstancias
> con el quetzal y la anaconda
> los de bicho alto
> y los de palo alto
> aquí nomás nomás
> We're waiting for US marines
> los meros justos
> los justos meros
> los meros meros
> los meros machos
> los mandamás.[17]

to the humorous parody in "The Advertisement" where Mexican Americans for all occasions are offered for sale,

  (1) a familially faithful and fearfully factional folk-fettered fool
  (2) a captivating, cactus-crunching, cow-clutching caballero
  (3) a charp, chick-chasing, chili-chomping cholo
  (4) a brown-breeding, bean-belching border-bounder
  (5) a raza-resigned, ritual-racked rude rural relic
  (6) a peso-poor but proud, priest-pressed primitive
  (7) a grubby but gracious, grape-grabbing greaser[18]

to the upbeat, emphatically rhymed "La Causa," by Abelardo Delgado, reminiscent of the folksong:

> what moves you, chicano, to stop being polite?
> nice chicano, could be patted on the head and wouldn't bite
> and now, how dare you tell your boss, "Go fly a kite"?
> *es la causa, hermano,* which has made me a new man.[19]

Those poems that cultivate the theme of self-identity, in keeping with the subject at hand, typically have a more reflective, self-absorbed tone, as in Alurista's "We've Played Cowboys," quoted earlier in this chapter.

Yet all of these examples that I have cited have in common the fact of language switching, an alternation of codes that adjusts itself to the tone that the writer is seeking.

Imagery

The term imagery has been used variously in literary criticism. I restrict my usage in this portion of my paper simply to metaphor and simile, both of which appear in abundance in bilingual Chicano literature.

Examples of bilingual metaphors:[20]

> Brother, oh brother *vendido*
> you are hollow inside.
> (Raymundo Pérez, "Hasta la victoria siempre.")

> *la tierra* is *la raza's* kissing cousin,
> (Abelardo Delgado, "La tierra.")

> Reluctant awakenings a la media
> Noche y la luz prendida.
>
> **PRRRRRRINNNNGGGGGG!**
>
> A noisy chorro missing the
>   Basín.
> (José Montoya, "La jefita.")

Examples of bilingual similes:[21]

> Transparente como
> Una jolla, opaca como
> El Carbón, heavy like
> A feather—carga fija
> Del hombre marginal.
> (José Montoya, "Lazy Skin.")

> I am speaking of
> Entering Hotel Avila
> Where my drunk compadres
> Applaud like hammers,
> (Gary Soto, "The Vision.")

> sousing himself to perdición
> on gabo's gratis spirits
> at the well-lit crap table
> while he tarries for the man
> to develop his picture and
> his querida—two brown persons
> standing tween one million laminated smackers
> como el Cristo plastificado entre los dos ladrones.
> (El Huitlacoche, "Searching for La Real Cosa.")

The anonymous folk-poem, "The Night Before Christmas," a parody of the original, written in doggerel verse, is quite well known in the Southwest. It yields an additional bilingual simile:

> When Santa will come in un manner extraño
> Lit up like the Star Spangled Banner cantando,[22]

Rhetorical Devices

Chicano literature is also capable of expressing itself with a variety of rhetorical devices in a bilingual mode. A number of examples follow that give a sampling of bilingual rhetorical devices that can be found in Chicano literature.

CONGERIES. (Accumulation of phrases that say essentially the same thing)

Unable to speak a tongue of any convention, they gabbled to each other, the younger and the older, in a papiamento of street *caliche* and devious calques. A tongue only Tex-Mexs, wetbacks, *tirilones, pachucos* and *pochos* could penetrate.[23] (El Huitlacoche, "The Man Who Invented the Automatic Jumping Bean.")

ANAPHORA. (Repetition of a word or phrase at the beginning of a literary segment)

> Preso
> Locked inside a glass-like
> Canopy built of grief[24]
> (José Montoya, "In a Pink Bubble Gum World.")

Bilingual anaphoras (if you accept this designator for the phenomenon under consideration) are different from the monolingual variety in that, with the exception of identical cognates, the word that is repeated has two different spellings and pronunciations. Thus the anaphora is mostly at the semantic level. And yet the repetitive quality still remains. Bilingual anaphoras can be distinguished from mere word plays based on repetition. Consider, for example, the following, also from the poem cited above:

> Pero armado con estas palabras
> De sueños forged into files—
> "Las filas de la rebelión"
> Cantaban los dorados de Villa.[25]

This latter example, apart from the fact that it does not occur at the beginning of a passage, is properly classified a word play, not an anaphora. It is my contention that the bilingual anaphora will conserve some, although usually not all, of the phonic and rhythmic qualities of this rhetorical device.

CHIASMUS. (A contrast by reverse parallelism)

> pobre man
> hombre rich[26]

VERSE FILLER. (*Ripio;* element used to complete a line of verse, often to satisfy the requirements of rhyme; typically used in doggerel)

> Tis the night before Christmas, and all through the casa
> Not a creature is stirring, Caramba ¿qué pasa?
> The stockings are hanging con mucho cuidado,
> In hopes that Saint Nicholas will feel obligado
> to leave a few cosas, aquí and allí
> For chico y chica (y something for me).
> Los niños are snuggled all safe in their camas,
> Some in vestidos and some in pajamas,
> ("The Night Before Christmas," see footnote 22.)

ALLITERATION.

> under lasting latigazos[27]
> (Ricardo Sánchez, "and it . . .")

See also a relevant passage from "The Advertisement," cited earlier.

INTERROGATIO. (The "rhetorical" question that is posed for argumentative effect and requires no answer)

> —¿A dónde voy? —, pregunta.
> ¿A los *cucumber patches* de *Noliet,*
> a las vineyards de *San Fernando Valley,*
> a los *beet fields* de Colorado?
>
> Hay ciertas incertidumbres ciertas:
>   lo amargo de piscar naranjas
>   lo lloroso de cortar cebollas[28]
> (Tino Villanueva, "Que hay otra voz.")
>
> How to paint
> on this page

the enigma
that furrows
your sensitive
brown face
　a sadness,
porque te llamas
Juan, y no *John*
as the laws
of assimilation
dictate.[29]
(Angela de Hoyos, "Chicano.")

METONOMY. (Naming a thing by substituting one of its attributes or an associated term for the name itself)

Zapata rode in white
campesino white
　and Villa in brown
(Alurista, "We've Played Cowboys.")

APOSTROPHE. (Speaking to an imaginary or absent person)

Come, mother—
　Your rebozo trails a black web[30]
(Rafael Jesús González, "To An Old Woman.")

HYPERBOLE. (An exaggeration or overstatement intended to produce an effect without being taken literally)

stupid america, remember that chicanito
flunking math and english
he is the picasso
of your western states
but he will die
with one thousand masterpieces
hanging only from his mind.[31]
(Abelardo Delgado, "Stupid America.")

UNDERSTATEMENT. (A statement deliberately worded so as to be unemphatic in tone, often for ironic purposes)

Sometimes he bragged
He worked outside Toluca

> For americanos,
> Shoveling stones
> Into boxes.[32]
> (Gary Soto, "A Few Coins.")

GRADATIO. (A progressive advance from one statement to another until a climax is achieved)

> Last week,
> I had been white
>   ... we were friends
>
> Yesterday,
> I was Spanish
>   ... we talked ...
>   once in a while.
>
> Today,
> I am Chicano
>   ... you do not know me.
>
> Tomorrow,
> I rise to fight
>   ... and we are enemies.[33]
> (Margarita Virginia Sánchez, "Escape.")

Spelling Innovations for Stylistic Purposes

Bilingual Chicano literature, mostly in the area of poetry, displays a significant number of spelling variations for literary purposes. The spelling may be used to evoke a typical or normal state of affairs, socially or psychologically. For example, it may show the accent of a specific Hispano or Anglo character, evoke English-Spanish interference effects in societal bilingual speech, or represent a language variety or dialect within Spanish or within English. In Tomás Rivera's "El Pete Fonseca," one of the characters comments:

> En la labor también nos acercábamos a ella o ella se acercaba a nosotros y el Pete se soltaba con sus canciones. A veces hasta en inglés *sha bum, sha bum o lemi go, lemi go, lober* ...[34]

Jesús Maldonado uses the terms, "alcaweta," "weras," and "logo"[35] in his poetry, and Estupinián utilizes "los wíkens"[36] in one of his poems. The other basic reason for spelling license is for some thematic purpose. Often a political statement is involved. In Alurista's *Dawn* we have the following two passages:

> you call it profitable investment
> i call it yanki colonization
> your foreign aid[37]
>
> now, now
> you don't want to be
> like the meskins
> you in amerikkka now[38]

A common device in Chicano literature is to write English in lower case where the standard spelling would call for capitals. The intention is usually to undermine the oppressive status of English, to put it on a par with Spanish, which rarely uses capitals. In addition to Alurista, whom I have just cited, this sort of usage is typical of Ricardo Sánchez, Abelardo Delgado, and many others.

Of course the spelling variations employed to portray a character or set of social circumstances may also serve a second, thematic function. This is the case with the example of "meskins" (uttered by the treacherous Cocacóatl) from Alurista, or in the following from the play, *Noo Jork,* by Jaime Carrero.

Mother: *Es importante.*
Cop: Not here in New York.
Mother: Very important in Noo Jork.
Cop: *(Smiling and correcting her pronunciation.)* New York. N E W Y O R K.
Mother: That's what I say: NOO JORK!
Cop: *(To Gladys.)* Tell your mother that she's not saying it right.
Gladys: Ma, *se dice* NEW YORK.
Mother: *No me da la gana.*
Cop: *(To Gladys.)* What's that?
Gladys: Never mind.
Cop: *(To the Mother.)* I must show you how to pronounce it. Say YOKE.
Mother: JOKE.
Cop: No, no, no. Yoke. New York.
Mother: Noo Joke!
Cop: No. *(Smiles.)* Say YELLOW.
Mother: Jello. *(Fast.)* Hey, I get this one. Your head is full of *jello* hair.
Cop: No. *(Slow.)* My head is full of YELLOW hair.
Mother: You're full of jello.
Gladys: Ma, *tú no entiendes.*
Mother: Sure. I understand. He wants me to become Irish.[39]

CONCLUSION

In this paper we have taken an introductory look at the way Spanish and English are incorporated and alternated in Chicano bilingual literature and compared the literary phenomenon with the kind of code-switching that takes place in the community. We have noted that while there is often great similarity between literary bilingual techniques and Chicano bilingualism as it appears in the community, that just as often the literary code-switching obeys an aesthetic canon rather than a social, communicative function. We have also sought to establish the beginnings of a corpus or dictionary of bilingual literary entries. We have used these as paradigms in order to show how code-switching in Chicano literature serves the development of a theme, the portrayal of character, the establishment of either a cross-cultural or bicultural literary space, the expression of a tone or literary voice, the depiction of images, the expansion of artistic licenses to spelling, and the fashioning of a wide variety of rhetorical devices.

NOTES

1. Guadalupe Valdés-Fallis, "The Sociolinguistics of Chicano Literature: Towards an Analysis of the Role and Function of Language Alternation in Contemporary Bilingual Poetry," *Point of Contact/Punto de Contacto,* vol. 1, no. 4 (1977), pp. 30–39; Guadalupe Valdés-Fallis, "Code-Switching in Bilingual Chicano Poetry," *Hispania,* vol. 59 (1976), pp. 877–86.

2. Ernesto Galarza, *Barrio Boy* (New York: Ballantine Books, 1972), pp. 196–97.

3. Alurista, "We've Played Cowboys," in A. Castañeda-Shular, T. Ybarra-Frausto, and J. Sommers, eds., *Literatura chicana: texto y contexto* (Englewood Cliffs, N.J.: Prentice-Hall, 1972), p. 31.

4. Pedro Ortiz Vásquez, "Quienes somos," *The Bilingual Review/La Revista Bilingüe,* vol. 2, no. 3 (1975), p. 292.

5. Luis Valdez, *Las dos caras del patroncito,* in Castañeda-Shular et al., eds., *Literatura chicana,* p. 53.

6. El Huitlacoche, "Searching for La Real Cosa," *The Bilingual Review/La Revista Bilingüe,* vol. 5, nos. 1 and 2 (1978), p. 142.

7. Octavio Paz, *El laberinto de la soledad* (México, D.F.: Fondo de Cultura Económica, 1959).

8. Adaljiza Sosa Riddell, "Malinche," *El Grito* ("Chicanas en la Literatura y el Arte"), book 1, year 7 (1973), p. 76.

9. Lorenza Calvillo Schmidt, "Como duele," *El Grito* ("Chicanas en la Literatura y el Arte"), book 1, year 7 (1973), p. 61.

10. Anonymous, "Los animales," collected by Américo Paredes in Castañeda-Shular et al., eds., *Literatura chicana,* pp. 129–32.

11. El Huitlacoche, "The Urban(e) Chicano's 76," *The Bilingual Review/La Revista Bilingüe,* vol. 3, no. 2 (1976), pp. 185–86.

12. El Huitlacoche, "From the Heights of Macho Bicho," *The Bilingual Review/La Revista Bilingüe,* vol. 2, nos. 1 and 2 (1975), p. 192.

13. Angela de Hoyos, "Café con leche," *Chicano Poems for the Barrio* (Bloomington, Ind.: Backstage Books, 1975).

14. Nick Vaca, "The Purchase," in Américo Paredes and Raymund Paredes, eds., *Mexican-American Authors* (Boston: Houghton-Mifflin, 1972), p. 144.

15. For a better understanding of code-switching in Chicano society see: Guadalupe Valdés-Fallis, "Social Interaction and Code-Switching Patterns: A Case Study of Spanish/English Alternation," in Gary D. Keller, Richard V. Teschner, and Silvia Viera, eds., *Bilingualism in the Bicentennial and Beyond* (New York: Bilingual Press, 1976), pp. 53–85; Guadalupe Valdés-Fallis, "Code-Switching and the Classroom Teacher," pamphlet (Arlington, Va.: Center for Applied Linguistics, 1978); Guadalupe Valdés-Fallis, "Code-Switching Among Bilingual Mexican-American Women: Towards an Understanding of Sex-Related Language Alternation," *International Journal of the Sociology of Language,* vol. 17 (1978), pp. 65–72; Wendy Redlinger, "Mothers' Speech to Children in Bilingual Mexican-American Homes," *International Journal of the Sociology of Language,* vol. 17 (1978), pp. 73–82; Lenora A. Timm, "Spanish/English Code Switching: el porque y how-not-to," *Romance Philology,* vol. 28 (1975), pp. 473–82; and Carol Pfaff, "Syntactic Constraints on Code-Switching" (ERIC ED 127 828).

16. Ricardo Sánchez, "smile out the revolú," *Canto y grito mi liberación* (Garden City, N.Y.:Doubleday, 1973), p. 139.

17. El Huitlacoche, "From the Heights of Macho Bicho," *The Bilingual Review/La Revista Bilingüe,* vol. 2, nos. 1 and 2 (1975), pp. 192–93.

18. Steve Gonzales, "The Advertisement," in Castañeda-Schular et al., eds., *Literatura chicana,* p. 128.

19. Abelardo Delgado, "La Causa," in Philip D. Ortego, ed., *We Are Chicanos* (New York: Washington Square Books, 1973), p. 219.

20. The examples, in order of appearance, are from the following: Raymundo Pérez, "Hasta la victoria siempre," in Ortego, ed., *We Are Chicanos,* p. 202; Abelardo Delgado, "La tierra," in Ortego, ed., *We Are Chicanos,* p. 218; and José Montoya, "La jefita," in Octavio I. Romano-V., ed., *El espejo–The Mirror: Selected Mexican-American Literature* (Berkeley: Quinto Sol, 1969), p. 188.

21. The citations, in order of appearance, are from the following: José Montoya, "Lazy Skin," in Romano-V., ed., *El espejo–The Mirror,* p. 184; Gary Soto, "The Vision," *The Tale of Sunlight* (Pittsburgh: University of Pittsburgh Press, 1978), p. 58; and El Huitlacoche, "Searching for La Real Cosa," p. 139.

22. The Chicano version of "The Night Before Christmas" is often published in newspapers in the Southwest during the Yuletide season. However, there are a number of variations. The one that I am familiar with is the following:

Tis the night before Christmas, and all through the casa
Not a creature is stirring, Caramba, ¿qué pasa?
The stockings are hanging con mucho cuidado,
In hopes that Saint Nicholas will feel obligado
To leave a few cosas, aquí and allí,
For chico y chica (y something for me).
Los niños are snuggled all safe in their camas,
Some in vestidos and some in pajamas,
Their little cabezas are full of good things

They esperan que el old Santa will bring.
Santa is down at the corner saloon,
Es muy borracho since mid-afternoon,
Mamá is sitting beside la ventana,
Shining her rolling pin para mañana.
When Santa will come in un manner extraño
Lit up like the Star Spangled Banner cantando,
And mamá will send him to bed con los coches,
Merry Christmas to all and to all buenas noches.

23. El Huitlacoche, "The Man Who Invented the Automatic Jumping Bean," *The Bilingual Review/La Revista Bilingüe,* vol. 1, no. 2 (1974), pp. 193–200.
24. José Montoya, "In a Pink Bubble Gum World," in Romano-V., ed., *El espejo–The Mirror,* p. 184.
25. Ibid., p. 185.
26. This example (author unknown) is cited by Valdés–Fallis, "The Sociolinguistics of Chicano Literature," p. 37.
27. Ricardo Sánchez, "and it . . . ," *Canto y grito mi liberación,* p. 39.
28. Tino Villanueva, "Que hay otra voz," cited by Valdés-Fallis, "The Sociolinguistics of Chicano Literature," p. 37.
29. Angela de Hoyos, "Chicano," *Revista Chicano–Riqueña,* año 3, no. 4 (1975), pp. 23–24.
30. Rafael Jesús González, "To An Old Woman," in Ortego, ed., *We Are Chicanos,* p. 170.
31. Abelardo Delgado, "Stupid America," in Ortego, ed., *We Are Chicanos,* p. 216.
32. Soto, "A Few Coins," *The Tale of Sunlight,* p. 52.
33. Margarita Virginia Sánchez, "Escape," in Ortego, ed., *We Are Chicanos,* p. 208.
34. Tomás Rivera, "El Pete Fonseca," *Revista Chicano–Riqueña,* año 2, no. 1 (1974), p. 18.
35. Jesús Maldonado, "Oda al molcajete," in Castañeda-Shular et al., eds., *Literatura chicana,* pp. 119–20.
36. Estupinián, "Sonido del Teponaztle," in Octavio I. Romano-V., ed., *El espejo—The Mirror: Selected Mexican-American Literature* (Berkeley: Quinto Sol, 1969), p. 194.
37. Alurista, *Dawn,* in *El Grito* ("Chicano Drama") book 4, year 8 (1974), p. 68.
38. Ibid., p. 69.
39. Jaime Carrero, *Noo Jork,* in *Revista Chicano–Riqueña,* año 2, no. 4 (1975), pp. 6–7.

IV | Educational Perspectives

Overview

In February 1974, the U.S. Commission on Civil Rights submitted to the President, Senate, and House of Representatives the sixth and final report investigating barriers to equal educational opportunities for Mexican Americans in the public schools of the Southwest. The following summary remark is taken from that document:

> The findings of this report depict an educational system which ignores the language and culture of Mexican American students. In fact, because of prevalent practices, these students far too often find themselves retained in grades, placed in low ability groups, or shunted off to classes for the educable mentally retarded.
>
> Mexican-American students are usually taught by teachers of a different cultural background whose training leaves them ignorant and insensitive to students' educational needs. And when these students seek guidance, only rarely do they find a counselor trained to provide it.

According to the figures released in the "Directory of Public Elementary and Secondary Schools in Selected Districts, 1972" (Office for Civil Rights, HEW), the number of students affected in the above-mentioned manner is approximately 1.6 million. The education of these children is not a small problem. It is also important to note that 70 percent of Spanish surnamed families in this country fall below median income levels (Department of Labor Statistics, 1974). These same statistics indicate the extreme nonstratification of the Mexican-American labor force in low-skilled manual labor categories. This we point out in order to indicate that the problems confronting the Mexican American are not rooted in education alone. Therefore, we cannot expect educational change alone to solve those multifaceted problems confronting Chicano youth. In this light, we cannot expect education to solve the problems of young Chicanos. If education is not the solution to the identifiable social and economic problems, the following question must be raised and discussed: What can education do for Chicano children?

EDUCATIONAL NONACCOMMODATION

Before this important question can be answered, it seems necessary to discuss the development of educational institutions with respect to the Mexican-American population. Consider for a moment your own development from an epistemological/accommodative perspective. That is, how did you gain information about your "world" and how did you change as you gained that knowledge? This process is a complex one but two major points are consistently apparent: (1) you in fact did gain new and improved knowledge, and, (2) you began to use that knowledge in such a way that any detailed analysis of your behavioral interactions would reveal adaptive changes. Psychologically, we might suggest that if either (1) or (2) of the above did not occur then deviancy might result. Sociologically, any social institution which fails to accomplish (1) and (2) of the above can also be considered deviant.

Consider the above model during the following remarks concerning the present relationship between education and Chicanos. We are proposing that the "educational institution" has developed deviantly with respect to Chicanos, and that it has done so because it has failed to maximally accumulate information with respect to this population and when it has gathered information it has failed to respond to that information. The consequence has been a poorer quality and quantity of education for Chicanos. In addition, these failures have had a tremendous impact on the adaptive style of Chicano populations. It is silly to think that no-change produces no-effect. Instead the no-change condition of our educational institutions has led to changes in Chicano linguistic and cultural systems. Therefore, nonaccommodation by educational bodies has led to a series of accommodation measures by Chicanos. Some can be characterized as detrimental and others are still unavailable for evaluation. In summary, it seems as if the educational institutions of our society have practiced nonaccommodation with respect to Chicanos; at the same time this tactic has greatly influenced the Chicano.

Recall that the epistemological model suggests that educational institutions should take information from/about Chicanos and then adapt or change their systems in order to better serve these populations. Evidence seems to point to the failure of these institutions to receive the necessary input from/about Chicanos. Educational institutions might be characterized as receiving input from the following sources:

The Public. This can be conceptualized as the political component in education and is best defined by national and state legislative bodies as well as local boards of education. This public input comes from individuals who are elected to office.

The Staff. These can be identified as the actual service providers: the teachers, principals, and administrators. Input is provided at several individual levels as well as group levels within the educational establishment: teachers, principals, superintendents, or professional organizations such as the state educational association or the state school administrators association.

Parents. This segment is best identified as local or state chapters of PTA.

Students. These individuals are the target of the institutions and whose existence creates and maintains education as one of our most important institutions. Schools have student government matrices that allow student input (although usually minimal) into the system.

The courts. This is one additional and provocative source of input. Until 1954, the courts said little to the educational establishment, but since that time, court decisions have played, and will continue to play, an important role in the adaptive process of education.

Allow us now to provide an analysis of education and Chicanos within the context of the above input systems. For the first four (public, staff, student, and parents), we can see that Chicano influence has been nonexistent. Chicanos do not get elected to legislative positions or school boards; they make up less than 1 percent of the total professional education staff; they do not participate in PTA, and they do not hold office in student government. The reasons for each of the above are probably varied and complex. The important point is that as an input source at these levels, they are almost nonexistent. Yet, it is not quite fair to suggest that educational institutions have not received accommodation information about Chicanos. Education has been getting clear input on some Chicano issues at various levels. Parents, psychologists, and students have, for years, complained about the inadequacies of education for Chicano children. Education has received this input only to continue to respond to this population in the way it responds to others who are not like them: it has failed to adapt.

But changes are taking place and are expected to continue. This seems to be the case because of the inroads that are being made by Chicanos at each of the input levels. First, on a nationwide scale, in 1968, 1970, 1972, 1974, 1976, 1978, and again in 1980, Chicanos ran for political office and began to win. In addition, various Chicano advisory systems are operating out of local state Chicano organizations. Along staff lines, professional organizations, such as the National Association of Bilingual Education (NABE) and Association of Mexican American Education (AMAE), were born and continue to operate in various states. Along parental lines, Chicano parents have become involved in an advisory capacity in various educational programs: Title I, Title IV ESEA Desegregation, Title VII Bilingual-Bicultural Education, Headstart, Follow Through. Although most of this involvement has been mandated by federal directives rather than state or local initiative, it has become a source of input for education.

How have these input changes influenced education? Between 1968 and 1973 bilingual-bicultural education became a reality in many states. The number of Chicano professional staff has increased at every level including administrative positions at local (principals) and state levels. Universities have established professional training programs in bilingual-bicultural education as well as integrated programs in Chicano Studies. These are only some of the many varied accommodations reflected by educational institutions due to the inclusion of Chicano perspective within the input stream.

One institution that has recently involved itself in the educational system and cannot be ignored because it has had far-reaching effects must be mentioned: the courts. Although court decisions affecting education have not usually been localized in any particular state, what would schools be like if it were not for *Brown* v. *Board of Education* or *Rodriguez* v. *Board of Education* and, more recently, *Lau* v. *Nichols*. At the local level, these cases have led to an equalization school-finance formula in 1972 and have elucidated the plight of minority populations. It is important to point out that the courts not only directed input to educational policy change but provided consequences for those systems that refused to change. Loss of federal dollars became a stark reality for some school districts across the nation. Although this was not the case in most states, motivation for change became a reality as school districts suffered these consequences. The Chicano has yet to use the courts to their maximum effectiveness in securing educational justice, but their use is predictable if change does not continue to occur.

It seems appropriate at this time to conclude that Chicanos are increasingly providing input for educational institutions. This input has led to recent changes in school policy and practice; the system is attempting to adapt. There is some reason for optimism. Unfortunately, educational institutions have not responded with open arms to Chicano input nor is there any reason to believe that this interaction style will change. It is therefore a continuing challenge for all those involved in education to recognize these efforts and to encourage, maximize, receive and act judiciously upon them.

The following chapters deal with this challenge. They are meant to deal specifically with issues of direct importance to Chicano education: segregation, bilingualism, and bilingual-bicultural education. This information is to be used by all educators and students in reshaping the educational institutions of the past to deal with the Chicano students of present and future generations.

11 | The Origins, Development, and Consequences of the Educational Segregation of Mexicans in the Southwest

GUADALUPE SAN MIGUEL

INTRODUCTION

Although there is a vast amount of literature on the education of the Mexican American, much of it is characterized by biased, unsubstantiated generalizations, and unsophisticated methodology. Moreover, the focus of much of educational literature on the Mexican American is narrow in two respects. First, it attempts to explain only one aspect of the Mexican American's experience with the public schools, the pattern of poor school performance. Second, the literature pays little attention to the development of public school systems in the Southwest and ways in which these school systems adapted to the Mexican-American, school-age population. Consequently, little is known about the nature and extent of the educational services provided to Mexican-American children in the past by local school officials in the Southwest.

This article attempts to reconstruct the historical development of one aspect of public policy toward the education of Mexican Americans in the Southwest from the late 1800s to the late 1960s: the segregation of Mexicans in the public school systems of the Southwest. This article employs a theoretical framework based on the proposition that the educational system corresponds to the social, economic, and political institutions of our society and that the only way we can obtain major changes in education is to forge change in the overall social, economic, and political relationships that characterize the society. This approach assumes, then, that the schools are dominated and shaped by the society that created them and which sustains them. The most important tenet underlying this approach is the correspondence principle. As Henry Levin, in an article entitled "Educational Reform: Its Meaning," states:

> In brief, this principle suggests that the activities and outcomes of the educational sector correspond to those of the society generally. That is, all educational

systems serve their respective societies such that the social, economic and political relationships of the educational sector will mirror closely those of the society
of which they are a part.[1]

To a large extent, schools perpetuate and reproduce the social relationships
and the ideological framework of the society of which they are a part. In the
Southwest, the society is separate and unequal and Chicanos occupy a subordinate position in the socioeconomic structure of that society.[2] Separate classes
and schools for Mexicans reflect this social condition and help to reinforce the
dominant-subordinate relationships found there. But stating that schools reflect
the social, political, and economic relationships of the society says little about
the process of the development of the educational segregation of Mexican
school children. How did the educational segregation of Mexicans originate?
And how did it evolve over the years? These are the basic questions this paper
will attempt to answer.

THE ROOTS AND DEVELOPMENT OF EDUCATIONAL SEGREGATION

The policy of segregating racial-minority school children initially did not affect
Mexican school children. However, during the late years of the nineteenth century the policy was extended to them on several grounds. Initially, its scope
was limited to the elementary grade levels. But the policy was ultimately
applied throughout all grades. Throughout the twentieth century it has proven
detrimental to the interests of Mexican-American school children.

The practice of placing nonwhite students in separate schools in the Southwest began in the mid-nineteenth century when several states acted to establish
and maintain separate schools for two racial groups—black and white school-
age children. The process of separate school placement based on racial or cultural considerations was not uniform or universal. The laws of some states of
the Southwest constitutionally mandated that separate schools be built for
blacks and whites. The laws of other states did not include such a mandate.
The New Mexico, Arizona, and Colorado state constitutions, for instance, did
not specify the separate placement of blacks and whites in the public schools,
in large part because the absence of significant numbers of non-Spanish-speak-
ing racial and cultural groups in these states discouraged such measures. The
California and Texas state constitutions, on the other hand, incorporated provisions for the establishment of racially separate public school systems, which
were implemented by educational officials.

In California, for example, the state superintendent of public instruction in
1858 recommended to the state legislature that a portion of public monies be
devoted to providing separate schools for the "inferior races" as a way of dis-

couraging integration in the public schools of the state.[3] He also recommended that public monies be withheld from any school district that permitted the admission of "the inferior races—African, Mongolian, or Indian—into the Common Schools."[4] In Texas, the Constitution of 1876 specifically stated that "there must be separate schools for white and colored children."[5]

During these early years of the establishment of the common school system in the Southwest, Mexicans were not targets of discriminatory educational legislation; however, they became targets as their numbers in the Southwest increased rapidly in the late years of the second half of the nineteenth century. Mexican children were not denied the opportunity to secure an education, but, as more and more of them entered the public schools, local school officials, with the sanction of the respective state departments of education, broadened the concept of racial separation initially intended for blacks to include them. Encouraged by the explicit sanction of racial school segregation in different state constitutions and by custom and tradition, local educational authorities established separate "Mexican schools" as early as 1896. In Corpus Christi, Texas, for instance, as Paul Taylor noted in his study of Mexican-Anglo relations in this community, a separate school was built for Mexicans "practically coincident with the entry of Mexican children to the city schools in 1896."[6] Shortly thereafter, the Seguín Independent School District in central Texas also built separate schools for Mexican school children.[7]

By the turn of the century similar schools had been constructed in California. For example, according to James W. Cameron, the Los Angeles school system built and maintained an elementary school attended by many Spanish surname children.[8] Throughout early years of the century it remained the only school for Mexican school children.

The practice of constructing separate Mexican schools spread slowly during the first two decades of the twentieth century. During the 1920s, the "Mexican school" phenomena in the Southwest increased. Moreover, the pattern of segregation strengthened as a result of school board policies and changing demographic and socioeconomic conditions. In many cases local and state board actions were directly responsible for segregation; in others, circumstances compelled school officials to reaffirm existing patterns of social segregation in the community.

Corpus Christi and Los Angeles are illustrative of this discrimination in educational policy development. In Corpus Christi, school officials did not have an official policy of separating Mexicans from Anglos; nevertheless, they prompted the segregation of Mexicans through their school construction policy. From 1900 to 1915, the Corpus Christi Independent School District constructed six permanent school buildings. It constructed two of these permanent schools in the city's predominantly Mexican ward and designated them as schools for Anglos only.[9] In Los Angeles, on the other hand, the city school district pursued a policy "of maintaining *de jure* segregation in three elementary schools in the San Fernando Valley in the 1920s and 1930s. Mexicans were also often separated into special classes."[10]

The development and strengthening of educational segregation in the Southwest during these years were facilitated by immigration from Mexico and the migration of Mexicans from the rural to urban areas of the Southwest. As a result of American industrial and agricultural prosperity and political economic disorder in Mexico, immigration to the United States increased dramatically. Hundreds of thousands of Mexicans crossed the border during the first three decades of the twentieth century. For example, between 1910 and 1930, 661,538 Mexicans legally crossed the border. In addition to this official figure, a large but unknown number of "illegal" Mexicans also arrived from Mexico. The sharp rise in Mexican migration into the United States outstripped the rise in the white Anglo population. In the five southwestern states the Mexican community grew from 158,742 in 1910 to 1,282,882 in 1930. The total non-Mexican population grew from 8,604,670 to 13,396,647 during the same two decades. In absolute numbers the Mexican community grew eight times while the predominantly Anglo population grew a little over 50 percent. In terms of percentages, Mexicans accounted for 4.2 percent of the five state's population in 1910 and nearly 10 percent by 1930. The Mexican community had thus become much more visible and identifiable in one generation.[11] Coupled with this increased migration of Mexicans into the United States, there were also countless others who began to move to the major urban centers of the Southwest in search of better opportunities.

Although no precise statistics exist indicating the exact number of Mexican school-age children who entered the public schools of the Southwest as a result of the migration, data from some school districts suggest that the numbers were substantial. In several urban school districts, such as Los Angeles, the trickle of Mexican children entering the city schools turned into a flood. Here, during the 1890–91 school year only twenty-two of 413 new immigrant school children were Mexican. By the end of the decade, of the 621 immigrant school children only forty-nine were Mexican. However, during the 1903–04 school year Mexican immigrant school children increased six-fold to 364. Moreover, the number of Mexican immigrant school children almost doubled two years later. By the 1906–07 school year, there were 3,899 Mexican immigrant school children. In short, by 1910 Mexicans were enrolling in the Los Angeles public schools at the rate of approximately one thousand a year.[12]

At the same time that the numbers of Mexican school children were growing, the number and percentage of Mexican-American children between the ages of 7 and 17 also increased rapidly. In Texas in the 1920s, for example, a survey by Herschel T. Manuel revealed that the Spanish-speaking population in the public schools increased at an average of approximately 7,400 per year.

According to Manuel, between 1922 and 1928 "the percent of increase of Mexican scholastics was more than five times of other white scholastics, and more than nine times that of colored scholastics."[13] This increase was so great that some scholars such as Manuel were led to conclude as follows regarding the impact of growth of the Mexican school population:

> In terms of building alone it would require the erection of 18 ten-room buildings annually to care for *new* Mexican scholastics (school-age children) if all entered and were housed in this way. Putting the matter a little differently, one may say that the *increase* in Mexican scholastics each year is sufficient to require one new building for every 21 already in use.[14] [emphasis in original]

The large influx of non-English speaking and culturally different Mexican children into the public schools of the Southwest created problems for local school systems. Some local officials regarded the problem as a crisis, and requested assistance from state educational officials and researchers in universities. Consequently, in an effort to remedy the problems faced by school districts, state and federal education agencies, as well as universities and individual scholars began to initiate studies on the "Mexican" problem in the schools.[15] At the same time some public school agencies initiated studies on the organizational, curricular, and financial implications of Mexican enrollment in the public schools. Moreover, many local school officials expressed concern over the presence of "a considerable Mexican element" in the public schools, the magnitude of the non-English speaking student population, and the high failure rates of Mexican children in the traditionally Anglo schools. Almost invariably their concerns climaxed in additional segregation of Mexican school children. Throughout the Southwest local educational authorities argued that Mexican-American children came to school without knowing an adequate amount of English.[16] Because of this language "deficiency" they could not effectively participate in schools or classes with their English-speaking peers. Thus, in order not to hamper the instruction of the English-speaking children and to enable Mexican-American students to learn English, it was better to place them in separate facilities.[17]

Local school officials also developed a variety of other social, economic, and cultural rationalizations for the practice of segregating Mexican-American school children. Some openly argued that these students should be segregated from Anglos because they were genetically and physically inferior. As one school executive from South Texas declared: "We segregate for the same reason that the southerners segregate the Negro. They are an inferior race, that is all."[18] In contrast to this official, others justified the policy by citing certain personal attributes of the Mexican-American population. Some officials, for instance, used the standards of cleanliness among this population as excuses for placing Mexicans students in separate school buildings or classrooms. "I don't believe in mixing," one South Texas school board member declared: "They are filthy and lousy, not all, but most of them."[19] He was joined in his defense of the policy of segregation by a superintendent who noted: "The reason (for separation) is because of their filth. . . . As a class, they are dirty."[20]

Mexican-American educators, such as George I. Sánchez and other scholars, challenged the discriminatory placement of Mexicans in segregated schools. Sánchez, for example, argued that the rationale for segregating Mexican-American children rested on assumptions that were "either illogical, without foundation in fact, or contrary to sound educational theory and practice."[21] He declared that none of the reasons given to segregate Mexican-American children were valid. He argued that English, while essential for understanding basic subject matter, was not necessary for engaging in certain kinds of activities outside of the classroom, such as playground activities, drawing, music, and arithmetic computation. He also pointed out that, pedagogically, children learned a second language quicker by interacting with those who spoke the language well, rather than by being placed in separate facilities with others who did not speak the language of the school. He claimed that there was no evidence that Mexican Americans as a group were "deficient" in English or that they were also "deficient" in academic subjects. And, he declared that the pervasiveness of segregation throughout the Southwest and the degree of variation in segregation practices across grade levels indicated that the separate placement of Mexican-American children was arbitrary and illegal.[22] In a devastating critique of the policy, he declared:

> the educational destinies of these Spanish-name children are being made the butt either of amateurish, or wholly misguided (and inconsistent), or of careless and shallow, reasoning or of reasoning that has been vitiated by considerations other than those that should enter into management of a program of public schools designed in the best interest of all the children of the entire community.[23]

In a similar vein Arthur L. Campa declared that segregation deprived Mexican-American children "of the opportunity to achieve oral language efficiency"; moreover, it created "social maladjustments and mental blockages that no amount of adult education" could eradicate."[24] Likewise, Manuel called segregation a dangerous policy. He declared:

> Children (in segregated schools) do not learn readily the give-and-take of democratic living except by living, playing, and working together. Artificial lines of cleavage promote misunderstanding and distrust, with a tendency toward disregard of fundamental human rights by the more favored and a tendency toward emotional maladjustment, suspicion, and dislike by the less favored.[25]

However, in spite of these challenges to the soundness of this practice and the rationales used to support it, the policy of segregation gained prominence within educational circles during the second quarter of the twentieth century. Throughout the Southwest, school officials drew upon educational surveys, legislative mandates, legal and quasi-legal rulings by local and state leaders that supported the use of the linguistic argument in the segregation of Mexican Americans in the public schools. Officials in Texas assumed the lead in sanctioning segregation in the public schools. The Texas Education Agency, for example, recommended the following to state school officials:

> ... they (non-English speaking children) should be segregated in the first two or three grades, when they are unable to speak English. The problem of teaching children who already have a speaking control of the vernacular is different from teaching non-English speaking children. It is believed that both non-English speaking and English speaking children will make better progress if they are segregated in the early school grades.[26]

To make matters worse for Mexican Americans the state court in Texas also provided a judicial rationale to the separate placement of Mexicans in the public schools. In 1930 the court in *Salvatierra* v. *Independent School District* ruled that the 1876 Texas State Constitution did not authorize local school districts to segregate students based on national origin, but did permit the separate placement of Mexican children in different facilities on educational or linguistic grounds.[27] Its position was supported by three federal courts whose rulings between 1948 and 1955 sanctioned segregation based on linguistic grounds.[28] In these cases the courts declared that it was unconstitutional, illegal, and arbitrary to place students of Mexican ancestry in different school buildings simply because of their national origin. But the courts ruled that segregation in the first grades was permitted if it was solely for "educational purposes." The legal basis for segregation laid by these courts was aptly summarized by the Arizona court in 1955 in *González* v. *Sheely, et al.,* when it declared that:

> The only tenable ground upon which segregation practices in the respondent school district can be defended lies in the English language deficiencies of some of the children of Mexican ancestry as they enter elementary public school life as beginners, but such situations do not justify the general and continuous segregation in separate schools of the children of Mexican ancestry from the rest of the elementary school population as has been shown to be the practice in the respondent school district.[29]

Shortly after these rulings, many school districts began to segregate Mexican children under the pretense that the separate placement was for educational purposes. Some augmented the segregation permitted by the courts by expanding the scope of discriminatory practices that initially were primarily aimed at groups other than Mexicans. For instance, during the early 1920s the California legislature aimed its discriminatory efforts at Japanese immigrants and Indians.[30] But in 1935, the segregation of Mexican children became permissible under the California Education Code when the California attorney general's office issued an opinion that categorized Mexicans as "Indians," thus allowing local school officials to place them in separate school facilities. As a result of this opinion the Education Code of 1935 came to read:

> The governing board of the school districts shall have the power to establish separate schools for Indian children, accepting children of Indians who are wards of the United States, and for children of Chinese, Japanese or Mongolian parentage.[31]

In some cases quasi-legal mandates by local leaders also bolstered the discriminatory treatment of Mexicans and other nonwhites in public schools. In Santa Ana, California, for example, affirmative discriminatory practices in educational policy were sanctioned and condoned by the city attorney's office as early as 1919. In January of that year the Mexican Pro-Patria Club, a local Mexican organization, challenged the local board's practice of segregating Mexican children. In response to the challenge local school officials solicited a legal opinion on the matter from the city attorney. While acknowledging that there were no constitutional or statutory provisions empowering local school officials to maintain separate schools for Mexicans or other nonwhites, the city attorney ruled:

> I desire to advise the Board that under the present arrangements in classification of the pupils entering the schools of Santa Ana, it is entirely proper and legal to classify them according to the regularity of attendance, ability to understand the English language and their aptness to advance in the grades to which they shall be assigned.[32]

Many cities in California as well as Texas and other communities throughout the Southwest pursued similar kinds of discriminatory practices in education. The official publications, the legal and quasi-legal mandates, racist attitudes, as well as internal school board practices, such as the use of intelligence tests, the establishment of gerrymandered attendance school zones, and restrictive transfer policies, encouraged the establishment and maintenance of numerous "Mexican" schools throughout the Southwest. For example, in Texas, "Mexican schools" existed throughout the state:

> The number of Mexican Ward Schools in independent school districts alone, doubled between 1922–1923 and 1931–1932, to a total of forty. By 1942–1943 separate schools for Mexican-Americans were maintained by at least 122 districts in fifty-nine widely distributed and representative counties across the state.[33]

The rise and growth of the "Mexican" school phenomena was apparent in California as well. In a study on public policy toward the education of nonwhites in California, Irving G. Hendrick noted that by the late 1920s, at the height of Mexican immigration, there were seventy-four regular elementary schools operating specifically for Mexicans and another twenty-five elementary schools serving the migratory Mexican population. Most of the segregated schools were found in counties in southern California such as Los Angeles, San Bernardino, Imperial, Orange, Riverside, and Ventura. Hendrick also found approximately 85 percent of California schools reporting in one survey acknowledged the separate placement of Mexicans in separate educational facilities. "Those not choosing to segregate Mexican children in separate buildings," he added, "generally relied on at least isolating them in separate rooms."[34]

After World War II larger number of Mexican children began to enroll in secondary institutions. Between 1945 and 1955, less than 15 percent of all Chicanos ages 16 to 18 enrolled in high school.[35] By by 1960, approximately 60–80 percent were enrolled in secondary schools.[36] Although the majority of Chicanos did not graduate from high school (approximately 60 percent of all Chicanos from Texas, for example, did not graduate from high school in 1960) most of them were enrolled in high school. With the enrollment of Chicanos in the higher grades, local and state school systems expanded the scope of the coverage of the policy of segregation by constructing "Mexican" junior and senior high schools.

The case of Corpus Christi, Texas is illustrative of this process. Between 1900 and 1930, there were a total of nine schools constructed in this city's school district. Seven of these were elementary and two were secondary schools. One of these seven elementary schools was predominantly Mexican, the other one was black. There was no junior or senior high school enrolling large numbers of Mexican children. By 1960 the situation had changed. There were a total of fifty-one public schools—thirty-eight elementary, eleven junior high, and three senior high. Twelve of the elementary and three of the junior high schools were all Mexican; three elementary, one junior high, and one senior high school were black. In 1968, the Corpus Christi Independent School District built a new senior high school in the barrio. Initially, the student population of this school was supposed to have included some Anglo students; Anglo parents protested and pressured the local school district to change the attendance zones so that their children would not have to attend the barrio school. As a consequence of Anglo pressure and with the consequent change in the attendance zones, the final enrollment of the new high school turned out to be 100 percent minority. Approximately 90 percent of the student population was Mexican American and 10 percent was black. The construction of the new senior high school thus completed the crowning of the "Mexican" school phenomenon begun in 1896 in Corpus Christi[37] and assured that a large proportion of Mexican children remained isolated in the district.

Children in other communities throughout the Southwest were likewise segregated. During the late 1960s the U.S. Civil Rights Commission conducted a
study on the education of Mexican Americans to find out the extent to which
educational segregation had developed in the Southwest in the absence of statutory or constitutional mandates. The commission discovered that there were
two million school age children of Spanish surname.[38] Approximately 70 percent of these attended school in the five southwestern states of Arizona, Colorado, California, New Mexico, and Texas. Mexican Americans comprised 17
percent of the total student enrollments in two states: California and Texas.
More importantly, the report found that the majority of them were concentrated in specific regions, and severely isolated by school district and by school
within individual districts.

THE CONSEQUENCES OF EDUCATIONAL SEGREGATION

The establishment and expansion of segregated and substandard schools has
had profound consequences for the education of Chicano children and for relationships between Anglo Americans and Chicanos. In the Southwest the segregation of Chicanos to a large degree has served to perpetuate and reinforce
the unequal relationships found between Anglos and Mexicans in many towns.
By so doing, the policy of segregation has discouraged sustained, equal status
interactions between Mexican-American and Anglo students, helped to insti-
tutionalize racism, and aided in the reproduction and strengthening of the
caste-like social structure that exists in the Southwest.[39]

Educational segregation has also discouraged cultural understanding among
different racial and cultural groups, fostered antagonisms among the different
groups, and perpetuated myths concerning the education of Mexican-American children and the need to place them in facilities separate from Anglos.[40]
Separate and inferior schooling for Chicanos has also helped to maintain the
existence of anti-Mexican attitudes among Anglos, especially Anglo parents of
school children, who have continued to perceive Mexicans as being culturally
and linguistically deficient, indifferent to schooling, and hygienically unfit to
mingle with Anglos,[41] as several scholarly studies and practical experience in
highly segregated school systems have demonstrated. One result of the perpetuation of such attitudes has been the failure of Anglos to accept Chicanos as
peers, even in those cases where Chicanos have attended schools with Anglos.
This nonacceptance by Anglos in the public schools in turn has had a devastating psychological impact on Mexican-American children. It has engendered
a sense of shame among them toward their history, their heritage, and their
cultural and personal identity.[42]

Segregationist practices have also had negative consequences on the achievement patterns of Mexican-American school children. Unwanted in school by

their Anglo peers, made to feel inferior by the teachers, and pressured by administrators to learn English and "American" ways, many Chicano children have found it difficult to continue their education.[43] Study after study over the past half century has shown that Chicanos have slower rates of progress in school when compared to Anglos. For example, during the early 1970s, the Civil Rights Commission, in its study of the education of Mexican Americans, found that 40 percent of the Chicanos dropped out before graduation and those that remained achieved lower levels than their Anglo classmates.[44]

Although most of the consequences of segregation have been negative, there is some evidence to indicate that it has had some positive impact on Chicano culture and on legal issues. For instance, the pervasiveness of educational segregation in this country has led to the evolution of legal doctrines which have successfully challenged the constitutionality of this practice in education.[45]

With respect to the education of Mexican Americans, moreover, there is some evidence indicating that segregation has contributed to the strengthening of a cultural identity among Chicanos, and aided in maintaining the Spanish language in an English-speaking environment. Empirical evidence on second-language acquisition indicates that the attitude of the dominant group toward the status of the minority group and its language is an important factor in learning the second language.[46] By historically ignoring, excluding, or suppressing the language and culture of Chicanos and failing to encourage the intermingling of different racial and cultural groups in the classrooms through the policy of segregation, educational authorities have discouraged Mexican Americans from learning English and helped to maintain Spanish language use in the public schools.[47] Nevertheless, despite the unintended positive consequdnces of educational separation on Spanish language use and Mexican cultural identity, school segregation has primarily had detrimental consequences on the education of Mexican-American children.

Today the segregation and discrimination against Mexican Americans is still widespread in the Southwest. A recent report on this segregation has indicated that if the present trend of segregation continues Chicanos will be the most segregated group in the public schools in the 1980s and will remain among the poorest educated groups in the country.[48] Thus, if Chicanos are to make progress educationally new strategies will have to be conceived to overcome a barrier that has denied Mexican Americans equal educational opportunity.

NOTES

1. Henry Levin, "Educational Reform: Its Meaning," in Henry Levin and Martin Carnoy, eds., *The Limits of Educational Reform* (New York: David McKay Company, 1976), p. 25.

2. For general overviews of the position of Chicanos in American society, see the following: Rodolfo Acuña, *Occupied America: The Chicano's Struggle Toward Lib-*

eration (San Francisco: Canfield Press, 1972); David J. Weber, *Foreigners in Their Native Land: Historical Roots of the Mexican American* (Albuquerque: University of New Mexico Press, 1973); Paul Rodman, "The Spanish Americans in the Southwest, 1848–1900," in John G. Clark, ed., *The Frontier Challenge* (Lawrence, Kansas: University of Kansas Press, 1971). See also Leonard Pitt, *The Decline of the Californios* (Berkeley: University of California Press, 1966); Alberto Camarillo, *Chicanos in a Changing Society: From Mexican Pueblos to American Barrios in Santa Bárbara and Southern California, 1848–1930* (Cambridge: Harvard University Press, 1979); Mario García, *Desert Immigrants: The Mexicans of El Paso, 1880–1920* (New Haven: Yale University Press, 1981); Richard Griswold del Castillo, *The Barrio of Los Angeles* (Berkeley: University of California Press, 1979).

3. Irving G. Hendrick, principal investigator, *Public Policy Toward the Education of Non-White Minority Group Children in California, 1949–1970,* final report, National Institute of Education Project No. NE-G-CC-3-0082, School of Education, University of California, Riverside, March 1975, p. 14.

4. Hendricks, *Public Policy,* p. 17, notes that California's first active state superintendent Moulder lashed out against the "Negrophilist school of mock philanthropists" who allegedly had found their way into California. "In several of the counties," stated superintendent Moulder, "attempts have been made to introduce children of Negroes into our public schools on an equality with whites. Until our people are prepared for practical amalgamation, which will probably not be before the millenium, they will rather forego the benefits of our Schools than permit their daughters—fifteen, sixteen and seventeen years of age plus to affiliate with the sons of Negroes. It is practically reduced to this, then, that our School must be maintained exclusively for whites, or they will soon become tenanted by blacks alone."

5. Texas Constitution, Art. 7, Section 7 (1876). *CF* Free Schools, ch. 124, section 93–96 (1905) Tex. Laws (repealed by Acts 1969, 61st Leg., ch. 129, section 1), quoted in Jorge C. Rangel and Carlos M. Alcalá, "Project Report: De Jure Segregation of Chicanos in Texas Schools," *Harvard Civil Rights—Civil Liberties Law Review,* vol. 7, no. 2 (March 1972), p. 312.

6. Paul Taylor, *An American-Mexican Frontier* (Chapel Hill: University of North Carolina Press, 1934), p. 216.

7. Rangel and Alcalá, "Project Report," p. 313.

8. James W. Cameron, "The History of Mexican Public Education in Los Angeles, 1910–1930," Ph.D. dissertation, University of Southern California, 1976.

9. Guadalupe San Miguel, Jr., "Endless Pursuits: The Chicano Educational Experience in Corpus Christi, Texas, 1880–1960," Ph.D. dissertation, Stanford University, 1978, p. 78.

10. Cameron, "History of Mexican Public Education," p. 153.

11. Annie Reynolds, *The Education of Spanish-Speaking Children in Five Southwestern States* (Washington, D.C.: U.S. Government Printing Office, 1933), pp. 5–8.

12. Cameron, "History of Mexican Public Education," p. 30.

13. Herschel T. Manuel, *The Education of Spanish-Speaking Children in Texas* (Austin: The University of Texas, 1930), p. 38.

14. Ibid., p. 50.

15. One of the earliest studies on the "Mexican problem" in the public schools was

conducted by the Texas Legislature. See, for example, George A. Works, "Non-English Speaking Children," in George A. Work, ed., *Texas Educational Survey Report, Vol. I: Organization and Administration* (Austin: Texas Educational Survey Commission, 1925), pp. 236–45.

16. See Gilbert George González, "The System of Public Education and Its Function Within the Chicano Communities, 1920–1930," Ph.D. dissertation, University of California at Los Angeles, 1974, pp. 95–121, for a comprehensive discussion of the articles published on the language issue in the public schools of the Southwest during the 1920s.

17. This rationale for segregation was articulated as early as 1920. See, for example, Grace C. Stanley, "Special Schools for Mexicans," *Survey*, vol. 44 (September 1920), pp. 714–15.

18. Taylor, *An American-Mexican Frontier*, p. 219.

19. Ibid., p. 217.

20. Ibid.

21. G. I. Sánchez, "Concerning Segregation of Spanish-Speaking Children in Texas," *Inter-American Education: Occasional Papers*, vol. IX (Austin: University of Texas, 1951).

22. Ibid., p. 25.

23. Ibid., p. 26.

24. Ibid., p. 55.

25. Ibid., pp. 49–51.

26. Texas Education Survey Commission, *Texas Educational Survey Report* (Austin: Texas Education Agency, 1925), p. 213.

27. *Salvatierra* v. *Independent School District* (Texas Civil Appear 33 S.W. 2nd 790, 1920).

28. One of these rulings was rendered in California. A second occurred in Texas. For the results of the court case in California, see *Méndez* v. *Westminster School District*, 64 F. Supp. 544 (S.D. Cal. 1946), aff'd, 161 F. 2nd 744 (9th Cir. 1947). The Texas Court case can be found in *Delgado* v. *Bastrop Independent School District*, Civil No. 388 (W.D. Tex. June 15, 1948).

29. *González* v. *Sheely, et al.*, (Civil No. 1473, U.S. District Court, D. Arizona, March 26, 1951), p. 1007.

30. Hendrick, *Public Policy*, p. 178.

31. California States 1935, c. 488, sec. 33.

32. Santa Ana, "School Board Minutes," Jan. 13, 1919.

33. Rangel and Alcalá, "Project Report," p. 313.

34. Hendrick, *Public Policy*, p. 185.

35. For statistics on the number of Mexican-American children enrolled in public schools in 1950, see U.S. Bureau of the Census, *U.S. Census of Population: 1950*, vol. IV, *Special Reports*, part. 3, ch. C, "Persons of Spanish Surname" (Washington, D.C.: U.S. Government Printing Office, 1953). For enrollment date on Mexican-American children in Texas during the 1955–56 school year, see Texas Education Agency, Division of Research, *Report of Pupils in Texas Public Schools Having Spanish-Surnames, 1955–1956* (Austin: 1957).

36. See U.S. Bureau of the Census, *U.S. Census of Population: 1960*, vol. II (Series

PC (2) Reports), *Subject Reports, Persons of Spanish Surname* (Washington, D.C.: U.S. Government Printing Office, 1961) for further data on the educational characteristics of the white population of Spanish surname in the five southwestern states.

37. For a history of the extension of school segregation in Corpus Christi, Texas, see San Miguel, "Endless Pursuits," Ch. II, pp. 58–92.

38. U.S. Commission on Civil Rights, *Mexican American Education Study,* Report I: *Ethnic Isolation of Mexican Americans in the Public Schools of the Southwest* (Washington, D.C.: U.S. Government Printing Office, 1971). The commission also found that Mexican Americans in general were underrepresented on school and professional staffs and on boards of education.

39. Theodore W. Parsons, Jr., "Ethnic Cleavage in a California School," Ph.D. dissertation, Stanford University, 1965, pp. 6–7. For another similar finding, see Ozzie G. Simmons, "Anglo-Americans and Mexican-Americans in South Texas: A Study of Dominant-Submissive Group Relations," Ph.D. dissertation, Harvard University, 1952.

40. Thomas P. Carter and Roberto Segura, *Mexican Americans in School: A Decade of Change* (New York: College Entrance Examination Board, 1979).

41. For a historical account of educators' views on Mexican Americans in the public schools, see Nick Vaca, "The Mexican American in the Social Sciences, 1912–1970," *El Grito,* vol. 4 (Fall 1971), pp. 17–51.

42. For a penetrating and sympathetic understanding of the impact racism has had on Chicanos who have attended public schools in South Texas, see especially, Taylor, *An American-Mexican Frontier,* pp. 191–226, and San Miguel, "Endless Pursuits," pp. 184–223.

43. See, for example, the following reports: U.S. Commission on Civil Rights, *Mexican American Education Study,* Report I: *Ethnic Isolation of Mexican Americans in the Public Schools of the Southwest* (1971); Report II: *The Unfinished Education: Outcomes for Minorities in the Five Southwestern States* (1971); Report III: *The Excluded Student: Educational Practices Affecting Mexican Americans in the Southwest* (1972); Report IV: *Mexican American Education in Texas: A Function of Wealth* (1972); Report V: *Teachers and Students: Classroom Interaction in the Schools of the Southwest* (1973); Report VI: *Toward Quality Education for Mexican Americans* (1974).

44. For further statistics on the educational attainment of Chicanos, see Ibid., especially Report II.

45. For an analysis of the history of legal challenges to the segregation of Mexican Americans, see Rangel and Alcalá, "Project Report," and Gaudalupe Salinas, "Mexican-Americans and the Desegregation of Schools in the Southwest," *El Grito,* vol. 4, no. 4 (Summer 1971), pp. 36–69.

46. See, for instance, Wallace E. Lambert and Robert C. Gardner, *Attitudes and Motivation in Second Language Learning* (Rowley, Mass.: Newbury House, 1972).

47. See U.S. Commission on Civil Rights, *Mexican American Education Study,* Report I: *Ethnic Isolation of Mexican Americans in the Public Schools of the Southwest,* for data on Spanish use in the Southwest.

48. Rafael Torres, *Hispanics and Desegregation* (Washington, D.C.: Aspira Center for Educational Equity, 1980).

12 | Early Childhood Bilingualism

EUGENE E. GARCÍA

The issues surrounding bilingualism are of specific interest to a large segment of this nation's population (U.S. Commission on Civil Rights, 1974) and of general interest to those individuals studying the general phenomenon of language acquisition (McNeil, 1966). Other reviews of bilingualism have dealt with the definition of bilingualism, amount of linguistic overlap, linguistic "interference," and theoretical issues related to each of these areas (see MacNamara, 1967; Riegel, 1968; and Vildomec, 1971). For the past ten years, numerous educationally related research and program-development efforts have been initiated. For example, the 1976 budget for bilingual education project was projected at near $100 million. An important aspect of this development has been the emphasis placed on developing models relevant to the formal teaching (and learning) of more than one language (Dissemination Center for Bilingual-Bicultural Education, 1974). The purpose of the present review will be to discuss some of these same issues in light of more recent theoretical research and applied information specific to bilingual development in young children. Therefore, this review should (a) serve as an update of earlier reviews in this area, (b) provide some functional information to those persons concerned with early childhood bilingualism, and (c) elucidate certain researchable areas that are in need of immediate attention in the context of language training. Additionally, different strategies for the investigation of multilingual development will be addressed.

LANGUAGE ACQUISITION

As one searches for a comprehensive definition of bilingualism, a continuum of definitional attempts unfolds. On one end of the continuum are general definitions such as "the practice of alternately using two languages" (Weinrich, 1953), or "knowledge of two languages" (Haugen, 1972). At the other end of this continuum are the operational definitions common to the field of experimental psychology ("subjects answered positively to questions concerning their use of two languages"; "subjects scored 90 percent correct on a standardized test of language proficiency in each language"; and so on). Regardless of the definition adopted for any empirical or theoretical treatment of bilingualism, "bilinguals" come in a variety of linguistic shapes and forms. Therefore, any

209

definition worthy of consideration must address this built-in linguistic diversity. But to consider only linguistic diversity would be an error. Thorough definitions of bilingualism must additionally consider cognitive and social domains: language or languages must be acquired and achieve maturity and use within a definable social context.

The following discussion will attempt to introduce a definition relevant to bilingual acquisition during early childhood. In doing so, early childhood bilingualism will necessarily be defined with considerations of linguistic, social, psychological, and to some extent physiological issues in mind. Bilingualism cannot presently be defined to the satisfaction of the theorist, researcher, or educator but an attempt is necessary here on pure communicative grounds. In perceiving quite well that I will fail to meet all demands placed on this definition, I offer the entire subject matter of this manuscript as a definition of sorts.

Early Childhood Bilingualism Defined

The term bilingualism here suggests the simultaneous acquisition of more than two languages during the first five years of life. This definition utilizes the traditional term language and requires the following conditions:

(a) Children are able to comprehend and/or produce some aspects of each language beyond the ability to discriminate that either one language or another is being spoken. The intent of this precondition is to confer the term bilingualism to children who can handle other than the most basic attributes of symbolic communication (that one set of symbols (languages) is the same or different than another). This is not a limiting condition since it allows many combinations of linguistic competence to fall within the boundaries of bilingualism (the most "simple" to include might be the child who has memorized one or more lexical or syntactic utterances in a second language).

(b) Children are exposed "naturally" to the two systems of languages as they are used in the form of social interaction during early childhood. This condition requires a substantive bilingual environment in the location of the child's first three to five years of life. In many cases this exposure comes from within a traditional nuclear family network but this need not be the case (relatives, visitors, and extended visits to foreign countries are examples of alternative environments).

(c) The simultaneous character of development must be apparent in both languages. This is contrasted with the case in which a native speaker of one language, who after mastery of that language, begins on a course of second language acquisition. The boundaries of this definitional precondition are somewhat strained due to the ongoing developmental nature of language. Therefore, it is probably the case that any child meeting the two above preconditions will also meet the present one. The present precondition indicates the importance of psychological (cognitive) and physiological development during early childhood as they might relate to bilingual acquisition.

It is therefore these *combined* conditions that define the present population of interest. It is clear from this definition that an attempt is made to include the child's linguistic abilities in conjunction with his social environment during an important psychological part of his life. An idealized definition follows from the three conditions stated above: A child, prior to the age of five, is able to function in two languages at some level of social interaction. In this way, the concentration on linguistic social competence redefines the traditional linguistic base of previous definitions.

Prior to leaving this definition, let us consider briefly each of the conditions identified as important. Linguistically, it is necessary to borrow from theoretical and empirical work on "single" or native language acquisition. Figure 12.1 presents an extension of single language terminology to the notion of bilingualism. In doing so, the primary features of language are placed in a three-dimensional perspective. That is, each language can be characterized by phonology, lexicon, morphology, syntax, and semantics. In addition each of these categoreis can be considered at receptive (ability to understand) and expressive (ability to speak) levels. Therefore, the study of language acquisition by children must consider the development of each of these segmented features. But as the second condition of the previous definition implies, these linguistic attributes are imbedded in a social (cultural) milieu (environ). Therefore, it is imperative to consider the cultural context as it relates to social variables, which influence both acquisition and use of a bilingual repertoire.

The linguistic and social variables alluded to above can be related to any bilingual; yet, our concern here is with early childhood bilingualism. Two important differences are related to the meaningful distinction between this form of bilingualism and others. First, early childhood is characterized traditionally as a time of considerable physiological transformation. Of special interest here is the development of neurostructures related to language acquisition. Therefore, any serious consideration of early childhood bilingualism must include an awareness of early brain development and its relationship to multiple-language acquisition. Penfield and Roberts (1959) assert that only young children can "generate" a new center, physiologically, for a second language system. These assertions are based on studies of brain lesions to the left hemisphere of the brain. At birth the cerebral hemispheres are considered to be equipotential for language localization. Progressive cerebral lateralization

Figure 12.1:   An Interactive Description of Bilingualism

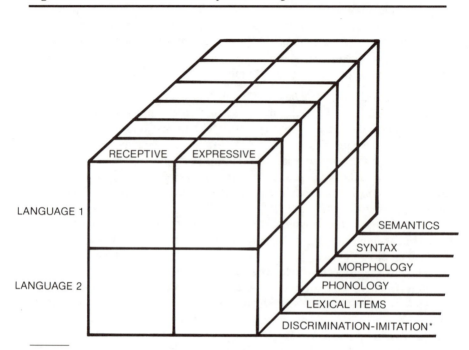

*This particular descriptive category relates only to the issue of comprehension (Receptive Speech). Expression in this case requires the ability of the subject to imitate, correctly, instances of each language.

occurs after about thirty-six months of age, leading finally to the restriction of language function to the dominant cerebral hemisphere (usually considered to be the left hemisphere) at about fourteen years of age. As the cerebral cortex matures postnatally, certain linguistic functions become increasingly restricted to the left hemisphere. Lesions of this hemisphere result in linguistic impairment whose severity is correlated with the maturity of the developing cerebral cortex.

As Jacobson (1976) suggests, "Formal linguistic analysis, divorced from its biological substrates, is unlikely to be a profitable approach to the problem of how the brain generates language and purely psychological approaches to that problem are equally unlikely to succeed." This is certainly a strong case for a keen awareness of physiological variables as they relate to early language acquisition in general and to the task of bilingual acquisition in particular. Unfortunately, the dependency of this work on brain dysfunction and the unavailability of an experimental technology for investigating the causal relationship between cerebral development and language acquisition leaves us with little more than an awareness of possible interrelationships:

> The task of finding causal relations between neurobiology and language has met with serious difficulties. Cerebral localization of language function, although a necessary preliminary step, falls short of a neurophysiological explication of language. If our expectations include such an explication, we have to admit that little progress has been made toward its realization. Indeed, it is not yet possible to describe any complex type of behavior in terms of a program of neural events, and many decades will pass before the neurophysiological mechanisms of cognitive processes in man are understood. (Jacobson, 1975, pp. 105–06)

Therefore, although it is necessary for us to be aware of and empirically concerned with the physiology of early-childhood bilingualism, we are left to concentrate only on the linguistic, social, and psychological aspects of the phenomenon. This may not be the case in the near future.

The psychological aspects of bilingualism are left untreated in the above discussion. This aspect of bilingualism in early childhood further differentiates its character from other forms of bilingualism not considered in our earlier definition. A specific example is the case of second-language acquisition. Typically, this effort is begun after near-complete development of the native language. But early childhood bilingualism takes place during the same temporal period as native language development in monolinguals. This temporal period is marked by parallel cognitive growth. Therefore, the relationship between bilingual development and cognitive development must be considered.

Recent information in the cognitive growth area has suggested an interactive relationship between cognitive structures and language acquisition (Brown, 1973). A similar interactive relationship must be considered for bilingual development during early childhood. Although direct research in this area is only beginning to emerge, its theoretical relevance has been historically noted (Leopold, 1947). Ervin-Tripp (1973) summarized some of the major differences, considered psychological, between children and adults as they relate to language acquisition:

a. Children show a greater readiness to learn the language of their contemporaries in a new linguistic environment.
b. Children enjoy rote memorization, while adults prefer solving intellectual problems.
c. Adults emphasize the content of language often neglecting its formal system.
d. Children are more perceptive to the sounds of a language, adults to its meaning.
e. Children relate speech more to the immediate context.

   f. Children usually learn new words through sensory activity, adults in a purely verbal context.

   g. Children can make linguistic abstractions—learn about structures never directly presented to them, but adults have a greater capacity to remember stated grammatical rules.

   h. Children seem less subject to interference from their native systems than are adults. (p. 63)

In summary, I have presented a definition of bilingualism specific to early childhood that considers more than pure linguistic features. Instead, it is concerned with traditional linguistic features in concert with social, psychological, and, to some extent physiological parameters. Additionally, although these parameters have been discussed separately (and will be divided along these same lines in the discussions that follow), they must not be seen as static entities. Instead it is important to view them within an interactive perspective such that their treatment theoretically, empirically, or educationally cannot be totally separated. The impact of each variable influencing bilingualism in early childhood must be evaluated within this perspective. It is this nonstatic model that will be of benefit in a clearer understanding of early-childhood bilingualism.

BILINGUAL DEVELOPMENT

It is common for an adult bilingual to be considered "educated" (Macky, 1967). But, as Haugen (1972) indicates, the converse may also be true. Independent of the social perceptions of bilingualism, it is clear that a child can and does learn more than one linguistic communicative form in many societies throughout the world. Sorenson (1967) describes the acquisition of three to four languages by young children who live in the northwest Amazon region of South America. Although the Tukano tribal language serves as the *lingua franca* in the area, there continue to exist some twenty-five clearly distinguishable linguistic groups in this Brazilian-Colombian border region. Skrabanek (1970) reported on the continued acquisition and support of both English and Spanish language systems among preschool children of our own Southwest for the last hundred years with no indication that this phenomenon will be disrupted. Unfortunately, little is known either descriptively or causally about the process of this linguistic development, although several studies tackled this phenomenon with linguistic description as their primary goal.

One of the first systematic investigations of bilingual acquisition in young children was reported by Leopold (1939, 1947, 1949a, 1949b). This author set out to study the "simultaneous" acquisition of English and German in his own daughter. These experimentally "rough" but initial descriptive reports indicate that although the subject was exposed to both languages during infancy, she "seemed" to weld both languages into one system during initial language production periods. Language production during later periods (ages two years two months to two years six months) indicated that the use of English and German grammatical forms developed independently.

More recent studies have systematically addressed several issues relevant to multiple language acquisition. Carrow (1971, 1972) has restricted her study to the receptive domain of young bilingual Mexican-American children in the Southwest. Children (ages three years ten months to six years nine months) from bilingual, Spanish-English home environments were administered the Auditory Test for Language Comprehension. This test assesses language comprehension without requiring language expression. The test consists of a series of pictures representing referential categories that can be signaled by words, morphological constructions, grammatical categories, and syntactical structures. The categories include verbs, adjectives, adverbs, nouns, pronouns, morphological endings, prepositions, interrogatives, and syntax complexity in both languages. A comparison of English and Spanish comprehension on this task for bilinguals revealed (Carrow, 1971) that: (1) linguistically, children were very heterogeneous, some scored better in one language than another, others were equal in both; (2) a greater proportion of children scored higher in English than in Spanish; and (3) older children scored higher on these measures in both languages. This was the case even though Spanish was not used as a medium of instruction for children who were in educational programs.

In a cross-sectional comparison of English comprehension among monolingual English and bilingual Spanish-English children (ages three years ten months to six years nine months), Carrow (1972) reports a positive developmental trend for both Spanish and English in bilingual children. Additionally, bilingual children tended to score lower than monolingual children on English measures during ages three years ten months to five years nine months; bilinguals did not differ significantly on these same English measures. These combined results seem to indicate that at the receptive level, Spanish-English bilingual children were: (a) progressing (increasing their competence) in both Spanish and English; (b) heterogeneous as a group, favoring one language (typically English) over another; and (c) behind monolingual children in their acquisition of English but eventually "caught up." Although there are obvious constraints to the specific conclusions reported above and their generalizations to other populations of bilingual children, they do offer some empirical information relevant to the study of early childhood bilingual development.

With respect to expressive development, Padilla and Leibman (1975) report on the longitudinal analysis of Spanish-English acquisition in two three-year-old bilingual children. These researchers followed the model of Brown (1973) in recording linguistic interactions of these children over a five-month period. By an analysis of several dependent linguistic variables (phonological, grammatical, syntactic, and semantic characteristics) over this time period, they observed gains in both languages although several English forms were in evidence while similar Spanish forms were not. They also report the differentiation of linguistic systems at phonological, lexical, and syntactic levels. They conclude:

> The appropriate use of both languages even in mixed utterances was evident; that is, correct word order was preserved. For example, there were no occurrences of "raining está" "ah, es baby" but there was evidence for such utterances as "está raining" and "es a baby." There was also an absence of the redundance of unnecessary words which might tend to confuse meaning. (p. 51)

Although these conclusions indicating the parallel development of the two languages must remain tentative due to the small sample of subjects and linguistic productions studied, they again serve as an empirical base from which similar research in the area of bilingual acquisition can be launched. Beyond the basic descriptive research discussed above, a second more popular form of research has considered the interactive influence of multiple-language acquisition.

LANGUAGE TRANSFER

When referring to the interactive phenomenon between languages of the bilingual, the term "interference" is often used. This term has gained multiple meanings as is shown by its gain of various modifiers: "linguistic interference," "psychological interference," and "educational interference" (Saville and Troike, 1971).

This interactive process might be considered both general and specific in nature. That is, it is possible that the requirements imposed on a child with respect to multilingual acquisition would lead to a general linguistic lag compared to a child whose communicative requirements center on one distinct language. Carrow's (1971, 1972) work is relevant to this notion of general "interference." Measures across languages indicated that English outdistanced Spanish for bilingual children and that English for these same bilinguals was lower than English for monolingual children of the same age. This English lag was evident during early ages (three to five years) but not at later ages (six to seven years). Although these data suggest a possible causal relationship between bilingualism and the initial "rate" of language acquisition, this is far from conclusive. In fact, Padilla and Liebman (1975) report contradictory evidence. Their analysis of two three-year-old bilingual children's linguistic development suggested no general language lag in either language. By comparing these subjects' utterances to those reported by Brown (1973) for monolingual English children and those reported by González (1970) for monolingual Spanish children they were able to conclude:

> There is no evidence in the language samples that might suggest an overall reduced or slower rate of language growth for the bilingual children of other studies. (p. 51)

Because the notion of a general lag does not consider the possible importance of similarities and differences of specific language forms, it does not seem to hold much promise for identifying important levels of interaction operating during bilingual acquisition. Therefore a more specific analysis of linguistic interaction that considers such differences and similarities is necessary.

This form of analysis has been of continued importance in the study of the second-language acquisition that occurs when an individual with a skilled ability in one language is introduced to and begins to learn a second language. For example, Milon (1972) has examined the development of negation in a longitudinal study of a seven-year-old Japanese child learning English. His observations indicate that the child progressed through the same phases as an English child acquiring this linguistic ability.

Experimental studies of specific instances of "interference" or lack of it have also been done with bilingual children. For instance, Evans (1974) reports the comparison of word-pair discriminations and word imitations in Spanish and English for monolingual English and bilingual Spanish-English children. Elementary school children were asked to discriminate between words containing English sounds considered difficult for Spanish speakers. Examples are the phonemes /b/ and /v/, which are clearly separate in English but not so clearly separate in Spanish. Additionally, children were requested to imitate in each language a series of words that considered this same "difficult" characteristic. Bilinguals did not differ from monolinguals on any of the English tasks. But as expected, bilinguals scored significantly higher than monolinguals on all Spanish tasks. García and Trujillo (1977) report a similar finding when they compared bilingual (Spanish-English) and monolingual (English) three, four, five, six, and seven year-olds on high error-risk phonemes (phonemes Spanish adult speakers mispronounce in Spanish), and simple-to-complex syntactic forms (sentences containing plural, possessive, and adjective morphemes). Bilinguals did not differ from monolinguals on English imitation tasks (both groups scored near 100 percent correct) but did differ significantly (made less errors) on Spanish tasks. This was the case across all age levels.

These experiments represent strategy that compares monolingual and bilingual subjects across specific linguistic categories represented in Figure 12-1. These studies are meant to empirically test a specific "interference" hypothesis during early childhood bilingual acquisition. They suggest that at the levels presently studied, little "interference" is substantiated.

Typical evidence of the "interference" phenomenon in bilingual children is taken from naturalistic language samples. As Ervin-Tripp (1973) suggests, "interference" in these samples is exemplified by performance errors in the learners linguistic system as they relate to a contrastive analysis of both languages involved. Padilla and Liebman's (1975) recent longitudinal work has addressed the issue of transfer through the analysis of linguistic errors. They were able to conclude that after an initial, short, undifferentiated phase (prior to two years six months), bilingual children tended to keep languages, Spanish and English, separate. More recent error analysis data allow Padilla (1977) to conclude that:

> Children reared in bilingual environments learn to differentiate their two linguistic systems relatively early. When linguistic interactions do occur there may be several possible explanations ranging from lack of familiarity with the word in one language to the child's acquisition of discourse strategies which demand a switch in language. (p. 11)

This type of investigation requires one major assumption: Any "interference" sample is causally related to an interaction effect of the two identified languages. Unfortunately, this assumption is in need of empirical verification. For instance, linguistic observations of a young child may produce the following utterances: "Did you see *ese carro*," or "*El* boy is going with us." Given our previous guide, each of these might be considered an example of "interference." Yet, a closer analysis of the child's total system might indicate that this type of linguistic format is his only model (it is not a function of one of the child's languages acting upon the other). Therefore, it would seem totally inappropriate to consider these utterances as forms of, or symptoms of, "interference."

LINGUISTIC INPUT AND SOCIAL CONTEXT

As Riegel (1968) suggests, any chronological record of the child's linguistic output coupled with linguistic input information would allow an important correlational analysis of language development. Although such extensive information remains unavailable, some systematic semblance of this type of data is becoming available for monolingual English children (Schacter, Kirshner, Klips, Friedricks, and Sanders, 1974). Unfortunately, little information of this calibre is available on young bilingual children.

Although this absence of empirical data is theoretically crippling, some cautious notions of bilingual input seem justifiable. If one considers the eventual bilingual product, it seems appropriate to suggest that some percentage of the child's linguistic information is in one language and some other percentage is in a second language. One might tie the acquisition of either language to the general theoretical notion of "degree of linguistic input." Mathematically, the extent of bilingualism would be directly related to the proportion of language information made available.

This simple relationship must be qualified due to several theoretical and empirical considerations. The traditional qualifications in this area have been expressed by the concepts of compound and coordinate bilingualism (Weinrich, 1953; Ervin and Osgood, 1965; Lambert and Rawlings, 1969). With respect to linguistic input, this distinction refers to the simultaneous or sequential input of two languages: compound bilinguals have learned their languages during the same temporal period while coordinate bilinguals have acquired their languages sequentially, during separate temporal periods. This distinction is usually applied to adults who have equal bilingual competencies but who have acquired language under these different circumstances. This traditional view is not applicable to our defined conceptualization of early childhood bilingualism. Recent data support this assertion.

For instance, Edelman (1969) reports the differential use of Spanish and English vocabulary in Puerto Rican children on a word-naming task as a function of the different contexts (school, home, neighborhood, church) the children were asked to describe. Skrabanek (1970), in a study of Spanish maintenance among Mexican Americans, found that the use of Spanish differed as a function of the age of the speaker. Older subjects spoke more often in Spanish although both young and old alike used Spanish a substantial proportion of the time. Kuo (1974) reports the differential use of language by Chinese-American children as a function of age and other socialization variables.

These data have specific implications for the earlier formulation of an input analysis. That is, linguistic input may differ for each language across settings and across individuals. Of course, the qualitative nature of the input may also differ (the phonetic, morphological, syntactic, and semantic characteristics). For instance, Harris and Hassemer (1972) found that complexity (in terms of length of sentence) of Spanish and English syntax usage for bilingual children was affected by direct Spanish and English models exemplifying complex syntax. Recent sociolinguistic formulations of bilingual use, especially the consideration of codeswitching (the alternating use of more than one language by the bilingual), further elucidate the importance of considering more than the simple notion of linguistic input (Hymes, 1967).

Useful accounts of early childhood bilingualism must, therefore, take into consideration more than the linguistic nature of the child's language. They must consider the child's surrounding environment. These surroundings must be further differentiated according to social contexts as well as the quality and quantity of linguistic input for each language. This type of analysis should allow a more complete relationship to be drawn between linguistic input systems and bilingual development in young children.

INTELLECTUAL FUNCTIONING AND COGNITIVE DEVELOPMENT

Intelligence

After one considers the typology of linguistic input, the relationship of its processing with respect to the language learner is of extreme relevance. Based on information relating childhood bilingualism to decreased performance on standardized tests of intelligence, a statement linking the two events is tempting. As Darcy (1953, 1963) indicates, the methodological problems of studies investigating this type of relationship are serious and any conclusions concerning bilingualism and intellectual functioning (as measured by standardized individual or group intelligence tests) are extremely tentative in nature.

An extensive study reported by Lambert and Tucker (1972) comes closest to answering questions regarding multilingual acquisition and intellectual functioning (as measured by standardized tests). They report exposing English-speaking Canadian children to a four-year, French-only educational program (grades K–4). After this exposure, children's measures on standardized tests of intelligence as well as academic achievement were compared to English-speaking monolinguals (tested in English) and French-speaking monolinguals (tested in French). No significant differences were found between these linguistically different populations. This study was able to control the multitude of variables (socioeconomic group, attitude toward language, quantity and quality of educational experience) that Darcy (1963) has previously reported as common confounds in earlier studies of this type. It seems appropriate to conclude that bilingualism alone does not lead to any decreased intellectual performance as measured by standardized tests of intelligence or academic ability.

With respect to nonlinguistic tasks, a number of theoretical implications have also been generated by the compound/coordinate distinction. For instance, Saville and Troike (1971) suggest that a compound bilingual first formulates his thoughts in one language and then translates these into a second language. Cárdenas (1972) suggests that there is less mental interference in the coordinate bilingual than in compound bilingual. John and Horner (1971), after reviewing the educational literature pertaining to bilinguals, recommend the compound bilingual as the model for bilingual educational programs. As López (1977) points out, these types of statements based on an empirically weak theoretical formulation have led to a general state of confusion. Unfortunately, the byproduct of such confusion has resulted in the implicit conclusion that bilingualism is a cognitive liability.

Yet, recent theoretical and empirical attention has led to a differing view-point independent of the compound/coordinate distinction. Leopold (1939), in one of the first investigations of bilingual acquisition with young children, reported a general cognitive plasticity for his young bilingual subject. He suggested that linguistic flexibility (in the form of bilingualism) generalizes to development of cognitive tasks. Peal and Lambert (1962) in a summarization of their work with French-English bilinguals and English monolinguals also contend that the intellectual experience of acquiring two languages contributed to an advantageous mental flexibility, superiority in concept formation, and a generally diversified set of mental abilities. Padilla (1977) reasons that bilinguals must be cognitively advanced because they are able to process information in more than one language. Additionally, many bilinguals are capable of receiving information in one language, processing that information, and producing allied information in another language. I refer here to the ability of a child to understand the statement of a problem in one language, solve the problem, and produce the answer in a second language. For example, Keats and Keats (1974) report a study in which German-English bilinguals who did not exemplify weight conservation were trained to conserve in one of the two languages. Results from English and German post-tests indicated that the concept was acquired in both languages. This suggests the possible increased flexibility of bilinguals during conceptual acquisition.

Unfortunately, strong empirical support for the above theoretical formulation is scarce. Feldman and Shen (1971), Ianco-Worall (1972), Carringer (1974), and Cummins and Gulatson (1975) have begun to provide relevant evidence. Feldman and Shen (1971) report differential responding between Spanish-English bilinguals and English monolinguals across three separate cognitive tasks. The first, an object constancy task, required subjects to identify an object (a cup) after its shape had been altered (smashed) in their presence. The second, a nonsense labeling and switched-name task, required subjects to label familiar items with either nonsense words ("wug") or to switch the names of these familiar items (label a cup a "glass" and vice versa). The third, an associative sentence task, required subjects to use familiar, nonsense, and switched labels (from the second task) in a sentence describing a relation between the labeled items ("the wug is on the plate"). Results indicated significantly increased cognitive flexibility for bilinguals. Ianco-Worall (1972) compared matched bilinguals (Afrikans-English) and monolinguals (either Afrikan or English) on separation of word-sound, word-meaning tasks. Comparison of scores on these tasks indicate that bilinguals concentrated more on the meaning of the words than on the sounds. Padilla (1977) reports similar research comparing German-English and French-English bilinguals to English monolinguals on tasks of mathematical ability and verbal analogies. In each of these tasks bilinguals outperformed monolinguals. The implication of these results includes the conceptual notion of heightened semantic flexibility. The bilingual does not seem to be tied to one particular "meaning" for any one symbol but is able to generalize a functional semantic class.

A similar line of research (Carringer, 1974) examined the relationship of bilingualism to creative thinking. Four subtests of the Torrence Tests of Creative Thinking were administered to Spanish-English bilinguals and Spanish monolinguals. Comparisons indicated that flexibility, verbal originality, and figural originality were significant in favor of the bilingual. Cummins and Gulatson (1975) compared sixth-grade children in Canadian French-English bilingual programs and monolingual English programs across several measures of reasoning and divergent thinking. These children were matched for sex, socioeconomic status, and age. Bilinguals scored higher on each measure than did monolinguals.

Another interesting example of research in this general area was reported by Lambert and Tucker (1972). This study attempted to assess whether bilinguals were more "flexible" in special cases of language learning. Specifically, they asked, "Can French-English bilinguals recognize and acquire (phonetically) a third language (Russian) more effectively than English monolinguals recognize and learn (phonetically) a second language (Russian)?" Their results indicated no significant advantage on this task for bilinguals. Yet, any advantage (or disadvantage) may very well be dependent on the levels of similarity and difference between the languages. This same conclusion may be appropriate for the above-mentioned studies relating bilingualism to specific cognitive tasks. That is, *any cognitive flexibility may be associated with the particular task of interest*. Future research should more clearly delineate this formulation.

One note of caution must be expressed here. Ramírez and Castañeda's work (1974) introduced the notion of differing cultural experiences as they relate to cognitive style. In young children, bilingualism and "biculturalism" are easily confounded. As Price-Williams (1975) suggests, the study of cultural differences as it relates to psychological processes is in its infancy. It awaits the challenge of new theoretical, methodological, and technical advancement. Yet, any researcher concerned with relationships between bilingualism and cognitive development must be aware of these possible confounds.

SUMMARY

Theoretical and empirical work within bilingualism has not usually addressed early childhood bilingualism. Additionally, it has dealt with only specific instances of a bilingual's repertoire (the structural linguistic and/or semantic attributes and their development within and between languages). More recently, the influences of social and psychological cognitive processes have become important factors that must be considered. Figure 12.1 presents a descriptive account of traditional bilingualism that is in need of social and psychological expansion if it is to serve as an important theoretical and research guide. That is, any thorough theoretical proposition that is to serve as a useful research directive should consider each of these traditional linguistic attributes within an interactive model. This is not to say that individual research efforts within the designated areas will not be fruitful, but any overall view of bilingualism in childhood can only profit by joint consideration of these three areas in some form of interactive network.

Recent research with young bilinguals has been relatively compartmentalized and has taken on three distinct forms: (a) language samples are gathered; these samples are analyzed phonologically, morphologically, syntactically, and semantically for development changes correlated with age; and an analysis of language transfer is performed to indicate if, when, and how errors in either language might indicate transfer; (b) a series of linguistic problems are presented to bilingual and monolingual children in two languages and comparisons are made between languages and between subjects; (c) bilinguals and monolinguals are compared on a series of nonlinguistic tasks (for example, Piagetian conversation tasks) and/or semantically related linguistic tasks in order to identify cognitive processing differences.

This research has allowed the following tentative conclusions concerning early childhood bilingualism.

A. Bilingual Development
  1. Bilingual children are heterogeneous in the development (rate and quality) of each language.
  2. The effect of learning two languages instead of one remains unclear although no deleterious effects have been reported (except at the expressive level).
  3. Language usage in the bilingual child seems to be related to context, age, and other social variables. Linguistic input in each language also varies across these and other variables.
B. Intellectual Functioning and Cognitive Development
  1. Bilingualism (alone) is not related to decreased intellectual functioning (as measured by standardized tests of intelligence or academic achievement).
  2. Bilingualism may interact positively with some specific cognitive tasks, possibly increasing semantic flexibility.

REFERENCES

Brown, R. A. *A First Language: The Early Stages*. Cambridge: Harvard University Press, 1973.

Brown, R., and Fraser, U. "Three Processes in the Acquisition of Syntax." *Harvard Educational Review,* vol. 34, 1963, 133–51.

Cárdenas, D. N. "Compound and Coordinate Bilingualism/Biculturalism in the Southwest." In R. W. Ewton, Jr. and J. Ornstein, eds., *Studies in Language and Linguistics, 1972–73.* El Paso: The University of Texas at El Paso, 1972.

Carringer, D. C. "Creative Thinking Abilities of Mexican Youth: The Relationship of Bilingualism." *Journal of Cross-Cultural Psychology,* vol. 5, 1974, pp. 492–504.

Carrow, E. "Comprehension of English and Spanish by Preschool Mexican-American Children." *Modern Language Journal,* vol. 55, 1971, pp. 299–306.

Carrow, E. "Auditory Comprehension of English by Monolingual and Bilingual Preschool Children." *Journal of Speech and Hearing Research,* vol. 15, 1972, pp. 407–57.

Cummins, J., and Gulatson, M. "Bilingual Education and Cognition." *Alberta Journal of Educational Research,* vol. 20, 1975, pp. 259–69.

Darcy, N. T. "A Review of the Literature of the Effects of Bilingualism Upon the Measurement of Intelligence." *Journal of Genetic Psychology,* vol. 82, 1953, pp. 21–57.

Darcy, N. T. "Bilingualism and the Measurement of Intelligence: Review of a Decade of Research." *Journal of Genetic Psychology,* vol. 103, 1963, pp. 259–82.

Dissemination Center for Bilingual-Bicultural Education. *Guide to Title VII.* ESEA Bilingual Bicultural Projects, 1974.

Edelman, M. "The Contextualization of School Children's Bilingualism." *Modern Language Journal,* vol. 53, 1967, pp. 179–82.

Ervin, S. M., and Osgood, H. "Second-Language Learning and Bilingualism." *Journal of Abnormal and Social Psychology,* vol. 49, 1965, pp. 139–46.

Ervin-Tripp, S. *Language Acquisition and Communicative Choice.* Stanford, Calif.: Stanford University Press, 1973.

Evans, J. S. "Word–Pair Discrimination and Imitation Abilities of Preschool Spanish-speaking Children." *Journal of Learning Disabilities,* vol. 7, 1974, p. 573.

García, E., and Trujillo, A. "A Developmental Comparison of English and Spanish Imitation Between Bilingual and Monolingual Children." In J. V. Martínez, ed., *Chicano Psychology.* New York: Academic Press, 1977.

Harris, M. B., and Hassemer, W. G. "Some Factors Affecting the Complexity of Children's Sentences: The Effect of Modeling, Age, Sex, and Bilingualism." *Journal of Experimental Child Psychology,* vol. 13, 1972, pp. 447–55.

Haugen, E. *The Ecology of Language.* Stanford, Calif.: Stanford University Press, 1972, pp. 307–24.

Hymes, D. "Models of the Interaction of Language and Social Setting." *Journal of Social Issues,* vol. 23, 1967, pp. 8–28.

Ianco-Worall, A. "Bilingualism and Cognitive Development." *Child Development,* vol. 43, 1972, pp. 1390–400.

Jacobson, M. "Brain Development in Relation to Language." In E. Lenneberg and E. Lenneberg, eds., *Foundations of Language Development: A Multidisciplinary Approach,* vol. 1. New York: Academic Press and Paris: UNESCO Press, 1975, pp. 105–119.

John, V. P., and Horner, V. M. *Early Childhood Bilingual Education.* New York: Modern Language Association of American, 1971.

Keats, D. M., and Keats, J. A. "The Effect of Language on Concept Acquisition in Bilingual Children." *Journal of Cross-cultural Psychology,* vol. 5, 1974, pp. 70–79.

Kuo, E. C. "The Family and Bilingual Socialization: A Sociolinguistic Study of a Sample of Chinese Children in the United States." *Journal of Social Psychology,* vol. 92, 1974, pp. 181–91.

Lambert, W. E., and Rawlings, C. "Bilingual Processing of Mixed-Language Association Networks." *Journal of Verbal Learning and Verbal Behavior,* vol. 8, 1969, pp. 604–09.

Lambert, W. E., and Tucker, G. *Bilingual Education of Children: The St. Lambert Experiment.* Rowley, Mass.: Newbury House, 1972.

Leopold, W. F. *Speech Development of a Bilingual Child: A Linguist's Record.* Vol. I: *Vocabulary Growth in the First Two Years.* Evanston, Ill.: Northwestern University Press, 1939.

Leopold, W. F. *Speech Development of a Bilingual Child: A Linguist's Record.* Vol. II: *Sound Learning in the First Two Years.* Evanston, Ill.: Northwestern University Press, 1947.

Leopold, W. F. *Speech Development of a Bilingual Child: A Linguist's Record.* Vol. III: *Grammars and General Problems in the First Two Years.* Evanston, Ill.: Northwestern University Press, 1949(a).

Leopold, W. F. *Speech Development of a Bilingual Child: A Linguist's Record.* Vol. IV: *Diary from Age Two.* Evanston, Ill.: Northwestern University Press, 1949(b).

López, M. "Psycholinguistic Research and Bilingual Education." In J. V. Martínez, ed., *Chicano Psychology.* New York: Academic Press, 1977.

MacNamara, J. "The Bilingual's Linguistic Performance—A Psychological Overview." *The Journal of Social Issues,* vol. 8, 1967, pp. 58–77.

McNeil, D. "Developmental Psycholinguistics." In Frank Smith and George Miller, eds., *The Genesis of Language: A Psycholinguistic Approach.* Cambridge, Mass.: M.I.T. Press, 1966, pp. 15–84.

Milon, J. P. "The Development of Negation in English by Second Language Learners." *TESOL Quarterly,* vol. 8, 1972, pp. 137–43.

Padilla, A. M., and Liebman, E. "Language Acquisition in the Bilingual Child." *The Bilingual Review/La Revista Bilingüe,* vol. 2, 1975, pp. 34–55.

Peal, E., and Lambert, W. E. "The Relation of Bilingualism to Intelligence." *Psychological Monographs General and Applied,* vol. 76, 1962, pp. 1–23.

Penfield, W., and Roberts, C. *Speech and Brain Mechanisms.* Princeton, N.J.: Princeton University Press, 1959.

Ramírez, M., and Castañeda, A. *Cultural Democracy, Bicognitive Development, and Education.* New York: Academic Press, 1974.

Riegel, K. F. "Some Theoretical Considerations of Bilingual Development." *Psychological Bulletin,* vol. 70, 1968, pp. 647–70.

Saville, M. R., and Troike, R. C. *A Handbook of Bilingual Education.* Washington, D.C.: TESOL, 1971.

Schacter, F. F.; Kirshner, D.; Klips, B.; Friedricks, M.; and Sanders, K. "Everyday Preschool Interpersonal Speech Usage: Methodological, Development and Socio-linguistic Studies." *Monographs of Society for Research in Child Development,* 1974, p. 39.

Skrabanek, R. L. "Language Maintenance Among Mexican-Americans." *International Journal of Comparative Sociology,* vol. 11, 1970, pp. 272–82.

Sorenson, A. P. "Multilingualism in the Northwest Amazon." *American Anthropologist,* vol. 69, 1967, pp. 670–84.

U.S. Commission on Civil Rights. *Toward Quality Education for Mexican Americans: Report IV: Mexican American Education Study.* Washington, D.C.: U.S. Commission on Civil Rights, 1974.

Vildomec, V. *Multilingualism.* Leyden, Holland: A. W. Sijthoff, 1971.

Weinrich, R. *Languages in Contact.* New York: Linguist Circle of New York, 1953.

13 | The "Culture" in Bilingual/Bicultural Education

JOHN L. AGUILAR AND CARLOS J. VALLEJO

INTRODUCTION

It has been said that in attempting to provide equal educational opportunities for all citizens, regardless of their cultural backgrounds, society has assigned its schools a virtually impossible task. Unquestionably, much of the difficulty experienced in this regard is due to the clinging by educational institutions to procedures and orientations geared to the education of a unicultural society. But, like it or not, we live in a culturally plural society, and this condition demands effective and equitable educational procedures and policies.

In his book, *Blaming the Victim,* William Ryan (1976, p. 8) charged that despite the many proposed changes in educational programming, institutions of public education (including elementary and secondary schools, as well as colleges and universities) continue to occupy themselves with the development of compensatory programs for the "culturally deprived," programs that do little more than shield them from critical examination of their existing programs. Multicultural, or bilingual/bicultural, education represents a major effort to meet the challenges posed by our environment of cultural pluralism. However, it too must guard against a retreat into noncritical defensiveness. This paper reflects what we feel is a needed policy of perpetual self-criticism and evaluation intended to maintain for bilingual/cultural education a consistently growing capacity to meet the educational needs of individuals from all cultural or language populations.

Among the major responsibilities of bilingual/bicultural education are (1) the provision of a relevant educational experience for students of all ethnic backgrounds, (2) the provision of training and research activities for educators involved in bilingual/bicultural education, and (3) the delineation of differences in the cultural characteristics of particular groups and in the ways their members' needs differ from those of participants in the majority culture. The last reflects the goal of bilingual/bicultural education to adapt, at least in part, its educational strategy to the perspective of sociocultural anthropology. Given this, a central task of research must be the adaptation of anthropological tools, such as the culture concept and the ethnographic method, to the needs and circumstances of bilingual/bicultural education.

We shall argue that it is not sufficient for bilingual/bicultural education to rest its instructional program on understandings about global or modal cultural characteristics of groups. Psychology's value to education lies primarily in its ability to address individual needs, but its value for bilingual/bicultural education is limited by its failure to address the cultural environment of such needs. While anthropology does address this environment, there is, we suspect, an incompatibility between its traditional group-oriented culture concept and the technical and philosophical goals of bilingual/bicultural education, at least insofar as these pertain to the education of individuals.

More specifically, we feel that, while more compatible with the reality of cultural pluralism and the accommodation of the educational system to this reality, the traditional notion of culture may deter recognition of minority students' individuality by losing them within a conceptual framework pertaining only to properties of their ethnic group. There is, in fact, a danger that the culture concept may form the basis for sophisticated, yet erroneous, stereotypes. An example of the operation for such a stereotype in politics is seen in Stoddard's report (noted in Feagin, 1978, p. 296) that Arizona officials planning a War on Poverty program were so oriented to the anthropological model of the passive, fatalistic Chicano that they were forced to explain Chicano political activism in terms of outside agitators.

As a remedy to this situation, we propose an alternative conception of culture that better serves the educational needs of the minority student. We wish to stress, however, that we are not minimizing the value of bilingual/bicultural education's long-standing concern with inter*group* cultural differences; we wish, instead, to advance a concept of culture that permits a dual focus on both intergroup and interindividual differences (as well as similarities). We shall proceed by way of a comparison between the group- and individual-oriented concepts of culture.

THE GROUP-ORIENTED CULTURE CONCEPT

When we speak of "the culture" to which an individual belongs, our reference is generally to the system of understandings (values, prescriptions, proscriptions, beliefs, and other constructs) characteristic of that individual's society, or some subgroup within his society—that is, ethnic minorities, social classes, countercultures, generations, sexes, and occupational groups. This is the traditional notion of culture employed by functionalist anthropologists in their analyses of the behavioral patterns and normative customs of groups.

The culture concept, with its technical anthropological meaning, was first defined by Edward Tylor in 1871 as "that complex whole which includes knowledge, belief, art, law, morals, custom, and any other capabilities and habits acquired by man as a member of society . . ." (Kroeber and Kluckhohn, 1963, p. 81). Since Tylor's time a great variety of definitions of culture has been advanced by anthropologists (cf. Kroeber and Kluckhohn). These definitions commonly attempt to encompass, as did Tylor's, the totality (or some subset of the totality) of humanity's achievements, dispositions, and capabilities. And virtually every anthropologist considers culture to be something that is learned, as it is transmitted from generation to generation.

Most definitions of culture include another social dimension, the notion that culture is something that members of a group share in common. A recently published anthropology textbook states, for example, that behaviors and ideas may be considered cultural only insofar as they are shared among members of a social group (Nanda, 1980). This formulation is useful for anthropological comparisons between societies or subgroups within societies. Its basic assumption, however, is that of uniformity in the cultural equipment of individual members of societies and their subgroupings. In this formulation, the ontological locus of culture is some kind of group.

At the same time, all anthropologists acknowledge that members of all sorts and sizes of societies display differences in their behaviors and ways of thinking and valuing. That is to say, societies are characterized to some extent by intracultural heterogeneity. But such discussions remain most often at the level of the group, as in statements about the "looseness" or "tightness" of societies' cultural systems. When these researchers proceed to write their ethnographies, they tend to igmore interindividual variations as they abstract what they apparently consider to be "an essential homogeneity from the background noise of insignificant diversity" (Schwartz, 1978, p. 419).

Along these lines, anthropologist Ralph Linton defined culture as "the sum total of ideas, conditioned emotional responses and patterns of habitual behavior which the members of (a) society have acquired through instruction or imitation and which they share to a greater or less degree" (quoted in Kroeber and Kluckhohn, 1963, p. 82). Although acknowledging that cultural items (ideas or learned behavioral habits) need not be totally shared by everyone in a group, in this concept it is, nevertheless, the property of sharing that defines the domain of culture.

This emphasis on shared traits is relevant to any consideration of the conceptual requirements of bilingual/bicultural education in that, as we have indicated, there may be an incompatibility between the goals of bilingual/bicultural education and the culture concept as it has been developed for the analysis of phenomena at the group level of abstraction: It leaves little, if any, room for the conceptual recognition of each student's individuality within the framework of the culture concept. Individuality becomes the domain of psychology, relevant only to discussions of personality, while the culture concept is reserved for behavioral and ideational features of the individual's group. The latter might be appropriate to the goal of educating (or re-educating) a group, as in modernization programs applied by developing countries to their peasant populations; but, we repeat, the focus of bilingual/bicultural education is the individual student, not his or her ethnic group.

The relevance of this problem lies in the possible consequences of the group-oriented culture concept for the perceptions and expectations of teachers in their interactions with minority children. It is our contention that a group-oriented notion of culture may serve to detract the teacher's attention from the minority student's individuality and, in consequence, hinder the educational process. The connection between teacher-student interaction and the culture concept derives from the fact that assumptions about the student's "culture"—whether right or wrong—may serve to stereotype the student and thus preclude the flexible, realistic, and open-minded quality of teacher-student interaction needed for effective instruction. This possibility becomes more apparent when one realizes that the educational process is fundamentally a process of social interaction.

Picture, if you will, a situation where a teacher is perplexed by some action or response on the part of a minority student. If the teacher has studied some of the anthropological ethnographies of the student's ethnic culture he or she may leap to an interpretation of the student's behavior in terms of the idealized or modal characteristics attributed to that culture. To construe an individual's behavior solely on the basis of generalizations about group traits is to stereotype the individual, no matter how valid the generalizations or how disinterested one's intentions may be. It would be better for the teacher to pursue the meaning of the student's behavior in the way ethnographers most often come to understand the people they study. Even though they write about cultures in collective terms, they come to know about them through observations of individuals. Of course, the teacher's effort to understand the individual student could (and should) benefit from a knowledge of cultural orientations that are widely, or typically, held in the student's ethnic community. But this fund of knowledge should be viewed only as background information. The question of its applicability to the particular student should be treated as inherently problematical. Many studies (for example, Cuellar, 1980, p. 200; Avendano, 1979, p. 133) also caution educational personnel against hasty "ethnographic/cultural" generalizations on the grounds that all linguistic–cultural groups are continuously undergoing significant cultural changes.

Thomas Carter's research (1968) into the effects of teacher's expectations on student learning and classroom behavior—namely that Chicano students may sometimes actualize in their behavior the negative expectations held for them by teachers—confirms the concerns expressed here. It may be expected, of course, that this pattern would be less likely among teachers who have elected to teach in bilingual/bicultural settings. It should be noted, however, that many teachers teach in bilingual/bicultural settings even though they may not be formally designated as such. And even minority teachers may be considered to be in some ways "culturally different"—generational and acculturational differences—from the children of their own ethnic group. Guerra (1979) points to linguistic and other cultural variations both within (student-student) and between (student-teacher) generations of bilingual populations. And Cuellar (1980, p. 198) argues that one's understanding of the meaning and value of culture and language must take account of the fact that "a community's characteristics reflect the composition of the different generational cohorts in the different age strata."

THE INDIVIDUAL-ORIENTED CULTURE CONCEPT

Fortunately, anthropological theory contains a parallel individual-oriented conception of culture developed and used by a number of psychologically oriented anthropologists (for example, Devereux, Goodenough, Hallowell, Sapir, Schwartz, Spiro, and Wallace). As Ted Schwartz notes, these theorists "invoked the individual in critical response to the superorganic view of culture, which often chose metaphors which would lead one to imagine culture as floating somehow disembodied in the noösphere or, at best, carried by human beings as a conductor might carry an electric current containing information" (Schwartz, 1978, p. 434).

An early expression of the individual-oriented concept of culture is seen in the work of a now-forgotten anthropologist, J. O. Dorsey. Sapir (quoted in Pelto and Pelto, 1975, p. 1) wrote the following of Dorsey's orientation:

> Living as he did in close touch with the Omaha Indians, [Dorsey] knew that he was dealing, not with a society nor with a specimen of primitive man . . . but with a finite though indefinite, number of human beings, who gave themselves the privilege of differing from each other not only in matters generally considered as "one's own business" but even on questions which clearly transcended the private individual's concerns.

Advocates of the individual-oriented approach to culture frequently describe a society's culture as a "pool" of constructs (rules, beliefs, values) by which the society's members conceptually order the objects and events of their lives. The participation of individuals in this pool is seen as variable. Spiro (1951), for example, has distinguished between the cultural "heritage" of all members of a society (that which has been made available to them by their predecessors) and each individual's particular cultural "inheritance" (that portion of the group's heritage that he or she has effectively received, or "internalized," from the past). Ted Schwartz has stressed that the individual also manipulates, recombines, and otherwise transforms his inherited constructs. This, together with the outright creation of new constructs, is a major source of culture change (Schwartz, 1978). The individual's own portion of a society's culture is termed by Goodenough as a "propriocept" (1981), by Wallace as a "mazeway" (1970), and by Schwartz as an "idioverse" (1978). This constitutes for these anthropologists the ontological locus of culture.

For some of the anthropologists employing an individual-oriented concept of culture, "the private system of ideas of individuals *is* culture" (Pelto and Pelto, 1975, pp. 12–13). Other individual-oriented anthropologists, however, reject the implication in such a notion of "individual cultures." As they see it, the contents of one subjective system cannot be considered a culture. Like Schwartz, these theorists consider a cultural system to consist of all the constructs available to a society's members. Nevertheless, the society is itself not the locus of culture; its individual members are. The culture is a distributive phenomenon in that its elements are variably distributed among the individual members of a society. A major implication of this distributive model of culture is a rejection of the traditional assumption of cultural homogeneity; it implies that each individual's portion of the culture differs in some ways from those of the other members of the society.

At the same time, Wallace (1970) argues for what seems to be a situation of total cultural heterogeneity. To him, the traditional anthropological conception of culture connotes what he terms the "replication of uniformity," that is, through the socialization process a society's total culture is replicated within each individual. Schwartz refers to this as "swallowing one's culture whole." In this "microcosmic metaphor," to use another of Wallace's terms, all members of a society are similar in that each contains within his head the same culture. According to the individual-oriented anthropologist, this is contradicted by the fact of individual differences in every known society. Wallace argues that the task of anthropology is, therefore, not to explain how culture is replicated within individuals through socialization but to explain how diversity is organized. This includes the various psycho-cognitive mechanisms that serve to coordinate social interaction in the face of massive nonsharing between individuals.

According to Schwartz, Wallace's antidote to the homogenous view of culture is an overdose in that it leads to the opposite malady of ignoring the degree of cultural sharing that in fact *does* occur between individuals. Schwartz's own model of culture takes into account both the sharing and nonsharing of cultural constructs between members of a society, and he argues that both are functionally essential to the viability of any society. Diversity, he argues, increases a society's cultural inventory—what any individual could contain within his head would make up a very small culture pool—and commonality permits communication and coordination in social life. In Schwartz's words, "it makes as little sense to depict the distribution of a culture among the members of a society as totally heterogeneous and unique in each individual as it did to argue for complete homogeneity. We must dispense with the *a priori* assumption of homogeneity, but, similarly, we are not served by an *a priori* assumption of heterogeneity" (Schwartz, 1978, p. 438).

We view Schwartz's formulation as the most appropriate model of culture for bilingual/bicultural education since it permits, within the framework of culture, simultaneous recognition of the minority student's ethnic culture (that is, such students share with their ethnic peers constructs that are not shared with out-group members) and those characteristics that define each person as a relatively unique individual (all individuals are in some ways different from their ethnic peers). It also permits recognition of traits shared with members of the larger culture, such as those acquired through acculturation.

Schwartz's formulation stands in contrast to the traditional functionalist anthropology and sociology that, in Richard Brown's words, "presupposes a system of socially shared symbols, expectations, and protocols and then explains items of behavior in terms of this already posited system" (1977, p. 19). The distributive model of culture understands the individual to participate in the creation of meaning. Rather than taken as unambiguous, the meaning of most, if not all, of the norms and social roles of the individual's culture are continuously interpreted, and this often occurs in opposition to interpretations of his or her fellow social members. The role of culture in the behavior and thinking of the individual must therefore always be treated by the social scientist as problematic.

Acculturation is a crucial variable in the analysis of ethnic minorities in plural societies and its process contributes significantly to the fact of the heterogeneity of ethnic cultures. Writing of Chicano culture, Bell, Kasschau, and Zellman (1976) note, for example, that among Chicanos "many have ancestors who came to North America several centuries ago, but others are themselves recent immigrants. Hence, a simple cultural characterization of [this] ethnic group should be avoided" (1976, p. vii). These authors also caution against a simplistic view of the process of acculturation, noting that it "may not be linear, in the sense that one simply loses certain Mexican attributes and replaces them with Anglo attributes" (1976, pp. 31–32). The process may be characterized more by complex patterns of combination and by ongoing recombination than by simple substitution and, in addition to the fact of degrees of acculturation among individuals, would contribute to the cultural heterogeneity of the Chicano population, which is to say, the relative uniqueness of its members.

We might add, parenthetically, that some people are likely to respond to the individual-oriented conception of culture with the question, "What about customs?" Chicanos, for example, might point out to us that they recognize certain *costumbres* that distinguish them as a group from the larger society. This points to a realm of culture that is highly shared and more likely to belong to the public sphere rather than the individual's subjective orientation. Referring to the "layered" nature of culture, anthropologist Benjamin Paul (1965, p. 200) has observed that

> What we call customs rest on top and are most apparent. Deepest and least apparent are the cultural values that give meaning and direction to life. Values influence people's perceptions of needs and their choice between perceived alternative courses of action.

What we are emphasizing in this paper is the problematical nature of the variability and sharing of values and other constructs as internalized by individuals. As Schwartz and Goodenough stress, the individual's participation in culture reflects his or her unique set of life experiences. This variable participation and the relative uniqueness of the individual that it engenders is, we believe, no less important for bilingual/bicultural education than the generalized cultural differences between ethnic groups. Bilingual/bicultural education must deal with both.

At the same time we hasten to add that teachers who work with children from linguistic and/or cultural minority populations must be keenly aware of not only the instructional objectives of bilingual/bicultural education but must also be knowledgeable about and sensitive to the impact that culture and language have on the student. These affect the student both as an individual and as a member of an ethnic group. Again, bilingual/bicultural education must deal with both.

REFERENCES

Avendano, Faustino. "The Spanish Language in the Southwest: Past, Present, and Future." In Arnulfo Trejo, ed., *The Chicanos: As We See Ourselves.* Tucson: University of Arizona Press, 1979, pp. 37–39.

Bell, Duran; Kasschau, Patricia; and Zellman, Gail. *Delivering Services to Elderly Members of Minority Groups: A Critical Review of the Literature.* Santa Monica: Rand Corporation, 1976.

Brown, Richard. *A Poetic for Sociology.* New York: Cambridge University Press, 1977.

Carter, Thomas P. "The Negative Self-Concept of Mexican-American Students." *School and Society,* vol. 96, 1968, pp. 217–19.

Cuellar, Jose B. "A Model of Chicano Culture for Bilingual Education." In Raymond Padilla, ed., *Ethnoperspectives in Bilingual Education Research,* Vol. II: *Theory in Bilingual Education.* Ypsilanti, Mich.: Department of Foreign Languages and Bilingual Studies, Eastern Michigan University, 1980.

Feagin, Joe R. *Racial and Ethnic Relations.* Englewood Cliffs, N.J.: Prentice-Hall, 1978.

Goodenough, Ward H. *Culture, Language, and Society* (2nd ed.). Menlo Park, Calif.: Benjamin/Cummings Publishing Co., 1981.

Guerra, Manuel H. "Bilingualism and Biculturalism: Assets for Chicanos." In Arnulfo Trejo, ed., *The Chicanos: As We See Ourselves.* Tucson: University of Arizona Press, 1979, pp. 129–36.

Koeber, A. L., and Kluckhohn, Clyde. *Culture: A Critical Review of Concepts and Definitions.* New York: Vintage Books, 1963.

Nanda, Serena. *Cultural Anthropology.* New York: D. Van Nostrand, 1980.

Paul, Benjamin. "Anthropological Perspectives on Medicine and Public Health." In James K. Skipper Jr. and Robert C. Leonard, eds., *Social Interaction and Patient Care.* Philadelphia: J. B. Lippincott, 1965.

Pelto, Perrti, and Pelto, Gretel H. "Intra-Cultural Variation: Some Theoretical Issues." *American Ethnologist,* vol. 2, no. 1, 1975, pp. 1–45.

Ryan, William. *Blaming the Victim* (rev. ed.). New York: Vintage Books, 1978.

Schwartz, Theodore. "Where Is the Culture? Personality as the Distributive Locus of Culture." In George Spindler, ed., *The Making of Psychological Anthropology.* Berkeley: University of California Press, 1978.

Spiro, Melford E. "Culture and Personality: The Natural History of a False Dichotomy." *Psychiatry,* vol 14, 1951, pp. 19–46.

Wallace, Anthony F. C. *Culture and Personality* (2nd ed.). New York: Random House, 1970.

14 | The Impact of Bilingual-Bicultural Education Programs on the Local School District

JOHN J. HALCÓN

The signing into law of Title VII of the Elementary and Secondary Education Act in 1968 marks the beginning of bilingual-bicultural education in this country. Passage of this legislation was greeted by ebullient educators, lawmakers, and community members as one of the greatest educational innovations ever devised. The Spanish-speaking community, in particular, was enthusiastic because this legislation represented the vehicle by which the Hispano community would at last achieve equality of educational opportunity.

But, after thirteen years, the dream of bilingual-bicultural education is mired in a web of disillusionment. Not only have bilingual programs been racked by controversy since their inception, but renewed attacks on the very efficacy of bilingual instruction have gained such momentum that many advocates fear for its ultimate demise. The purpose of this paper is to explore one such controversy, the one believed to be at the core of the question of the efficacy of bilingual instruction.

THE CONTROVERSY

The dominant controversy in bilingual education policymaking today is whether or not bilingual programs meet the needs of limited- and non-English-speaking (LES/NES) pupils: Does bilingual instruction make a difference in the achievement of these pupils? This question has remained the most perennial. After ten years of experimentation in the field and reported evaluations of achievement outcomes, it has reached a new intensity with the publication of the Final Report of the Evaluation of the Impact of 38 ESEA Title VII Spanish-English Bilingual Education Programs (1978) by the American Institutes for Research (AIR). This report essentially concludes that Title VII bilingual programs are ineffective and that the programs reviewed failed to significantly improve the academic achievement levels of participating students.

Opponents of bilingual education will no doubt use these findings to justify their abhorence of utilizing a language of instruction other than English in the classroom. Proponents of bilingual education, on the other hand, have begun to react in a predictably outraged and defensive manner. One proponent (Cervantes, 1978, pp. 6–8) has attacked the finding of the report by citing everything from methodological inconsistencies to irregularities in the awarding of the contract to AIR, and a connection with the Watergate affair. This is a response in part to the AIR findings.

One has only to peruse individual program evaluation reports, professional journal articles, or the propaganda literature on bilingual education to realize the paradoxical nature of the controversy. Opponents can "prove" that bilingual education does not work by citing the AIR Report (1978). Proponents, on the other hand, can "prove" that students who are bilingual or limited speakers of English profit from instruction in their dominant language (Lambert, 1977, p. 39), and that bilinguals perform at a significantly higher level on measures of both verbal and nonverbal ability (Cummins and Gulatson, 1974 a & b). Proponents argue that if properly implemented, programs of bilingual instruction are the *modus operandi* that will guide the Spanish-speaking community toward equality of opportunity.

In the context of these arguments the development of bilingual educational policy remains controversial: (a) about the effectiveness of current policy; and (b) the direction of future policy. Policy based solely on achievement scores without consideration of other possible factors may be a narrow and inefficient perspective from which to derive bilingual program policy. Instead, I believe that additional information is needed concerning resources internal to the school district, upon which the impact of bilingual programs depends. There is no question that in bilingual education programs achievement levels of participants are not uniformly high. The AIR Report (1978) very clearly demonstrated this. Yet, individual programs—Carpintería (1977), Santa Barbara (1978), and Goleta (County Superintendent of Schools, 1978) in California, and Sante Fe (National Assessment and Dissemination Center, 1978) in New Mexico—each report significant progress in achievement in their respective programs. Accordingly, the questions that need to be answered are: Which resources when delivered to LES/NES pupils account for achievement gains? What factors affect the delivery of these resources?

The main argument of this article is as follows: between the legislation that mandates bilingual education programs and the expected outcomes of these programs, there stands the complex organization of school districts, which acts as a powerful intervening variable. Rather than viewing achievement outcomes as the primary basis upon which bilingual educational policy is derived, we should explore the antecedents to these achievement outcomes. By understanding which resources are most effective in producing learning gains among LES/NES pupils and by accounting for the conditions within the school district organization that affect the delivery of those resources, we may be in a position to develop more cogent policy for bilingual education. The provision of information concerning the organizational factors that affect the flow of pertinent resources to LES/NES pupils may begin to dissipate the controversy surrounding the efficacy of bilingual instruction.

To focus more clearly and productively on the complex dynamics of the school district, a political economy framework is utilized (Zald, 1970, p. 222). This framework for the study of change in complex organizations is a middle-range theory of organizational dimensions. Moreover, it is a useful theoretical framework for comparative study.

THE EFFECT OF CLASSROOM RESOURCES UPON PROGRAM IMPACTS

A review of the literature indicates that the allocation of some resources are highly correlated with positive achievement gains among LES/NES pupils. Further, a review of various evaluation reports of successful[1] Title VII Bilingual Projects indicates that in individual programs, there exists a high correlation between positive achievement gains and the utilization of these resources.

Teacher Competence

There have been many attempts to relate teacher process variables to pupil gain scores (Rosenshine and Furst, 1971; Medley and Mitzel, 1959; Brophy, 1975; and Calkins et al., 1976). In fact, Wideen et al. (1959, p. 1) report that there is a long history of studies attempting to identify characteristics of teachers whom students perceived as "good teachers." But in many cases, research on teacher effects have been inconsistent in their conclusions (Brophy, 1975; Calkins et al., 1976; Shavelson and Dempsey, 1977). There have been consistent results, however, when pupil achievement has been related to teacher competency variables.

Calkins et al. (1976, p. 5) report that one line of research on teaching is the "effectiveness paradigm," which uses achievement outcomes as a measure of teacher effectiveness. Importantly, Burstein and Linn (1977, p. 2) specify that regarding the effects of the school, the resources an individual receives, the individual's background, and the influence of his community setting are phenomena that also affect pupil outcomes. Shavelson and Dempsey (1977, p. 5) suggest that under certain conditions some teachers may be more effective than others, and some teachers may also be more effective with particular groups of students. Cruickshank (1976, p. 59) and Brophy (1975, p. 11) both support these notions. By comparing task situations in both low and high socioeconomic status (SES) schools, they suggest that the teaching approach for either type of school may be vastly different. They found that successful teachers in high SES schools were task-oriented and had high expectations for their pupils, while in low SES schools, the successful teacher had to be more willing to take up personal matters with pupils and had to be more supportive of them. They were also found to have high expectations for their pupils.

Coupled with the trend for accountability in teaching and competency-based education programs, the relationship between effectiveness in teaching and achievement scores takes on a new significance for the classroom teacher. Cruickshank (1976, p. 59) argues that among the most promising variables related to reading and math achievement are: (1) use of small group interaction; (2) maximum direct interaction, which includes monitoring and individual feedback; and (3) the use of a variety of instructional materials.

Roberts and Becker (1976, p. 193) in a study of teaching effectiveness in industrial education suggest that measures of communication including dynamism, presentation skills, time spent interacting with students, and frequency of praise and banter are important variables. They find (p. 195) that "effective teachers constantly move from group to group, . . . the relationship between teachers and pupils is warm and supportive, . . . there is a great deal of positive reinforcement . . . and teachers tended to display confidence in the ability of their students."

Goodman and Hammond (1977, p. 208) in a study of learning-disabled children strongly imply that (special education) teachers need to be especially adept in their field in order to successfully teach academic skills. They argue that this cannot be done if the teacher does not have a thorough understanding of the skills they intend to teach. Roberts and Becker (1976, p. 196) conclude that personal example is an important variable that modifies the behavior of students and influences their work. "Whether consciously or unconsciously, students tend to model themselves after the teacher, whether the teacher is good or bad."

Dual-Language Competence of the Staff

Consistent as a criterion of effectiveness of the Title VII Programs surveyed is the dual-language competency of the staff. Each of the successful programs reported that the majority of their staff was bilingual, and either currently held a bilingual credential, a certificate of competency or were enrolled in a program leading to the certificate. In the Santa Fe project, all staff, instructional aides, teachers, principals, the project director, the instructional materials coordinator, and the project secretary were bilingual. The Goleta project reports that all staff, with the exception of four pre-school teachers, were bilingual. The Carpintería project reports that of eight teachers in the project, five were bilingual, and all eleven aides were bilingual. The Santa Barbara project reports that of the fifteen teachers in the program, nine were bilingual; and of the sixteen instructional aides, fourteen were bilingual. A perusal of the AIR project descriptions (1977b) indicates that the majority of the staff in each program are reported to be either bilingual or of Hispanic origin. Unfortunately, the programs fail (as does the AIR report) to operationally define the extent of "bilinguality" of the staff. The fact of the matter is, according to Cervantes (1978, p. 19), that "no more than 23% of the programs' staff evaluated by AIR actually hold bilingual credentials."

Parent Involvement

The literature suggests that the active involvement of parents in the school district is highly correlated with the achievement outcomes. Fischer, Frederickson, and Rosa (1976, p. 1) find that the active involvement of parents in the operation of bilingual education programs as teacher aides, school/community representatives, and members of advisory councils was one measure of the success of a bilingual program.

The Title VII projects reported a high degree of involvement of their "program" parents. Carpintería (1977) reports that there is good community support for its program, and the Goleta project (1977–78) conducts a very active parent education program. The remaining programs also report active participation by their respective parent groups and community.

The majority of programs evaluated by AIR (February, 1977b) indicated that the involvement of project parents was minimal. In those programs where parents were involved, they were limited to participating in social activities and outings. One project did report that there is significant parent participation in school board and bilingual advisory committee meetings, and another reported that many of the parents are involved directly in the classroom.

Bilingual Curriculum as a Medium of Instruction

One of the most controversial issues encountered in education is a question of the efficacy of a bilingual curriculum as a medium of instruction. Cummins and Gulatson (1974b) report that bilinguals perform significantly higher on measures of both verbal and nonverbal intelligence. And, on tasks of concept formation, Liedke and Nelson (1968) found that bilingual children performed significantly better than monolingual children. Lepke (1974) further suggests that children generally achieve high levels of competence in their dominant language when there is no danger of replacement by a second language. Her analysis (1977, p. 5) also suggests that a child's cognitive learning experiences are affected by the level of competency that the child achieves in both languages.

The Title VII projects surveyed report findings supportive of these research studies. The Carpintería project (1977, p. 80) reports that achievement in reading is not suffering as a result of project participation and perhaps is being enhanced. The Santa Barbara project (1978, p. 183) reports that the bilingual students performed better in English than either the Spanish-dominant and the English-dominant student, and they performed better in Spanish than the Spanish-dominant student. The Goleta project (County Superintendent of Schools, 1978, p. 152) concludes that the results of its evaluation report tend to support the concept of developing the child's dominant language well before introducing the second language as a viable approach to educating their children. The Santa Fe project (National Assessment and Dissemination Center, 1978, p. 4) reports that the use of Spanish as a medium of instruction oscillated between 30 percent and 50 percent of the day. The strong correlation of the use of two languages as a medium of instruction between the "positive" research findings and the evaluation reports of successful programs suggest that this particular variable may be one important indicator of the relative success or nonsuccess of bilingual programs.

Classroom Methods and Structure

The relative value of certain classroom methods to the success of a program is highlighted by the Title VII Bilingual Projects. The Carpintería (1977, p. 19), Santa Barbara (1978, p. 27), and Goleta (County Superintendent of Schools, 1978, p. 25) projects each report the development of domain-referenced achievement tests that are especially useful because students in the respective projects were at different levels of development and thus they stressed individual instruction.

The literature suggests that varying classroom strategies are necessary for different learning styles of individuals, and the literature also reports on the various impacts of classroom methods/structures on achievement. Giordano (1977, p. 39) believes that there are optimal methods of teaching bilingual children to read. Ideally, an optimal method would build on basic communicative strategies that are compatible with the major channel of language processing. Marshall (1977, p. 9) reports that classroom structure and adequacy of implementation appear to be associated with reading scores.

Stability of Staff

An important indicator of a successful bilingual program, as suggested by the Title VII programs analyzed, is the stability of the staff, or the number of years the particular staff has worked with the respective programs. The Goleta project (County Superintendent of Schools, 1978) reports that its director has been operating the program for the last seven years, while the Carpintería project

(1977, p. 18) reports that the director has been with the project since the inception of its program. In turn, the Santa Barbara project (1978, p. 25) felt that one of the weaknesses in the district's bilingual program was lack of consistent leadership, while the Santa Fe bilingual program (National Assessment and Dissemination Center, 1978, p. 3) reports that the year-to-year improvement of its project can be attributed to the great stability enjoyed by its staff. In this particular case, the director has been with the project since its inception (seven years).

AIR (1977b) reported that the overwhelming majority of teachers in the project evaluated had been with their respective projects three years or less. And a significant portion of those were in their first year of teaching in the bilingual program.

Length of Student Involvement in the Bilingual Program

Another important resource or indicator of a "successful" program is the actual number of years that the pupil has been involved with the respective project. The conclusions reached by the Santa Fe Bilingual Project (1978, ii) indicate that over time, the Title VII students showed increasing capability in English language skills (particularly in reading) and in mathematics. The Title VII students over time also outperformed, in the majority of cases, the non-Title VII students in reading and math, and one group studied surpassed and/or matched national norms in reading and in math. The Santa Barbara project (1978) reports that after four years of bilingual instruction test results show that the pupils appear to be meeting program expectations (p. 41) and that, as the grade level increases, more students in the programs are reading at higher levels as measured by the CLOZE tests (p. 80). Moreover, the third-year Spanish-surnamed students seemed to do better than did first- or second-year students, and in a number of instances, the English-dominant students were performing at higher levels as the number of years in the program increased. The Carpintería project (1977, p. 51) reports that there is a slight increase in performance for number of years in the program. And, the Goleta bilingual project (County Superintendent of Schools, 1978, p. 89) reports that, generally, the third-year pupils, in all comparison groups, achieved at a higher level than did the second-year students at the same grade level.

The review of the literature on classroom resources and their impact on program outcomes suggests that strong relationships do exist. Achievement gains are influenced by the allocation and utilization of particular resources. A survey of several Title VII projects suggests that particular resources are effective indicators of successful programs. Specifically, the following resources appeared consistent in their association with program success as measured by individual student outcomes:

1. teacher competence
2. dual-language competencies of the staff
3. parent involvement
4. bilingual (English/Spanish) as a medium of instruction
5. classroom methods and structure
6. stability of staff
7. number of years the student has been in the project

It is not my position that these resources are the only indicators of "successful" bilingual projects nor do I mean to imply that, in and by themselves, they will constitute a successful program. These are, at best, some indicators of success, and it is reasonable to assume that there exists a universe of resources, as yet unexplored, that would serve a similar purpose.

Granting that certain resources do affect achievement gains, let us now shift focus and explore how the school district organization affects the delivery of these resources to their clients. It is our hope that if we can understand the conditions under which an organization makes decisions to allocate or to utilize particular resources, then we can more clearly begin to understand the strengths and weaknesses of that organization when success of a program is measured by achievement outcomes.

THE POLITICAL ECONOMY OF THE LOCAL SCHOOL DISTRICT

The local school district can, of course, be characterized as a complex organization. As such, it can be analyzed from various perspectives. The political economy approach to the analysis of complex organizations leads us to focus on the school district as an organization in which change arises as a result of both internal and external processes (Wamsley and Zald, 1973, p. 16). The dominant concern of this model is with the political and economic processes of the organization. This model of analysis is concerned with the interactions of various properties of the organization such as the values of those in power; the supply of resources; the demand for services by clients; and organizational responses to a changing society (Zald, 1970, p. 224). More traditional concerns of organizational analysis are subordinated and are only important insofar as they articulate with the political and economic process (Zald, 1970, p. 225). Thus, the school district is conceptualized as consisting of an internal and external polity and of an internal economy. (See figure 14.1 for a model of the political economy of the school district organization).

It is important to clarify at this point that it is not our interest, nor is it necessary for the present purposes, to present an exhaustive theory about the political economy of the local school district. Our purpose is a more limited

Figure 14.1: Model of the Political Economy of the School District Organization

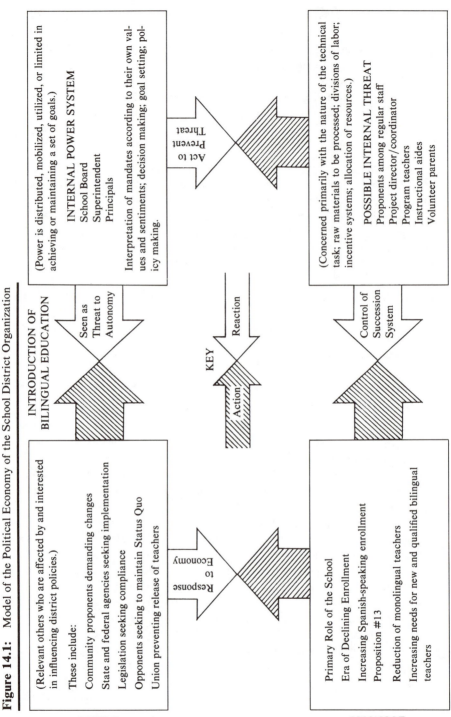

POLITY

(Relevant others who are affected by and interested in influencing district policies.)

These include:

Community proponents demanding changes
State and federal agencies seeking implementation
Legislation seeking compliance
Opponents seeking to maintain Status Quo
Union preventing release of teachers

INTRODUCTION OF BILINGUAL EDUCATION

Seen as Threat to Autonomy

(Power is distributed, mobilized, utilized, or limited in achieving or maintaining a set of goals.)

INTERNAL POWER SYSTEM

School Board
Superintendent
Principals

Interpretation of mandates according to their own values and sentiments; decision making; goal setting; policy making.

Act to Prevent Threat

KEY

Reaction

Action

Response to Economy

Control of Succession System

ECONOMY

Primary Role of the School
Era of Declining Enrollment
Increasing Spanish-speaking enrollment
Proposition #13
Reduction of monolingual teachers
Increasing needs for new and qualified bilingual teachers

(Concerned primarily with the nature of the technical task; raw materials to be processed; divisions of labor; incentive systems; allocation of resources.)

POSSIBLE INTERNAL THREAT

Proponents among regular staff
Project director/coordinator
Program teachers
Instructional aides
Volunteer parents

one: to illustrate the pertinence of the mechanisms of this particular model for the study of bilingual educational programs. In effect, I am asking the question: How does the school district react to the introduction of bilingual-bicultural education programs?

In utilizing this model, the aim is to illustrate how the political economy of the local school district affects the delivery of those resources within the school district that, in turn, determine the success or failure of a bilingual instructional program. Since space does not permit a detailed illustration of how the political economy of local school districts affects the various resources, the focus will be on one type of resource, namely staff competency.

Medley (1977, p. 6) suggests that observed measures of effectiveness are indicators of teacher competence; teachers who are more effective are also more competent. Therefore, a strong relationship between teacher effectiveness and a particular behavior can be interpreted as indicating that such behavior is characteristic of competent teachers. Shavelson and Dempsey (1977, p. 607) believe that certain teaching behaviors are more effective with certain groups of students; they suggest that teacher effectiveness, as measured by pupil outcomes, may depend on the luck of matching a teacher with a particular group of students.

Internal Polity and Bilingual Programs

The internal polity of an organization is defined as the internal power system of the organization (Zald, 1970, p. 237). It is the systematic manner in which power is distributed, mobilized, utilized, or limited in achieving or maintaining a set of goals or values. When a bilingual program is introduced to a district, organizational elites (school boards, superintendents, principals) often view it as a threat to the internal environment of the organization. In particular, when changes are advocated by minority groups, they are often perceived as politically motivated and institutionally threatening (Teitelbaum and Hiller, 1977, p. 11).

The threat to the internal structure of the organization posed by bilingual programs has two sources: first, there are the external sources such as community proponents of the program, state or federal agencies, and legislation (the external polity); second, there are the internal sources such as program proponents among the regular staff, the project director, teachers, aides, and volunteer parents (the internal economy). The external sources limit the options of the executive elites and, in so doing, pose a threat to their autonomy. However, it is the internal sources that are the most threatening to the school district.

Organizational change is inevitable when bilingual programs are introduced to the school district. The nature of its client group, the goals of its curriculum, the sources of its funding, and the character of its advocates all require change.

Change, in turn, affects district policy, products, educational goals, existing technology, and interunit relations. But district elites, not wishing to lose control of their power and, in response to threats to their long-held values and sentiments, will oppose any change. One way in which they oppose it is through the process of succession. When changes in district policy by state and federal legislation are mandated, the district elite (though bound by the law) will interpret those mandates (as much as their power will allow) in favor of their own values and sentiments. This process of interpretation does not preclude attempts on their part to sabotage the spirit and intent of the legislation. In no place is this sabotage more apparent than in the structures and processes of the succession system.

The standard pattern of recruiting key personnel is determined both by the perceived requirements of top officers and the opportunities to develop those competencies provided in the organization (Zald, 1970, p. 247). District elites recruit both project directors and teachers whose values and inclinations most closely resemble their own. Very often competent bilingual teachers will not be hired if the district elite see them as a potential threat to the internal polity. It is not surprising, therefore, that the state of California reports that only 37 percent of all bilingual classroom teachers were able to demonstrate skill awareness and applicability in the students' primary language.

Project directors are often brought up through the ranks into a directorship directly from the classroom with little or no administrative experience. And more often than not, they have no say in the decision-making process of the program activities, have no control over the budgets, hiring of program teachers or aides, or even the goals of the program. Given this pattern of recruitment in bilingual programs, a pattern that has its basis in the internal polity of school district organizations, it is clear that bilingual programs have, at least in this respect, been programmed to fail on the basis of administrative incompetence.

The Internal/External Economies and Bilingual Programs

Economies of an organization are systems for producing and exchanging goods. The internal economy of the school district is mainly concerned with the nature of the technical task, that is, with the raw materials to be processed, the divisions of labor and incentive systems necessary to task accomplishment, and the allocation of resources.

In an era of declining enrollment (less and less children, overall, are attending school), and teacher reduction (Commission for Teacher Preparation and Licensing, 1978, p. 2), there is an increasing need for new and qualified bilingual teachers. McCurdy (1978) reports that the steady decline in overall enrollment will continue in California. The Office of the Superintendent of Public Instruction (1978, p. 10) estimates that while the Anglo student population is steadily declining, the LES/NES student population is gradually increasing. Moreover, with the recently proposed cutback in state spending caused by Proposition 13, the teachers' unions are increasingly pressuring the school districts not to release teachers who otherwise would be laid off because of declining enrollment. Instead, there is pressure to place them in other programs. These "other programs" are actually the bilingual program classroom.

The utilization of monolingual (English-speaking) teachers for bilingual programs has been, and continues to be, a very real option for the overwhelming majority of school districts of California. Federal bilingual legislation makes no requirement that bilingual program teachers actually be "bilingual"; it does, however, recognize the lack of "adequately trained" professional personnel. Schneider (1977, p. 184) has estimated, from a sampling of Title VII projects across the country, a total need for roughly 35,000 trained bilingual teachers, while there were only 9,000 teachers in Title VII projects. Similarly, in the case of the state of California there is a projected high level of demand for bilingual teachers and a projected substantial shortfall of such teachers (Commission for Teacher Preparation and Licensing, 1978, p. 27). While California (Chacón-Moscone, 1976) does not require that bilingual program teachers be "competent" in light of the teacher shortage, the law permits districts to waive the competency standard for a period of two years provided that nonqualified teachers are enrolled in programs of competency development.

The consequence of this situation is that in some districts choosing not to teach in the bilingual program is tantamount to not teaching at all. In at least one district of which I am aware, most monolingual teachers did not want to be in the bilingual program and were opposed to the concept of bilingual instruction. Yet, given declining enrollment in this particular district, and because they were not seen as an internal threat by the district, they were given the option of teaching in the bilingual program or not teaching at all. Needless to say, they chose to teach. Thus, for the monolingual teacher, having to teach in a bilingual classroom became a negative incentive, which was also interpreted as a negative sanction; in effect, they were "dumped" into the program. Given these conditions, under which many monolingual teachers are transferred into bilingual programs, there appears to be operating, in effect, a system of negative incentives that may be importantly undermining the effectiveness of bilingual programs.

External Polity and Bilingual Programs

The external polity of an organization is defined as those groups or positions that have an active and somewhat organized influence on the process of decision-making (Zald, 1970, p. 233). The relationship between "relevant others" (in this case proponents and opponents of bilingual instruction, who are affected by and interested in influencing the policies for which the district has primary responsibilities) forms the basis for the external polity.

The introduction of bilingual programs into a school district affects the external political environment of the school district. Where once the amount and distribution of limited resources to district-approved and community-sanctioned programs were the political norm, the imposition of mandated programs of instruction designed primarily for the nontypical pupil has upset the balance of the existing political relationship of the district. The "relevant others" that make up the policy subsystems are forced to reassess their political "niche" (Wamsley and Zald, 1973, p. 26). That is, they are forced to choose between the lesser of the two evils, irrespective of the effect on the program children. A case in point is the conflicting interests of the school district in relation to teachers' unions and bilingual proponents. Whose interests take precedence, those of the mandated bilingual program, and the needs of its clients, or those of the powerful teacher union and its client, the classroom teacher? In this political question, there exists a dilemma.

As mentioned previously, (a) the State Bilingual Education Act (Chacón-Moscone, 1976) stipulated that all teachers in bilingual educational programs in California must be "competent," and (b) Anglo student enrollments in California are declining significantly, while LES/NES students are increasing dramatically. In its relationship with the teachers' union, this situation affects the school district in a most pernicious manner. The district finds itself in the position of either violating a legal mandate or of violating a legitimate and legal contract with the teachers' union. In its relationship to the external policy, the school district is under pressure to fulfill its primary mission, that of teaching the children, while trying to satisfy its political and legal responsibilities. Assuming that the district decides to hire additional competent teachers, the unions will balk at the possibile release of member teachers who are not effective but are tenured. Among other things, this raises serious questions about the commitment of the school district to bilingual education. If, on the other hand, the district moves ineffective teachers into bilingual programs, it can expect the state or "relevant others" to raise questions of noncompliance, which is exactly what prompted the signing into law of AB-1329 (the Chacón-Moscone Bill) in 1976, and the subsequent controversies surrounding its competency requirements. What options are left to the school district? Whose interests will the district serve? At what expense?

This discussion of the political economy of the local school district and bilingual programs is meant to illustrate the complexities of the effects of bilingual education on the school district. Clearly, it is not meant to be an elaboration of the parameters of that complexity, but only serves to highlight, from a complex organizations' perspective, a limited number of potential processes and problems, whose interrelationships must be understood if policy makers are to derive useful data from which to make clear decisions about bilingual policy. It is entirely too simplistic to look exclusively to educational program impact, as measured by achievement gains, as the single valid basis of policy decisions.

The political economy model of change in complex organizations provides a useful perspective because it allows a more "inclusive" view of the organizational dynamic, which takes in limited- and non-English-speaking pupils and is expected to "teach" them. Unfortunately, knowing that an impact has been positive only tells us that whatever we are doing may be working; if the impact is negative, however, we only know that what we are doing is not working. This is insufficient for the purposes of determining policy. The questions that need to be answered are, Why does a program work? What are the characteristics of a program that account for achievement gains? Under what conditions can we expect a program to "succeed"?

When we begin to answer these questions, then the larger issue of the efficacy of bilingual instruction as an educational alternative for the LES/NES pupil will be better understood. Until such time, we can expect the controversies that have surrounded bilingual education since its inception to continue.

NOTE

1. The following criteria were established by the California Title VII programs as indicators of "success" in their respective programs: (1) The bilingual program is helping and/or at least not interfering with academic achievement; (2) The program is enhancing the achievement of all students, English-dominant as well as Spanish-dominant and bilingual.

REFERENCES

American Institutes for Research (AIR). *Evaluation of the Impact of ESEA Title VII Spanish/English Bilingual Education Project.* Vol. 1: *Study Design and Interim Findings.* Palo Alto, Calif., February 1977(a).

American Institutes for Research (AIR). *Evaluation of the Impact of ESEA Title VII Spanish/English Bilingual Education Project.* Project Descriptions. Palo Alto, Calif., February 1977(b).

American Institutes for Research (AIR). *Evaluation of the Impact of ESEA Title VII Spanish/English Bilingual Education Project.* Final Report. Palo Alto, Calif., 1978.

Brophy, Jere E. *Teacher Behaviors Related to Learning by Low vs. High Socio-economic Status Early Childhood Students.* Report No. 75-5. National Institute of Education (DHEW), Washington, D.C., d. 75. Paper presented at the Annual Meeting of the American Educational Research Association, Washington, D.C., April 1975.

Burstein, Leigh, and Linn, Robert L. *The Identification of Teacher Effects in the Presence of Heterogenous Within-Class Relations of Input to Outcomes.* Paper presented at the 61st Annual Meeting of the American Educational Research Association, New York: April 4–8, 1977.

Calkins, Dick; Godbout, Robert; Lee, H. Poyner; and Kagle, C. L. *Relationships Between Pupil Achievement and Characteristics of Observed Teacher Behavior Distributions.* Research Report No. 6. Austin: University of Texas, Research and Development Center for Teacher Education, January 6, 1976.

Carpintería Unified School District, Carpintería, California. *Evaluation of the Carpintería Bilingual Project Funded Under ESEA Title VII, PL-89-10* (Project Number 403 CH 70085). Final Report 1976–77, November 1977.

Cervantes, Robert. "An Exemplary Consafic Chingatropic Assessment: The AIR Report." Paper presented at Association of Mexican-American Educator's Conference, San Francisco, California, October 26–28, 1978.

Chacón-Moscone, A. *Bilingual-Bicultural Education Act of 1976.* AB 1329. Section 1. Chapter 57.6 added to Division 6 of Education Code. Sub Section 5757.10 State of California, 1976.

Commission for Teacher Preparation and Licensing. *Report on the Supply of and Demand for Bilingual Teachers in School Districts in California.* Presented to the California State Legislature, September 1, 1978.

County Superintendent of Schools, Santa Barbara County, Santa Barbara, California. *Evaluation of the Goleta Bilingual Project Funded Under Title VII, PL-89-10* (Project Number 403 CH 80031). Final Report 1977–78, November 1978.

Cruickshank, Donald R. "Synthesis of Selected Recent Research in Teacher Effects." *Journal of Teacher Education,* vol. 27, no. 1, Spring 1976, pp. 57–60.

Cummins, J., and Gulatson, M. "Some Effects on Bilingualism in Cognitive Functioning." In S. Carey, ed., *Bilingualism, Biculturalism and Education.* Alberta, Canada: The University of Alberta, 1974(a).

Cummins, J., and Gulatson, M. "Bilingual Education and Cognition," *Alberta Journal of Educational Research,* vol. 20, 1974(b), pp. 259–66.

Fischer, Joseph; Frederickson, Charles; and Rosa, Carlos. *Parents' Career Aspirations for Their Children Enrolled in Bilingual Programs.* Monograph No. 2. Chicago: Chicago Board of Education, Department of Research and Evaluation, March 1976.

Giordano, Gerard. *Neurological Research on Language and the Implications for Teaching Bilingual Children to Read.* Carbondale, Ill.: Proceedings of the International Conference of Frontiers in Language Proficiency and Dominance Testing, Southern Illinois University, April 13–21, 1977.

Goodman, Gay, and Hammond, Brad. "An Assessment of Phonics Knowledge in Special Education Teachers." *Reading Horizons,* vol. 17, no. 2, Winter 1977, pp. 206–10.

Lambert, Wallace E. "The Effects of Bilingual Education on the Individual Cognitive and Sociocultural Consequences." Cited in Caroline A. Korn, *Teaching Language Through Science in a Primary Bilingual Classroom.* Master's thesis, University of San Francisco, 1977, p. 39.

Lepke, Helen S. "Discovering Student Learning Styles Through Cognitive Style Mapping." In Renata A. Schulz, ed., *Personalized Foreign Language Instruction*

Learning Styles and Teaching Options. Rowley, Mass.: Newbury House Publishers, Inc., 1974.

Liedke, W. W., and Nelson, L. D. "Concept Formation and Bilingualism." *Alberta Journal of Educational Research,* vol. 14, 1968, pp. 225–32.

Marchall, Hermine E. *Variations in Classroom Structure and Growth in Reading.* Paper presented at the Annual Meeting of the American Psychological Association, San Francisco, August 1977.

McCurdy, Mack. "Segregation in Schools Grows, Survey Reveals." *The Los Angeles Times,* October 19, 1978.

Medley, D. M. *Teacher Competence and Teacher Effectiveness: A Review of Process-Product Research.* Washington, D.C.: American Association of Colleges for Teacher Education, August 1977.

Medley, D. M., and Mitzel, H. E. "Some Behavioral Correlates of Teacher Effectiveness." *Journal of Educational Psychology,* vol. 50, 1959, pp. 239–46.

National Assessment and Dissemination Center, School of Education, California State University, Los Angeles. *Longitudinal Study of Title VII Bilingual Program,* Santa Fe Public Schools, Santa Fe, New Mexico, June 9, 1978.

Office of the Superintendent, Santa Barbara County School, Santa Barbara. *Planning and Implementing Bilingual/Bicultural Programs: A Handbook for School Administrators,* June 1976.

Public Law 90-247, Title VII ESEA. *The Bilingual Education Act of 1968.*

Roberts, Churchill L., and Becker, Samuel L. "Communication and Teaching Effectiveness in Industrial Education." *American Educational Research Journal,* vol. 13, no. 3, Summer 1976, pp. 181–97.

Rosenshine, B., and Furst, N. "The Use of Direct Observation to Study Teaching." In R. Travers, ed., *Second Handbook of Research in Teaching.* Chicago: Rand McNally, 1971.

Santa Barbara School District, Santa Barbara, California. *Evaluation of the Santa Barbara Elementary Schools Bilingual Project Funded Under ESEA Title VII, PL-89-10* (Project Number 403 DH 60186). Final Report, November 1978.

Schneider, Susan G. *Revolution, Reaction, or Reform: 1974 Bilingual Education Act,* New York: Las Americas, 1977.

Shavelson, Richard, and Dempsey, Nancy. *Generalizability of Measures of Teacher Effectiveness and Teaching Process: Beginning Teacher Evaluation Process.* Technical Series Reports No. 75-4-2. San Francisco: Far West Lab for Educational Research and Development, 1977.

Superintendent of Public Instruction. *Education for Limited English Speaking and Non-English Speaking Students.* Part II. Presented to California State Board of Education, July 1978.

Tietelbaum, Herbert, and Hiller, Richard J. "Bilingual Education: The Legal Perspective." *Current Perspectives: Law,* vol. 3. Rosslyn, Va.: Center for Applied Linguistics, September 1977.

Wamsley, Gary L., and Zald, Mayer N. *The Political Economy of Public Organizations: A Critique and Approach to the Study of Public Administration.* Lexington, Mass.: D.C. Heath, 1973.

Wideen, Marvin F.; Kennedy, Barry J.; and Bettschen, Catherine. "The Identification of Teacher Process Variables Affecting Student Outcomes in Two Alternative Science Curriculum Treatment Settings." Paper presented at the Annual Meeting of the American Educational Research Association, New York, April 4–8, 1977.

Zald, Mayer N. "Political Economy: A Framework for Comparative Analysis." In Mayer N. Zald, ed., *Power in Organizations*. Nashville, Tenn.: Vanderbilt University, 1970, p. 222.

V | Future Chicano Studies Research

Overview

Today, the discipline of Chicano Studies continues to develop and exert influence. In the absence of developments such as the elimination of Chicano Studies programs and through the persevering efforts of scholars in the field, such as those whose contributions are reflected in this volume, the discipline will continue to grow. The discipline will continue to shape knowledge and thinking about the experience, status, needs, problems, and aspirations of the Mexican population in the United States and influence the development of public policies toward Chicanos.

In the concluding article in this volume, Raymond Rocco addresses a number of questions related to aspects of the future of Chicano Studies research. These questions include: What should be the nature of research in Chicano Studies? Should it be theoretical or atheoretical? What conceptions of academic research should serve as its point of departure? What bodies of theory, if any, have the potential for enabling students of the Mexican experience to generate bodies of insights that will help to better understand the experience of the Mexican population, and facilitate the development of strategies for dealing with its problems?

In his article, Rocco calls for research informed by an understanding of the significance and role of theory in research. In the past, he argues, adequate attention has not been given to this issue. In an attempt to help correct this situation and stimulate discussion, Rocco clarifies the concept of theory, spec-

253

ifies the inadequacies of the popular conception of theory, and identifies the traditional approach to understanding the experience of people of Mexican descent in the United States and the approach's shortcomings. He then spells out the essential elements of an alternative to traditional theory. This alternative is rooted in the tradition of critical theory. It is an alternative, Rocco suggests, that can contribute to the development of the knowledge Chicano Studies has sought to produce since its creation, knowledge that can help us understand the experience of the Mexican population and facilitate efforts to improve its standing in American society.

15 | Chicano Studies and Critical Political Theory

RAYMOND A. ROCCO

The development of the field of Chicano Studies now seems to have reached a point where its legitimacy, at least among its practitioners, is no longer a primary animating question to be addressed. Scholars investigating the experiences of the Mexican people in the United States are now found in universities and colleges throughout the nation. Although small in number when compared to faculty in other fields, they nevertheless continue to add significantly to our knowledge-base regarding Chicanos. This does not mean, of course, that Chicano Studies centers or departments have finally been accepted by the traditional disciplines as their equal; it does not, moreover, imply that the blatant efforts on many campuses to either ignore or eliminate the teaching and/or research programs of Chicano Studies, have either ceased or diminished in intensity. If anything, the situation is quite to the contrary.

Despite the growth of Chicano Studies, the role of theory in research in the field has remained underexamined. Theory has not received the attention or study to insure that the efforts to develop Chicano Studies will in fact promote the values that we subscribe to and be methodologically grounded. We have uncritically, and in many instances unconsciously, accepted the assumption that the commitment to "objective" truths or "facts" will somehow automatically result in the expansion of liberties and/or opportunities for Chicanos. We have often not asked what this norm of "objective" truth means or if it is possible to attain. This question cannot be answered through the mere accumulation of information or discrete bits of data, but requires in essence a theoretical discussion. Therefore, this article not only attempts to suggest the role that theory plays in Chicano Studies, but it is also written with the intention of creating dialogue to discuss, dispute, and explore this issue collectively.

My primary purpose is to delineate the general role that theory plays in social inquiry and to suggest particularly how the perspective of critical political theory can illuminate issues and problems that might not otherwise be addressed in the area of Chicano Studies. As such, this study does not mean to deal with the substance of the Chicano experience, that is, with the history, politics, or economics of the Mexican population in the United States. Instead, it focuses on demonstrating what theory is and why it is absolutely necessary for us, as students of the field, to be familiar with the nature of theory as well as to know what is at stake in choosing a theory for our study. The primary goal is to explicitly address the often unspoken assumption that the only subject matter that ought to be included in the field of Chicano Studies is the substantive historical experiences of Chicanos. Since it is not possible to conduct these studies without *some* categories or theories, we need to discuss what theories and categories are, and how these—even before we begin the actual substantive study—incline us to define "problems" and "solutions" in specific ways. What follows is equally valid for all social inquiry, of which Chicano Studies is one component. Thus, the intent of this article is not to discuss some specific aspect of our history but to deal with what theory is and why we need to reflect on it.

I refer to the approach here as "critical" in order to pose the question of what it is we think we are doing when we assume we are developing or engaging in social inquiry. The term "political" will be utilized in the sense of asking what relationship exists between this "what we are doing" and the arena of power, considered as the primary defining characteristic or dimension of the political realm. This essay will concentrate on the nature of theory and method and conclude by briefly illustrating the significance of the discussion of theory by reviewing a couple of substantive issues affecting the Mexican population in the United States.[1]

THEORY: THE POPULAR VIEW, ITS USES, AND DEFINITION

In the United States, there is a negative bias toward the term "theory." This bias is expressed in popular adages like, "it works in theory but not in practice." It is also evident in the idea that a theorist is someone whose perspective and/ or concerns are divorced from the practical, everyday world. Expressed in this view, theory is thought to be somehow unrelated to reality, abstract and far removed from routine political and economic activities. Not perceived is the fact that this notion of theory is in itself a theoretical position: a hypothesis about the nature of "theory" or what constitutes a theory, and also of its relationship to our practical world. In fact, this image of the nature of theory as something divorced from practical concerns is a conception that reflects our society's or culture's perspective. The notion that theory is abstract, like all concepts, happens to be based on our cultural and historical experience. Part of this notion forms the basis of most Americans' pragmatic political outlook. Therefore, the value of a phenomenon, a thought, or concept becomes determined on the basis of its practical utility, specifically, how useful it is for a specific purpose. The "value" of theory is regarded as low because its practical utility is not readily apparent.[2]

This conception of theory is inadequate in two ways. First, it restricts us to a limited view of theory by defining it initially in terms of impractical, abstract characteristics. Second, it rests on a restricted, historical, and static concept of social reality. If we examine the root of the term "theory," we find that it derives from the Greek word *theoria,* which means "to see" or "to view."[3] Thus, in terms of its literal meaning, theory refers to the way in which we come to *see* or *view* the world around us, and, in fact, the sense of "seeing" in this context refers to the notion of a way of coming to *know* the world. Theory is that set of ideas through which we know the world.

This can be regarded as a more adequate and less restricted notion of theory than the one that informs our particular cultural use of the term. In this case theory is considered to be a particular mix of ideas that we rely on to know the world, to make sense of the world around us. The world, our social reality, is not given to us in a self-evident manner. The meaning of events, institutions, and processes is not provided by some outside source, a neutral observer. Their meaning is drawn from and rooted in a particular social reality; the context of our experience also supplies the ideas and concepts—or "theories"—by which we make sense of that context.[4]

Social historical experience is understood through learned prior categories, concepts, or theories in our socialization process, allowing us to recognize and categorize actions and events in a systematic fashion. The tendency is to rely on these notions routinely without scrutinizing them or thinking about them. In fact, we tend to accept these as "natural," "just the way things are—how could they be otherwise?" We embrace notions that contradict the learned categories, or experiences that cannot be deciphered through them, as unnatural, foreign, and/or incorrect.[5]

If we accept the broader meaning of the term theory discussed above, it becomes clear that theory is an indispensable, inherent feature of social experience. Everyone in this sense is a theorist, for we all rely on a set of ideas or a framework to interpret the world. Upon approaching any subject of study of Mexicans in the United States, there already exists at least a tentative theory—some idea about the phenomenon, its constituent elements, and how they relate to one another. The difference between most of us and those who have taken up the task of "doing theory" is one of degree and not of kind. The theorist's task involves trying to become self-conscious and critical regarding the concepts; the theorist adopts the task in order to know what the nature of these concepts are and whether in fact they are adequate to provide the type of understanding of that experience we seek.[6]

CONTRAST BETWEEN TRADITIONAL AND CRITICAL THEORY[7]

Both traditional theory and critical theory have been developed as alternative frameworks used in the social sciences in particular; they are based on extremely different assumptions about the nature of society, man, thinking and acting, and the nature and causes of social injustices and other evils; therefore they lead to very different ways of understanding and explaining these social phenomena as well as different strategies to overcome them.

Traditional Theory

The concept of theory that most works in the social sciences rely on is rooted in the pragmatism of the scientific method and the world view it is based on and reflects. The ideal of social scientists has been to develop the study of human society and behavior into a rigorous "science" patterned after the approach to inquiry developed in the natural sciences. The scientific method used in this perspective assumes that one can, through its use, observe or measure discrete "facts" in some way that our values or biases do not affect this process. Thus facts and values are completely separated. Facts are considered to be "neutral"—what we do as scientists is simply to record the facts. There is no interpretation or evaluation of the facts involved. The "facts" are seen as corresponding to objective reality. They are "out there"—independent of our perspective or relationship to them. Only what we can measure, or in some way establish as real in the world through the method of science, is considered fact in this approach and thus it is assumed that there is no difference between what is observed (i.e., appearance) and objective reality. There are no hidden dimensions. Everything is accessible to observation. The observed "facts" are reality. Thus, in this view, if we follow the method of science in the study of human behavior, our particular perspective or values will not affect what we study in any way. The method or approach can be applied to any phenomena without biasing either the analysis or conclusions.

What this would mean in Chicano Studies is that if we use the scientific method in our study of the history of the Mexican population in the United States, our biases would not influence the recording of the "facts" of that history. There would be no need for interpretation at all. Most critiques of social science studies of Mexicans that appeared several years ago were guided by these assumptions grounded on the view of traditional theory.[8] They were based on the mistaken belief that we could arrive at the "objective," nonbiased "facts" of Chicano history; we did not perceive that the basic problem was the restricted view of society and history stemming from traditional theory. The restricted and limited nature of our arguments would have been much more clearly visible had they been developed on the basis of some version of critical theory, for critical theory contains within it a basic critique of traditional theory.

Critical Theory

Critical theory is most closely identified with the works of thinkers like Hegel, Marx, and Nietzsche in the past, and more recently with Horkheimer, Adorno, Marcuse, Habermas, and others associated with what has come to be labeled the Frankfurt school of critical analysis.[9] Although all these writers have different formulations of what critical theory is, it is nevertheless possible to identify several common characteristics of the approach that can thus be considered as defining the basic and essential elements of critical theory.

In opposition to traditional theory, critical theory proceeds on the assumption that all elements or "facts" of social reality are by their nature interrelated or interconnected. Social reality does not resemble a series of discrete, that is isolated or externally related, "facts" that we can record through empirical observation. Rather, it is a process in constant motion or change with respect to each other. The facts of our world exist as a set of social relationships, and it is the network of relations within which any fact exists that gives it its meaning. A fact can only be understood if we see it in terms of its relationship to other elements or facts. In other words, the meaning of a particular social fact is provided by the other facts to which it is related. To distinguish the individual fact from the network of which it is a part would be to distort it and lose the total picture. This is exactly what, from the critical perspective, traditional theory does.

Critical theory holds that we need to look behind the facts, to see the network of relationships that give a particular fact or set of facts meaning. Thus, that which appears to us for immediate and obvious observation is not complete reality at all because reality is perceived as including the relationships that are not physically apparent but need to be discovered.

To illustrate the difference between traditional and critical theory, an example can be used. Upon meeting an individual for the first time, most acknowledge that we do not know that person, although the person is present in a tangible form. The person remains quite unknown because we do not know precisely what critical theory directs us to, that is, the network of relationships that make that person known. Individuals only make sense to us (in terms of "knowing" them) if we become aware to some degree of how and to whom each person is related in terms of dimensions, such as friendship, love, work, and recreational relationships. Individuals present only their appearance and not their reality. They remain an abstraction and not something concrete.

The critical perspective sees all facts or elements as socially interrelated in the sense outlined above. All elements of social reality are embedded in some type of network. The identity and actions of an individual, group, or class need to be understood not as isolated facts but as inherently interrelated phenomena, each acquiring meaning through the other elements in the context. As opposed to the isolationist mechanism of traditional theory, critical theory rests on a dialectical view of society and reality. To understand an experience or activity from this perspective, one must trace the ensemble or network of relationships that give the experience or activity a particular meaning.

The second important characteristic of the critical approach to the study of social activity encompasses the assumption that no form of knowledge, theory, or concept can be value neutral or free of commitments to certain values, or of interests to a social group. All knowledge, observed experience, or activity, according to this view, is inherently embedded in specific sociohistorical conditions. These conditions provide the ingredients for the theories and concepts we use to make sense of our reality. In other words, we cannot think without thinking about something—and that something is provided by the sociohistorical conditions forming the context for existence. For example, one cannot think about a Chicano Studies class without at the same time having some impression about its value, purpose, and objectives.

The process of thinking is not a passive process where the sociohistorical world imposes itself without our being involved in the world. Rather, all of our knowledge, of which theories and concepts are types, develops from human practice or activity, that is, our confrontation and interaction with nature and other humans, or with our natural and social environment. The critical theorist might well ask, Where else *could* knowledge come from if not from our activity in the world?

Critical theory further argues that all human action is purposive in nature, which means that all human activity is necessarily guided by values and interests. In other words, human activity is directed toward a certain end or goal by a particular value or interest. All human activity expresses some value or interest. If all knowledge derives from human activity, and all human activity expresses some value or interest, then the values and interests expressed in the activity from which our knowledge is derived are implicitly present in the categories of knowledge. So all forms of knowledge necessarily contain within them value predispositions or reflect the interests of some social group.[10] Any form of knowledge will necessarily correspond to some particular form of societal organization because knowledge cannot exist in isolation.

In a society where interests and values are promoted through power relations, power relations determine the values and/or interests pursued, sought, or reflected in policies, actions, or in the structure of societal institutions. Knowledge will also manifest a political dimension, for the interests and values promoted through this type of practice or human activity (for example, the use of power) are also going to guide the substance of the concepts and theories

Figure 15.1:   Dialectic Method

	Object of Study	
Active	S_1	S_3
Reflective	S_2	S_4

(a) historical conditions
(b) social and political interests and values
(c) philosophical presuppositions of approach

used. The relationship of activity (power relations), values/interests, and knowledge is the reason why critical theorists tend to focus their substantive studies on how ideologies function to obscure the link between power and knowledge or forms of thought, and to demonstrate how particular forms of thought or ideologies either support or oppose various interests in society. This constitutes part of our social reality that traditional theory cannot explain.

Since the perspective of critical theory is opposed to traditional theory, it is not surprising that the method of critical theory also differs from the scientific method relied on by those who adopt the framework of traditional theory. Before moving to a brief discussion of how critical theory can affect the study of Mexicans in the United States, it is imperative to present a brief review of the method considered appropriate to a critical perspective.

Although references to a critical methodology are often made, only a few works exist that attempt to systematically define what is involved in this method. However, there does seem to be somewhat of an agreement that the approach must be a dialectical one. The following draws on a few of these works to present an elementary model of what a dialectical methodology entails as basic assumptions.[11]

A critical dialectical method does not attempt to understand a phenomenon by breaking it down into its component parts, as traditional theory would. That is, there is no precise and specific step-by-step procedure to follow. A different assumption exists: that any particular object of study can be understood only by considering it in its active relationships with other phenomena. However, this does not prevent us from attempting to define in at least a general manner the essential steps that are involved and that help sustain the dialectical quality of the approach (see figure 15.1).

In the active stage (S_1 and S_3 in the figure 15.1), the researcher begins by focusing on a particular object of study. He explores it to see or expose the network of relationships of which the object is a part and give it its meaning.

This means, of course, that the knowledge gained by studying the specific phenomena never becomes complete in the sense of uncovering all relevant relationships; rather the acquisition of knowledge must be considered as an ongoing process. It seems more appropriate to say that knowledge is always an approximation of reality because even accurate information or description becomes untrue in the sense that the reality to which the information or description corresponds is constantly changing. Therefore, static or constant description and/or categories used to understand that reality will not be valid for very long. The result of dialectical analysis is not some ultimate truth but a process of successive approximations that attempts to change the categories in order to remain closer to the reality it seeks to understand.

The specific methods or techniques used to comprehend an object of study can include those that are traditionally used in the social sciences and humanities, such as statistics, historical biography, comparative institutional analysis, and textual exegesis. A commitment to dialectical analysis does not require a complete rejection of these traditional techniques for it is not the techniques themselves that are restrictive but rather the perspective that normally guides their use. In the active stage of analysis, for example, the immersion in the object of study, the researcher should draw on as many of the different techniques possible since each one will help expose more dimensions and levels of the structure of the object.

This effort to immerse oneself in the object of study must proceed in a manner that leads toward the reflective stage (S_2 and S_4 in figure 15.1). The researcher must incorporate a reflexive dimension by "turning back on oneself," by examining the nature and roots of the assumptions and categories of the framework used to study the object. After observation and study in the initial active stage, one must critically examine the "data" obtained by (1) examining the historical conditions from which and within which the investigation is developing, (2) exposing the social and political interests to which the object of study is inherently related and expressive of, and (3) delineating the philosophical assumptions or prior ground assumed by the approach. In stage three, one would return to the object of study to expose further aspects of its relation to other objects in light of what has been understood in stage two.

It is important to note that the process of moving from an active immersion in the subject matter to a reflective analysis of the ground on which the investigation is proceeding is not a static one, which means that we cannot stop, nor freeze, nor hold constant the developmental nature of social reality for the purpose of analysis. Rather, the entire process, the active and reflective activities, move through time. When one returns to the analysis of the substantive subject matter at stage three, one has to have absorbed the development of the entire process; each component in the relational framework will have changed and developed during stages one and two. We cannot think of these stages as discrete, separate entities. In other words, the object of study is changing even while we study it (S_1). And, while we think about its context (S_2), its characteristics will have undergone some alteration (S_3). Thus, there emerges the need to constantly reexamine the categories and theories as initially adopted in an effort to understand a particular phenomenon. Not only must we trace how the object of study changes, but also how the conditions are also changing that make it possible to understand and know it. Without this effort, concepts, categories, and theories become static or frozen at one particular stage. If we then attempt to apply these concepts without checking their possible inadequacy as instruments for understanding the changed, new nature of the object of study, our analysis will become abstract and invalid.

At the start of this essay, it was pointed out that its intent was to concentrate on the nature of theory and why an awareness of it is important to anyone studying society. Those of us committed to the continuing development of the field of Chicano Studies, particularly need to continually rethink what we are doing and why, if we are to achieve Chicano Studies' objective of contributing to the development of Mexican communities. We need to constantly be aware that ideology can masquerade as effectively as science, religion, politics, or philosophy might. We should not rely on the tradition of social science that limits instead of enhances our creative potential. And yet, because it is the dominant orientation taught in graduate courses as well as in introductory surveys and because it is so pervasive in our academic culture, there is an ever-present possibility of succumbing to the anesthetic effect of the traditional model of social science, which obscures the real relationship between power, interest, and knowledge.

In the field of Chicano Studies, the object of study, the active dimension or stage of our method, is the collective historical experience of the Mexican people in the United States. If a dialectical perspective is applied to the experience, we need to incorporate in the approach the reflective stage as well, not as an afterthought or peripheral concern, but in the internal structure of the analysis.[12] The facts discovered in the active engagement of Chicano history cannot in themselves provide their meaning. For this we need to to see them as consisting of active relationships with other facts. We also need to move to a careful, evaluative consideration of the historical conditions from which those facts developed, to see the interests and values reflected in those conditions and to examine the interests and values expressed in the assumptions of our approach.

We have from time to time dealt with some of these issues in the discussions of different approaches that have been published, for example, in the discussions and critiques of the internal colony model. But we have not incorporated the awareness of the immense significance of our choice of perspective and theory for our analysis into the very structure of Chicano Studies. We need to build into the structure of our analysis a consideration of what is at stake in choosing the respective categories, what consequences follow in terms of how to limit our perception of problems and their solutions. It is not simply a matter of making this clear and then moving on to the substantive discussion in our teaching to help students develop critical abilities. Rather, we should see that the activity of clarifying what is at stake is in itself something that needs to be taught and learned.

The following two examples should serve to illustrate the difference this critical perspective can make in our approach to Chicano Studies. One is an obviously relevant choice, but the other is chosen precisely to demonstrate the advantage of a critical approach.

The first issue is affirmative action. A traditional theory approach concentrates on the apparently clear actions involved and accepts a commonly provided meaning of affirmative action. Affirmative action is a practice that gives preferential standing to minority group members. But, does this concrete definition really provide us with its true social and political meaning? Why do some see it as a commitment to overcome the consequences of generations of institutionalized racism and explicit discrimination while others consider it to be a form of reverse racism? How do we begin to choose which of these is "valid" or "objectively" correct? Only an approach that looks beyond the apparent facts of the practice of affirmative action and views it in its relationship to (a) the historical conditions and factors that generated it as a practice or policy and (b) the interests and values of which it is expressive, and that continually reevaluates its own presuppositions regarding these factors, can begin to understand the dynamic and real nature of the phenomenon, and at the same time shed light on why some groups see it as legitimate governmental activity while others think of it as racism.

The second example is the 1970s trend toward a self-oriented, privatized psychological view of life represented by groups like Erhard Sensory Training (EST) for example. Some have labelled this phenomenon the "culture of narcissism" because of the great emphasis placed on the primacy of the self and the individual.[13] The concern manifests itself in the rapid growth in the number of encounter groups, courses focusing on the problems of coping with personal crisis, the appearance on the best-seller lists of books dealing with assertiveness training, and others reflecting the philosophy of "looking out for number one," "I'm OK, you're OK," and in general personal survival in the jungle of society.[14]

There is no doubt about the existence of such a trend in the current period. From the perspective of the economically and politically exploited Chicano population, such a phenomenon would not appear to be a particularly salient or relevant occurrence, for most of the techniques and programs of the "self-analysis" groups are so expensive that they are available primarily to middle- and uppermiddle-class individuals. In other words, because of the cost involved, this narcissism would primarily affect the non-Chicano sector, which in turn would involve less Chicano participation in this issue, at least in terms of its relevance to Chicano Studies.

Yet, a critical perspective, because of its insistence on placing the object of study within its broader context, and because it conceives of events and actions as well as institutions as being relational activities rather than static objects, would lead us to conclude that the worldview fostered by the primacy of self groups and books is in fact an ideology of narcissism with social content and implications in promoting the belief that the individual only needs to be responsible to himself, and that no societal or community responsibilities or obligations are required. Thus, only what affects one personally acquires any significance or importance. The criteria for evaluating political or policy proposals and positions immediately affect one's own interest to the complete exclusion of any consideration of their potential impact on the larger community. Whoever sees the world in this narcissistic way will approach policy issues from the stand point that as long as *I* do not need to rely on public schools, public transportation, public health care, public social and recreational programs, then why should *I* support them. Consequently, cutbacks in the budgets for such programs—precisely the services that are desperately needed by a significant segment of the Mexican population—will be given either implicit or explicit support. Peter Marin summarizes the political and social significance:

> What disappears in this view of things is the ground of community, the felt sense of collective responsibility for the fate of each separate other. What takes its place is a moral vacuum in which others are trapped forever in a "private" destiny, doomed to whatever befalls them. In that void the traditional measures of justice or good vanish completely. The self replaces community, relation, neighbor, chance, or God. Looming larger every moment, it obliterates everything around it that might have offered it a way out of its pain.
>
> The end result of this retreat from the complexities of the world is a kind of soft fascism: the denial, in the name of higher truth, of the claims of others upon the self. Our dedication of the self becomes equal in effect and human cost to what Nietzsche long ago called the "idolatry of the state." Just as persons once set aside the possibilities of their own humanity and turned instead to the state for a sense of power and identity no longer theirs, so we now turn to the self, giving to it the power and importance of a god.[15]

Each person is assumed to be responsible for his own condition and for his own plight. To correct one's plight all that is needed is to will it with enough intensity. Social structure and institutional practices fade far into the background. This is definitely an ideology, and one that will provide support for specific and concrete programs and policies that *directly* affect the Mexican population. Therefore, the spread of this ideology ought to be of primary concern to those attempting to understand the dynamic processes that structure the opportunities and everyday realities of Chicanos. If we were to rely on the view of traditional theory, however, it would be unlikely that we would see this connection because the immediate and apparent meaning of narcissism would seem to make it irrelevant to the concerns of Chicanos.

NOTES

1. I have dealt more specifically with how critical theory can serve as a corrective in the study of the Chicano politics in "A Critical Perspective on the Study of Chicano Politics," *Western Political Quarterly,* vol. 30 (Dec. 1977), pp. 559–73.

2. This conception of the relationship between ideology and theory is found in Kenneth M. Dolbeare and Murray J. Edelman, *American Politics* (Lexington, Mass.: D.C. Heath, 1979).

3. For a discussion of the classical notion of theory see Nathan Rotenstreich, *Theory and Practice* (The Hague: Martinus Nijhoff, 1977), ch. 1.

4. This notion is developed fully in Kenneth M. Dolbeare, *Political Change in the United States: A Framework for Analysis* (N.Y.: McGraw-Hill, 1974).

5. See Peter L. Berger and Thomas Luckmann, *The Social Construction of Reality* (Garden City, N.Y.: Anchor Books, 1966).

6. Sociologist Alvin Gouldner argues for the necessity to examine our concepts and frameworks reflexively in *The Coming Crisis of Western Sociology* (N.Y.: Basic Books, 1970).

7. The following discussion reflects the argument found in "Traditional and Critical Theory," in Max Horkheimer, *Critical Theory* (N.Y.: Herder and Herder, 1972), pp. 188–243.

8. See, for example, Mario Barrera, Carlos Muñoz, and Charles Ornelas, "The Barrio as an Internal Colony," in Harlan Hahn, ed., *People and Politics in Urban Society,* vol. 6 (Beverly Hills: Sage Publications, 1972), pp. 465–98; and Nick Vaca, "The Mexican American in the Social Sciences: Parts I and II," *El Grito,* vol. 3, no. 3 (Spring 1970), pp. 3–24.

9. An excellent analysis of the critical school is to be found in Trent Schroyer, *The Critique of Domination* (N.Y.: Braziller, 1973).

10. The argument that all knowledge is inseparable from human values and interests is found in Jurgen Habermas, *Knowledge and Human Interests,* trans. Jeremy J. Shapiro (Boston: Beacon Press, 1971).

11. Particularly Fredric Jameson, *Marxism and Form* (Princeton, N.J.: Princeton University Press, 1974); Jean-Paul Sartre, *Search for a Method* (N.Y.: Vintage Books, 1963); and a very difficult but worthwhile article by Michael Kosok, "The Systematization of Dialectical Logic for the Study of Development and Change," *Human Development,* vol. 19 (1976), pp. 325–50.

12. See some of the essays in Reynaldo Flores Macias, ed., *Perspectivas en Chicano Studies* (UCLA: Chicano Studies Center, 1977).

13. For perceptive analysis of the phenomenon of narcissism, see Peter Marin, "The New Narcissism," *Harper's,* vol. 251 (Oct. 1975) and Christopher Lasch, *The Culture of Narcissism* (N.Y.: W. W. Norton, 1978).

14. For a critique of these developments, see Edwin Schue, *The Awareness Trap: Self-Absorption Instead of Social Change* (N.Y.: McGraw-Hill, 1976).

15. Marin, "The New Narcissism," p. 48.

About the Editors and the Contributors

JOHN L. AGUILAR is Assistant Professor of Anthropology at Arizona State University. His social anthropological research has focused mainly on processes of social interaction and patterns of ethnic relations in the Mayan region of southern Mexico.

MARIO BARRERA is Associate Professor of Chicano Studies at the University of California at Berkeley. His professional interests encompass social theory, social class structure, and political change. He is the author of *Race and Class in the Southwest: A Theory of Racial Inequality* (University of Notre Dame Press, 1979). This book was selected by the American Political Science Association as the best book on ethnic and cultural affairs published in 1979. Dr. Barrera was the recipient of the Ethnic and Cultural Affairs Award awarded annually by the American Political Science Association. He has also published on educational change and political movements among Chicanos. He is currently at work on a book on the Chicano community in the twentieth century.

ALBERT CAMARILLO is Associate Professor of History and Director of the Center for Chicano Research at Stanford University. In 1979 he published *Chicanos in a Changing Society: From Mexican Pueblos to American Barrios in Santa Barbara and Southern California, 1848–1930* (Harvard University Press). He is currently completing a comparative study of the development of Chicano communities in cities across the United States in the twentieth century.

EUGENE E. GARCÍA is Director of the Center for Bilingual/Bicultural Education and Professor of Education at Arizona State University. He served as a faculty member at the University of Utah and the University of California, Santa Barbara, before joining the faculty at Arizona State University. He has published extensively in the area of bilingual development. His most recent book, *Early Childhood Bilingualism,* was published by the University of New Mexico Press (1983).

JUAN GÓMEZ-QUIÑONES is Professor of History and Director of the Chicano Studies Research Center at the University of California at Los Angeles. A student of Mexican labor in the American labor force, he pioneered the development of Chicano labor historical studies in the seventies and was a cofounder of the scholarly journal, *Aztlán: International Journal of Chicano Studies Research.* He has published extensively in scholarly journals, and his most recent major work is *The Development of the Mexican Working Class North*

267

of the Rio Bravo (Chicano Studies Research Center, University of California at Los Angeles).

JOHN J. HALCÓN received his Ph.D. from the University of California, Santa Barbara in Education. He serves as Director of Bilingual Education at California Lutheran College. His research evaluates the organizational character of bilingual education in local educational districts, with particular emphasis on the organizational structures devised by districts to incorporate bilingual education and the effect of these structures on the total educational environment.

MARÍA HERRERA-SOBEK is Associate Professor in the Spanish and Portuguese Department at the University of California, Irvine. Her fields of expertise include Chicano folklore, especially *corridos,* Chicano literature, Latin-American literature, bilingual education, and women's issues. Among her scholarly contributions, one work distinguishes her in the field of folkloristics, *The Bracero Experience: Elitelore Versus Folklore* (UCLA Latin American Center Publications, 1979).

JORGE A. HUERTA is Associate Professor in the Drama Department at the University of California, San Diego. He has been actively involved in all facets relating to theater as an actor, producer, director, and writer. A founder of Teatro de la Esperanza in Santa Barbara, California, he later organized a student theater group in San Diego. He has published extensively on all aspects of Chicano theater and has a landmark study, *Chicano Theater: Forms and Themes* (Bilingual Review, 1981).

GARY D. KELLER is Associate Professor and serves as Provost at the State University of New York, Binghamton. He has also been Graduate Dean at Eastern Michigan University. In charge of *The Bilingual Review/La Revista Bilingüe* and editor of Bilingual Press, he has been an instrumental force in the dissemination of scholarly studies and creative writings by Hispanics throughout the United States. His main area of emphasis is linguistics as it relates to bilingual education and literature. He also serves as editor of Teachers College Press's Bilingual Education Series.

FRANCISCO A. LOMELÍ is Assistant Professor at the University of California, Santa Barbara, in the Spanish and Portuguese and Chicano Studies Departments. His fields of study cover both Chicano and Latin-American literature. With Donaldo W. Urioste, he wrote *Chicano Perspectives in Literature: A Critical and Annotated Bibliography* (Pajarito Publications, 1976). Some of his research covers Southwest literary history, writings by Chicanas, and a translation of Argentine poet Rodolfo E. Braceli's *The Last Testament.* An interest in Chilean letters is evident in his *La novelística de Carlos Droguett* (Editorial Playor, 1983).

CARLOS MUÑOZ, JR. is Associate Professor of Chicano Studies at the University of California at Berkeley. In the early seventies he was one of the founders of the National Association of Chicano Studies. He has edited a special issue of the journal *Aztlán: International Journal of Chicano Studies Research* on politics in the Chicano community. He has also authored articles on various aspects of the Chicano movement. He is concluding the writing of a book on the Chicano student movement that will be published by the University of Notre Dame Press.

ISIDRO D. ORTIZ is Assistant Professor in the Departments of Political Science and Chicano Studies at the University of California, Santa Barbara. His research focuses on the political activism of Chicanos. In 1981 he received the Western Political Science Association's award for the best paper on Chicano politics. His articles have been published in several professional books and journals.

RAYMOND A. ROCCO is Associate Professor of Political Science at the University of California at Los Angeles. His interests embrace the development and role of ideology in scholarly research and social theory in the United States and Mexico. In 1977 he was the recipient of the Western Political Science Association's award for the best manuscript on Chicano politics. He has completed a major study of the political thought of Mexican philosopher Leopoldo Zea, and the development of the antipositivist tradition in social theory in Mexico.

CARMEN SALAZAR-PARR is Associate Professor at Los Angeles Valley College in Van Nuys, California, and has also served as visiting lecturer at the University of Southern California. She is highly regarded in the fields of Mexican and Chicano literatures with numerous key contributions. She has also co-edited language texts and readers for beginning literature students. One major contribution has been in the area of feminine literature aside from her active participation in the journal *Hispania*.

GUADALUPE SAN MIGUEL received his Ph.D. from Stanford University in Education. He serves as Assistant Professor in Education at the University of California, Santa Barbara. His research focuses on the historical aspects of school segregation in the southwestern United States with particular emphasis on the strategies adopted by Mexican Americans to overcome educational inequity.

CHRISTINE M. SIERRA is Assistant Professor of Political Science at Colorado College. Her professional interests include Chicano political organizational development, feminist politics, and socioeconomic and political change in the Southwest. She has completed a major study of the National Council of La

Raza, one of the major Latino organizations in the United States. She has been active in the National Association of Chicano Studies and the American Political Science Association.

Carlos J. Vallejo is Assistant Professor in the Department of Elementary Education at Arizona State University. His primary responsibilities include teaching and course development in the areas of bilingual and multicultural education.

Index